INTELLIGIBLE AND
RESPONSIBLE TALK ABOUT GOD

INTELLIGIBLE AND
RESPONSIBLE TALK ABOUT GOD

A THEORY
OF THE DIMENSIONAL STRUCTURE OF LANGUAGE
AND ITS BEARING UPON THEOLOGICAL SYMBOLISM

BY

ROBERT ALLEN EVANS

LEIDEN
E. J. BRILL
1973

ISBN 90 04 03683 0

PRINTED IN BELGIUM 74-610

Dedicated to :

Tom F. Driver, Paul L. Lehmann,
John Macquarrie and Daniel Day Williams

TABLE OF CONTENTS

PREFACE

The telephone on the pastor's desk rang. A voice on the other end of the line informed him that the daughter of one of his elders had been struck and killed as she stepped out from between two parked cars. She had just registered for her first day of classes at the State University. The car was driven by a fellow student. As the pastor hung up the phone, a series of thoughts flashed through his mind : Only child. Adopted after a long wait. Parents devoted to Carol. Devastating tragedy for parents. What can I say to Fred and Alice? How can I talk about God at a time like this? As the pastor fumbled for his car keys and started the trip toward the parents' home, an overwhelming sense of nausea drove all thoughts but one from his mind : "How can I say anything meaningful about God's grace and love to my friends?"

Arriving at the house with some anxiety, the pastor was met by Alice, only to be told that Fred had already left. "Left for where?" was the surprised response. She replied, "He has gone to the campus to find the boy who was driving the car that killed Carol. Fred wants to tell him that it's all right. We forgive him. We didn't want the boy to torture himself. God's grace will take care of him and us".

One meaning of God's grace was demonstrated. Suddenly the pastor understood and embraced Alice. Her response had allowed the pastor to be free and joyous in the midst of tragedy. The event obviously had a similar effect on Alice. The pastor felt the urge to dance and sing and praise the Lord whose presence he had just encountered. These words had provided not only illumination and insight about the meaning of God's grace and its presence in an unexpected situation, but the words also transformed him, changed him. They altered his relationship to Fred and Alice and eventually his relationship to other persons in his church and community. This moment of communication gave the pastor a new perspective on himself and on his God.

In this experience talk about God had been intelligible and responsible. The words resulted in understanding and insight. Perhaps more important, the conversation was a catalyst for change, the words did something; they influenced not only how one reflected about himself and his world, but how he responded to persons and situations he encountered. The story affected not only the pastor but others with whom he shared the story.

Most of us who share in a religious tradition can point to experiences similar to this, where language has come alive and made us aware of God's reality and His presence. However, we also know a number of instances in which talk about God is neither intelligible nor responsible. Not only does it fail to enlighten and transform, but it blocks understanding and snarls relations with others. It can be so frustrating as to lead people to reject the possibility of talking about God at all. Such language is meaningless and irrelevant.

The simple question is, Why? What accounts for the fact that sometimes talk about God comes alive, and other times it is stillborn? Are there any clues in the nature of language and experience which could begin to account for this capacity or power of language?

Research is undertaken and manuscripts published for any number of reasons. In each specific case the motives are probably mixed. It is important to be clear about some of the personal reasons which led me to this research and the publication of this work. As a parish pastor, campus minister and teacher, I have been plagued by the question of why and how talk about God functions. I am also frustrated by the inability of myself and those around me to give an answer to this question. The purpose of this study is not simply to satisfy my intellectual curiosity, to develop a theory of the nature of language that could provide a more satisfying account of why language functions as it does. I am also seeking avenues and models which would enable one to speak more coherently and significantly about God. How does one write and speak and share with others in concrete terms so that experiences which constitute the very foundation of one's humanity are disclosed, lit up, and exposed? The detailed and sometimes plodding nature of the manuscript belies the person and the passion that stand behind it. It is important therefore to read this preface, in which I try to explain in an informal style the reasons for this work and precisely what it claims to do.

The personal reasons for publication involve the attempt to share with the reader the directions in which this research has led me, the guidelines it has established for my own work and ministry. This research has persuaded me to focus attention on symbol, myth, and story as the keys to interpreting one's encounter with God. The present investigation required me to concentrate on the question of what it means to be human, to reflect on those thoughts and actions that characterize who I am. In two works published prior to this, but written as a consequence of this research, I argued that it is neither principles nor rationale which primarily determine man's reflection and action. Rather, it is symbols or myths about himself, his world, and his God that determine who one shall be. In recent course offerings I have examined the philosophical foundations and cultural implications of myths and symbols, especially those which shape my own life and the lives of my students. Also preaching has become for me revelatory story telling in which the task is to point to illuminating and transforming symbols which demand disclosure and interpretation. One is drawn to a kind of imagery by which it is possible to interpret our human experience and discover again the unexpected and undeserved presence of God in every component of our daily lives. This kind of theologizing, interpretation and proclamation is based on certain forms of ontology and epistemology. The present work attempts to expose those philosophical presuppositions which undergird my understanding of the nature of language.

The professional reason for publication is the hope that this research may be suggestive for others in the field. Perhaps a dialogue will ensue where the author may learn by the criticisms, corrections, and creative additions of others. The major thesis of the manuscript is that the conceptual and symbolic functions of language should be regarded as being on a continuum rather than in distinct or separate realms. The work constitutes a move toward a dimensional theory of language which is offered here as the tentative and experimental design of a clearing house for language.

As an exploration of the dimensional theory of language, the work makes some contributions which merit consideration. This investigation provides an interpretation of the symbolic dimension of language which is operative in every major universe of discourse. It also makes a contribution to the contemporary discussion of symbolism by providing a definition and discussion of symbol as a particular linguistic form with special linguistic functions. A preliminary sketch of this theory of language supplies a feasible rationale for symbols having an identifiable impact on persons and communities, namely, that symbols can be illuminating and transforming. The manuscript focuses particular attention on theological symbolism and demonstrates how a proper appreciation of its power can account for theological language coming alive, enlightening us, and redirecting us.

This theory of language demands that we take seriously the mysterious quality of language and confirms a "high evaluation" in which language is precious because it is in fact the key to God's self-disclosure. We need to understand language, particularly in its symbolic mode, as that which allows and accounts for revelation. I am calling for a new appreciation

of symbolism, particularly in light of the way in which it has been disparaged in analytic studies during the past decade. For many, language
is merely a convenient and arbitrary means of communication within
a particular group of people and does not merit special attention. If
in fact it does constitute the non-concealment of God to man, we must
face the charge that we have been using language too casually and
superficially. We have failed to see its power and potential for both
illuminating and transforming our human existence. It is in language
that Being discloses itself in and to man. Man is characterized therefore
by his openness to Being, and it is his encounter with Being that liberates
man for his full potential.

This study argues that language cannot be properly understood, particularly theological language, without referring to both the symbolic and
conceptual functions of language and seeing them in a dialectical relationship to one another. A dimensional theory of language also demands
a coherent understanding of the dimensions of thought or reason,
the appropriate forms of knowledge, and the means of confirmation
of these respective dimensions. The applicability of this understanding
of language to several different universes of discourse provides the foundation for an authentic interdisciplinary dialogue. This is opened up in a
preliminary way in regard to natural science and joins in the present
discussion of the relationship between science and theology.

Furthermore, the present study interprets the distinctive contribution
to an understanding of the nature of language and particularly the theory
of symbolism made by Wilbur M. Urban. He has been an important
resource for theologians such as Paul Tillich and John Macquarrie,
and the importance of his contribution to an understanding of theological language and symbolism has often been slighted or ignored.
(There has been some revival of interest in Urban's contribution in the
very competent study by Warren A. Shibles, entitled *Analysis of Metaphor
in the Light of W.M. Urban's Theories*. Dr. Shibles' study is an analysis
of the contribution of Urban to the theory of metaphor, whereas my
work proceeds to examine the implications of Urban's thought for
theological language in particular). I also give considerable attention to
the philosophical reflection of the later Heidegger, especially insofar
as his ontology provides a foundation for a dimensional theory of
language. Finally, the theology of Paul Tillich is utilized as an illustration
for theological symbolism. However, this study attempts to provide
an adequate foundation for Tillich's use of symbol and calls for necessary
additions and revision in Tillich's understanding of the nature of lan-

guage. This revised understanding, I maintain, is a prerequisite for symbols having the capacity Tillich claims for them. In general the critical examination of sources serves to expose the contributions of those who have been substantively affected by the idealist tradition in philosophy. This investigation therefore, contributes to the renewed appreciation of some of the insights of those influenced by idealism, particularly in regard to language, and attempts to call the attention of those laboring in the field to a reconsideration of this resource. The theory of language sketched here does not attempt to draw a detailed map of the entire terrain. What it does do is to point down what I feel is the right road and invite others to explore this route.

A work such as this, which has been in progress for a number of years, receives criticisms at various stages. I am grateful for those critiques; a number of revisions have emerged as a result. However, it is also prudent to attempt to forestall some criticism by being clear about the primary aims and limitations of this work.

As my primary goal was to develop a dimensional theory of language, I have not attempted to argue in detail with other contemporary positions on the philosophy of language. This was not thought necessary for two reasons. First, other authors have engaged in this dialogue in recent publications. For example, in reference to theological language, there is the work of Langdon Gilkey, *Naming the Whirlwind : The Renewal of God Language.* On the basis of what he describes as a modern secular mood Gilkey engages in a wide-ranging debate with those who seek to base intelligible language about God on speculative metaphysics, linguistic analysis of ecclesiastical discourse, phenomenological analysis of religious experience, or revelationist theology. Gerry H. Gill, in his work, *The Possibility of Religious Knowledge,* focuses on the epistemological issues particularly in reference to the work of Ludwig Wittgenstein and J.L. Austin. The contributions of anthropologists such as Claude Lévi-Strauss to the understanding of language and particularly the role of myth and symbol is critically interpreted by G.S. Kirk in his recent work *Myth : Its Meaning and Functions in Ancient and Other Cultures.* Finally, a substantive study of the existential and experiential basis of talk about God, employing the notion of God as agent, has been completed by Gordon D. Kaufman. *God the Problem* investigates the uses or significance of talk about God so that such language could be considered meaningful and important. My work does not attempt to duplicate or regurgitate this critical analysis on the nature of language nor does it attempt to answer shortcomings of these positions. However,

I hope this study will affirm my awareness and appreciation of the insights concerning language provided by the positions represented in these debates, which have significantly affected my own understanding of language.

Second, I have not argued extensively with current works on language because I wish to focus on the development of a dimensional theory of language in relation to particular formative figures. Such focus poses limiting boundaries, but this concentration is a self-conscious decision. The research is frequently dependent on the insights of Wilbur Urban and Martin Heidegger. Extensive documentation from these sources seemed imperative, but these authors are not intended to function as "authorities". This documentation may give the manuscript a rather "clogged" effect, like a pipe which does not draw smoothly because it is so tightly packed, and, as a Scotsman might note, often with someone else's tobacco. However, in the end this often produces a richer and more satisfying smoke. Despite the difficulty of the draw, I want to clearly indicate the contributions of Urban and Heidegger to this dimensional study of language. However, I have also sought to declare explicitly the points in which I differ from these germinal influences so that the distinctive component in the mixture becomes apparent.

Various stages of revision have not successfully concealed the fact that this is basically a doctoral dissertation (presented to the faculty of Union Theological Seminary, New York). Consequently, the style suffers somewhat from the origin of the manuscript. However, the declared qualification of this work is that it merits publication; therefore I take the decision of my examining committee seriously. If the reading goes slowly, do not slight Chapter IV. The core of the thesis is here. The summary portions of each chapter indicate this core and the consequences which emerge from it. Let me conclude these cryptic suggestions to the reader by noting that a diagram of the schematic proposal, which provides a graphic image of the theory, is presented at the end of Chapter V.

The emphasis on the development of the theory has resulted in fewer concrete examples in this specific work than I find ordinarily desirable. This deficiency has been remedied in more recent publications. My introductory essay in *The Future of Philosophical Theology* attempts to place the theory in a particular cultural setting and to demonstrate its influence and potential. In *Belief and the Counter Culture* I attempted to sketch quite concretely the determining symbols for an emerging culture. However this later work, directed toward the general reader, lacked the explication of the epistemological and ontological foundations for an understanding of language as set forth here. It is my hope that these works with different audiences in mind balance one another to present a coherent, integrated theory.

Finally, two transitions within my own thought sould be indicated. I do not see these as falling in the category of limitations, except insofar as the full impact of these transitions is not sufficiently reflected within the body of this work. The first is a broadening of the philosophical foundation on which I think this dimensional theory of language can be justifiably based. The impression may be given, particularly in Chapter II, of a rather fervent and devoted if not exclusive commitment to the ontological position of the later Heidegger. I do not wish to deny my enthusiasm for the ontological insights emerging from a fundamentally idealist component in Heidegger's thought. However, I do want to repudiate the inference that there is an exclusive claim, that this philosophical position is the only one in the contemporary philosophical scene which is either credible or competent to provide working presuppositions for a dimensional structure of language. My growing appreciation of the sensitivity and wisdom of the later Wittgenstein and a renewed appreciation for process philosophy, particularly as represented in Whitehead's work on symbolism, is present although this is not clearly indicated in the manuscript. My primary concern is that language be understood as having the capacity for access to Being. Heidegger's work presents one philosophical perspective which supports such a conclusion. However, it is clearly not the only philosophical position capable of providing this support.

The second point of transition is a fuller appreciation of the significance of the non-verbal context in which communication occurs. In the present manuscript emphasis is on the crucial role of language in knowing, communication, and confirmation. Testing this theory of language to see whether it is a viable account of how language functions, how it causes things to happen, I have become aware of the strategic nature of extra-linguistic factors and become appreciative of the role of physical objects, bodily activity, and human emotions in the process of genuine communication. The importance of the non-verbal context for language is suggested in this study, but not sufficiently accentuated.

Talk about God is multi-dimensional and therefore is often extremely difficult to understand. This is particularly true in the context of a theological seminary where every qualification and nuance seems so important. Genuinely illuminating and transforming communication is not only a mystery, but somewhat of a miracle. As ironic as it may be, this seems particularly true in communication between teacher and student. It is in gratitude for such encounters that this work is dedicated to four men who are both teachers and friends : Tom F. Driver, Paul L. Lehmann, John Macquarrie, and Daniel Day Williams. With each man I had the opportunity of being a colleague both in learning and teaching as I served in the positions of student and teaching assistant at Union Theological Seminary in New York.

The debt registered here is not a consequence of agreement, but rather emerged precisely out of the constructive, stimulating confrontation represented in their different theological positions and personal styles. I have argued in this work that dialogue is an essential component in intelligible and responsible talk about God. The lived experience with these friends confirms that judgment. Their existential struggle to find more satisfactory ways to talk about God manifested itself in a dialectic that forced me to find my own way. The theory presented here is not representative of any one of their positions, nor would they likely give unqualified support to my conclusions. Yet, that image of a critical continuum is a paradigm not only of the nature of language but of good teaching. However, the debts do not all fall in the category of assets. Some liabilities were also part of this encounter called "graduate education". In fact it has sometimes been suggested that it takes at least a couple of years for one to overcome the disabilities of a graduate education and become a good teacher. At least some of the pedantic and scholastic plodding of this work may be laid, directly or indirectly, at their doorstep as well. But it is my personal appreciation and affection for these partners is dialogue which leads me to take the privilege of public confirmation of my gratitude to them.

This stimulating encounter with men, manuscripts and models over a four-year period was made possible by the United Presbyterian Church, USA, through their Presbyterian Graduate Fellowship program which allowed me to pursue with intensity alternative solutions to the problem of theological language that had surfaced in the midst of a pastoral ministry in Tulsa, Oklahoma. It is a love for and commitment to the healing ministry of a community of believers which motivated this research and for them I hope it will provide some insight. The Fund for Theological Education granted a Rockefeller Doctoral Fellowship in Religion which made it possible to carry on a fruitful dialogue about this topic not only in the United States but in Germany and Switzerland as well. Many people have been involved by choice and chance in a supportive or critical response to the ideas in this manuscript which often contributed to modification or revision. Some of these people may prefer not to be mentioned; nevertheless, let me cite in addition to those to whom the book is dedicated, three who have been particularly significant : J.A. Martin, Gordon D. Kaufman, and a special friend and colleague at McCormick, Thomas D. Parker. The bulk of the typing was done speedily and cheerfully by Gladys M. Burkhart. A smaller but equally joyful contribution in typing and manuscript preparation was made by Caryl Estéves and Mary Lee Reed.

There is no conceivable way to adequately thank my wife and children for their contribution to this project. However, it seems inhumane and insensitive not to make a stab at it. Not only did Alice forbear my absence in body and mind, as a result of my affair with this paper mistress, but she abetted the liaison by editing, typing and proofreading. Far more significant, but indescribable, is their undaunted support and love for me. This perhaps contributed more than anything else to my personal wrestling with the question of responsible and intelligible talk about God. This is precisely because they mediated and shared with me God's gracious presence to and for us. So Alice, Judith and Mellinda join me in a farewell embrace of Dulcinea.

McCormick Theological Seminary   ROBERT A. EVANS
Chicago, Illinois
May, 1972

INTELLIGIBLE AND RESPONSIBLE TALK ABOUT GOD

How can we speak intelligibly and responsibly about God? This question poses one of the most compelling problems for contemporary theology : the problem of the nature and function of theological language. Philosophers and theologians alike recognize a kind of crisis in the understanding of theological language. According to Langdon Gilkey the present ambiguity about the "meaning" of God-Language, has at its core a concrete and crucial question, "Is faith in God a real possibility for a modern secular man; is it possible to speak meaningfully—to ourselves and to others—of God and what he has done for man ...?"[1]

The problem has been dramatized over the years by certain philosophers particularly in the analytic tradition. An early and extreme position is taken by A.J. Ayer, who considers theological language to be cognitively meaningless and therefore nonsense.[2] Alasdair MacIntyre is less rigorous in his condemnation than Ayer, but no less insistent on demanding that we know how talk about God is to be construed, and he even asks whether it is so idiosyncratic that we can hope for no philosophical account or it.[3]

Other philosophers, granting theological discourse a meaningful and cognitive role, have attempted to determine the particular function of theological language in terms of a recognition of patterns in sets of facts (John Wisdom),[4] an expression of a "blik" or a fundamental attitude toward the world (R.M. Hare),[5] or as a declaration of policy (R.B. Braithwaite).[6] Despite the variety of opinion represented here, the one point at which all these philosophers concur is in the need to

---

[1] Langdon Gilkey, *Naming the Whirlwind : the Renewal of God-Language* (Indianapolis : Bobbs-Merrill, 1969), p. 5.

[2] A. J. Ayer, *Language, Truth and Logic* (London : Victor Gollancz, 1936).

[3] *Metaphysical Beliefs*, Alasdair MacIntyre (ed.) (London : SCM Press, 1957).

[4] John Wisdom, "Gods", *Proceedings of the Aristotelian Society*, 1944-45.

[5] R. M. Hare, "Theology and Falsification", *New Essays in Philosophical Theology*, A.G.N. Flew and Alasdair MacIntyre (eds.) (London : SCM Press, 1955).

[6] R. B. Braithwaite, *An Empiricist's View of the Nature of Religious Belief* (Cambridge : Cambridge University Press, 1955).

investigate the nature and function of theological language if we are to talk about God intelligibly.

However, these philosophers are not alone in their recognition of this crisis in understanding in theological language. A theologian, Gordon D. Kaufman, in his work *God the Problem* explores "what we are trying to say when we speak of God". Acknowledging the controversy he declares, "In these explorations, though I also share in the profound cultural and philosophical confusions and doubts about such talk, I have attempted chiefly to see what can be said positively or affirmatively".[1] Other theologians have demanded a radical re-analysis of the conventional language of theology. Rudolf Bultmann has called for a "demythologizing" of certain language within the Christian tradition.[2] Paul Tillich notes the confusion of language in theology and philosophy and urges the recovery of the significance of the "symbol", especially the religious symbol. One of the more extreme positions on the part of a theologian is taken by Paul Van Buren when he asserts that this uncertainty about the meaning and significance of theological statements is so great that even "the word 'God' is dead".[3] Langdon Gilkey focuses the present debate over theological language by pointing to the fact that "current questions concern more the *meaning* than the *validity* of theological discourse".[4] There is an increasing acknowledgment among theologians themselves that if one is going to speak responsibly and intelligibly about God, an analysis of the nature and function of theological language is required.

Paul Tillich provides an apt summary of our contemporary predicament in regard to language :

> ... we are in a confusion of language in theology and philosophy and related subjects which has hardly been surpassed at any time in history. Words do not communicate to us any more what they originally did and what they were invented to communicate. This has something to do with the fact that our present culture has no clearing house such as medieval scholasticism was, Protestant scholasticism in the 17th century at least tried to be, and philosophers like Kant tried to renew. We have no such clearing house, and this is the one point at which we might be in sympathy with the present day so called logical positivists or symbolic

---

[1] Gordon D. Kaufman, *God the Problem* (Cambridge : Harvard University Press, 1972), p. 9.

[2] See Rudolf Bultmann, *Jesus Christ and Mythology* (London : SCM Press, 1960).

[3] Paul Van Buren, *The Secular Meaning of the Gospel* (New York : The Macmillan Company, 1965), p. 103.

[4] Gilkey, *Naming the Whirlwind*, p. 13.

logicians or logicians generally. They at least try to produce a clearing house. The only criticism is that this clearing house is a very small room, perhaps only a corner of a house, and not a real house. It excludes most of life.[1]

Today there is a real need for a new clearing house for philosophical and theological language—a clearing house that is adequate for the volume of business it must handle. Not a small room, but a real house that can encompass the full range of human experience. It is the task of the theologian in the contemporary situation to work at the design of such a clearing house for language, particularly in regard to those departments which deal with theological language. Although his special competence may be in one or two particular rooms, he must have some picture of the completed project where the various rooms adjoin one another to provide movement throughout the whole house. Some theologians are already at work on their design,[2] but I think it can be stated that the task has just begun.

According to John Macquarrie the analysis of theological language is a sophisticated and reflective form of God-Talk.[3] I am convinced that this analysis must focus on the various types or dimensions of theological assertions, on the cognitive status of these assertions, on the forms of knowledge these assertions are held to provide, and on the means of confirmation, if any, of the respective types of theological assertions. In response to these issues there has been a certain concentration on indirect forms of discourse, on symbol, model, or metaphor, as they are employed in theological language. God, insofar as he is the Ultimate, the Transcendent, the Holy, can only be spoken of indirectly or symbolically. The notion of inexpressibility is at the core of almost every religious experience. That which confronts us in

[1] Paul Tillich, "The Nature of Religious Language", *Theology of Culture*, R.C. Kimball (ed.) (New York : Oxford University Press, 1965), p. 53.

[2] Some representative and programmatic works in the area of the nature and function of theological language are : Ian T. Ramsey, *Religious Language* (London : SCM Press, 1957); Frederick Ferré, *Language, Logic and God* (New York : Harper & Row, 1961); John A. Hutchison, *Language and Faith* (Philadelphia : Westminster Press, 1963); D. M. Evans, *The Logic of Self Involvement* (London : SCM Press, 1963); William Hordern, *Speaking of God* (New York : The Macmillan Company, 1964); John Macquarrie, *God-Talk* (London : SCM Press, 1967); Langdon Gilkey, *Naming the Whirlwind : The Renewal of God-Language* (Indianapolis : Bobbs-Merrill, 1969); Gordon D. Kaufman, *God the Problem* (Cambridge : Harvard University Press, 1972).

[3] Macquarrie, *God-Talk*, p. 11.

the religious experience so transcends our normal means of understanding
and expression that we are forced either into silence or into the use of
special linguistic forms which seem appropriate to the reality which
has confronted us. Silence is an inadequate response if we are to claim
that there is a cognitive element in religion and that we have some
knowledge of the Holy. Knowledge, if it is to be that in any significant
sense, demands expression and communication. Thus words and linguistic
forms of some type are necessary. The question is what type of linguistic
form is appropriate. While recognizing their limitations, what forms are
most adequate to disclose the reality which encounters us? How can
we responsibly speak about God without abrogating his transcendence
or his mystery? The response given by many theologians is that we can
speak of God only symbolically or metaphorically. Paul Tillich, for example, maintains that symbols are the language of religion and this is the
only way in which religion can express itself adequately.[1] I am convinced
that theological symbolism is the key to responsible talk about God.

However, it is also necessary to speak about God intelligibly, and if
a theory of religious symbolism is going to avoid charges of subjectivism
and unintelligibility, it must ground itself in a coherent notion of symbolism. If in the last analysis that notion of symbolism is going to be comprehensible and comprehensive, it must in turn be rooted in an adequate
understanding of the nature of language. It is the thesis of this study
that a *dimensional* structure of language provides the basis for an adequate
notion of theological symbolism .Theological symbolism in turn supplies
the key to intelligible and responsible talk about God. In order to justify
this proposed theory of the dimensional structure of language, this
study must examine the nature of language itself. As John Macquarrie
reminds us :

> If we are to make any progress ... toward arriving at a more satisfactory account
> of theological language, we shall have to leave for a while the area of theo-
> logical debate and turn to an inquiry into the nature of language in general.
> This is one of many cases in which the theologian, whether he is willing or
> unwilling, is constrained to enlist the help of the philosopher. The theologian
> talks about language, and he must have some idea, explicit or implicit, of what
> language is. If he is wise, he will pay attention to what has been said on the subject
> by those who have made language the specific theme of their researches.[2]

---

[1] See Paul Tillich, "The Meaning and Justification of Religious Symbols", *Religious
Experience and Truth*, Sidney Hook (ed.) (New York : New York University Press,
1961), p. 3.
[2] Macquarrie, *God-Talk*, p. 54.

This study will focus primarily on the insights of two philosophers of language who are particularly important for my own theory of the dimensional structure of language; namely, Wilbur M. Urban and Martin Heidegger. No attempt has been made to be comprehensive in regard to these figures in light of the breadth and extraordinarily complex nature of their thought and work. The emphasis in this study is not on the defense of the presuppositions of these philosophers but rather on the refinement and application of their insights in an attempt to develop a feasible exploratory theory about the nature and function of language. The major concern of this investigation is with the development of my own systematic thesis. However, my debt to these philosophers is obviously very great.

The theory of a dimensional structure of language as proposed in this study is an attempt to provide a foundation for intelligible and responsible talk about God. It is my contention that an adequate understanding of the nature of language should be one that is cognizant of and can account for the symbolic element in human language while maintaining the interrelatedness of the symbolic and non-symbolic elements. The symbolic element has a bond with the non-symbolic by means of which the symbol is expanded and interpreted so as to be the basis for significant meaning and intelligible communication. Provisional definitions establish the context of my investigation of the theory of language by focusing on a specialized understanding of symbol as having the capacity to convey authentic awareness and significant insight about some aspect of reality (Chapter I). This capacity of the symbol is accounted for by acknowledging not just a theory of symbolism but a symbolic dimension in all language.

The illuminating and transformational power of the symbolic dimension is dependent on a "high evaluation" of language in which language is viewed as an adequate access to reality. Martin Heidegger's insight that "language is the house of Being" provides a clue to an ontological foundation for this capacity of language, this disclosure of Being in language. I maintain that this disclosure occurs specifically via the symbolic dimension of language (Chapter II). It is the symbolic element and the "high evaluation" which ultimately account for language as a bearer of meaning and a medium of communication. This analysis of the nature and function of language employs the insights and often the terminology of Wilbur Urban (Chapter III). The symbolic dimension, because it is a dimension and not a sphere of language, is dialectically related to and interdependent with the non-symbolic or conceptual dimension of language. It is in the conceptual dimension of language that the symbol is interpreted by expansion and evaluation (Chapter IV).

The theory of language developed in this study seeks to offer a coherent notion of symbolism and to ground that notion in an adequate understanding of the nature of language itself. Thus the schematic proposal set forth endeavors to meet the demands of a competent analysis of human language. This analysis is based on the identification of two principal dimensions of language, the symbolic and the conceptual, and points to the cognitive status of these dimensions as reflected in foundational and technical reason. These two types of reason result in two types of knowledge, receiving and controlling (Chapter V). Finally, the means of confirmation of assertions within these two dimensions is examined in reference to the authentication and verification of their respective assertions (Chapter VI).

A case is made for the comprehensive nature of the dimensional theory of language by demonstrating, in reference to the work of Karl Jaspers, that this theory is applicable to several representative universes of discourse : theology, history, and science (Chapter VII). Natural science is then taken as a paradigm case for the dimensional structure of language with special attention given to the role of scientific symbols or models (Chapter VIII).

In conclusion, the study focuses on the relationship between a dimensional structure of language and theological symbolism. The dimensional understanding as a comprehensive theory of language supports and makes intelligible the claims that theological symbols are illuminating and transformational (Chapter IX). The thought of Paul Tillich is employed as an illustration of such a theory of theological symbolism. However, in addition to providing support for Tillich's claims for theological symbols within the nature of language, this theory proposes a revision in Tillich's position which acknowledges not merely a "theory of symbol" but rather a symbolic dimension in *all* principal universes of discourse. It must be reiterated, however, that the symbolic and conceptual dimensions, of theological language are interdependent, for theological symbols must be interpreted and this occurs within the conceptual dimension of theological language (Chapter X).

If this dimensional understanding of language is applicable to all principal universes of discourse, including the theological, then our speaking of God in the symbolic dimension of language becomes not only meaningful but also significant. Recognizing the crisis in the understanding of theological language and particularly theological symbolism, this theory of the dimensional structure of language constitutes a schematic proposal, an attempt to work toward a clearing house for theological language which would make our talk about God both responsible and intelligible.

CHAPTER ONE

PROVISIONAL DEFINITIONS

The intent of this section is to establish some tentative definitions for terms with which I will have a primary concern. Hopefully, this will set the guidelines for further discussion. However, the frustrating thing about a study of language is that every term seems to demand clarification and thus qualification. Thus even the method of definition requires some explanation.

Serviceable definitions have in the first instance a *contextual* aspect. This means they are developed out of and are related to a particular subject or problem. When they pretend too extensive a scope they usually become so general as to have no significant meaning. In any complex theme a good definition is related to and consistent with the meaning of the other central concepts. Second, an adequate definition has a *historical* aspect. The concept or term has had previous meanings or at least its root term has, and thus there has been a development of meaning related to the historical context. Etymologies may be helpful if their import is not exaggerated.[1] The historical aspect may not always be explicitly developed here, but in accounting for certain variance in definition it is an important characteristic to keep in mind. Finally, constructive definitions have a *provisional* aspect. They should always be open to the possibility of adjustment and change. This may be necessitated by a transfer of the context in which they are employed, by a change in understanding of the historical situation which gave rise to the definition, or simply by a new insight or discovery within the same general or historical situation. A recognition of the importance of contextual, historical, and provisional aspects of definition may caution one against the too facile utilization of a term or concept used in another completely different context or historical situation.

As Wilbur Urban correctly notes, it is exactly concepts such as language

---

[1] The danger of excessive dependence on etymologies has been illustrated by James Barr in his *Semantics of Biblical Language* (London : Oxford University Press, 1961), pp. 107ff.

(or religion, too, for that matter) which defy definition.[1] This is due to the scope of their contextual application, depending, for example, on whether one is attempting to approach the problem primarily from a psychological, historical, philosophical, or theological perspective. Despite the problem of contextual plurality, it appears to me not only possible but necessary to draw certain distinctions between various terms used in the study of language. This may be done by determining a term's approximate meaning in relationship to the other terms employed in the context of this particular study via what I have called provisional definitions.

This definitional endeavor is further complicated by the historical aspect of definition because the terms used in the technical study of language have changed so radically over the years; presently there exists no general consensus concerning the meaning of key terms.[2] Perhaps an even more troublesome issue in the search for intelligibility in the use of language is that terms have sometimes been used in ways that are at variance with common usage or at least exceedingly confusing to the normal reader.[3] I have no illusions about overcoming these difficulties in this brief study. But I will endeavor to use terms which are reasonably distinguishable from one another and strive to apply them in a consistent way. These distinctions need to be drawn, I am convinced, even if the terms employed in this study are not the only alternatives. It is just this process of sorting out which is required to reduce some of the ambiguity and move toward the establishing of a clearing house for language.

Language, Discourse, and Articulation

Language — The term "language" should be employed as the generic term applicable to the widest span of considerations and problems involving human expression and communication. Language in the generic

---

[1] Wilbur M. Urban, *Language and Reality* (New York : The Macmillan Company, 1961), p. 70. (First published in 1939).

[2] An example of this historical change is given by Urban in reference to the complete alteration in the meaning of the term "connotation". *Ibid.*, pp. 138-139.

[3] This is particularly true of terms that are frequently used in ordinary conversation such as "sign" and "symbol". Both are important terms in the study of language and they require a more precise technical definition within the context of a particular study. It is almost inevitable that some contrast with what we call "ordinary usage" will result, but perhaps it should be kept to a minimum. Note Macquarrie's critique of Tillich's use of "sign" and "symbol" in John Macquarrie, *Principles of Christian Theology* (New York : Scribners, 1966), p. 123, n. 10.

sense may refer to issues of meaning, expression, communication, and confirmation. If the term language is going to be limited to a reference to the words and their relational ordering in a specific discipline, such as theology or natural science, then this should be noted by appropriate qualifiers and explanation; but it is both confusing and contrary to common usage *simply* to assume this more limited meaning of language.

The thrust of this comment is to assert my preference for the use of "language" as the generic reference in opposition to terms such as "speech"[1] or "discourse".[2] These terms are useful in making important distinctions, as will be demonstrated in this section, but these terms ought not to be interpreted as being wider in application than "language". I think the demands of intelligibility lead us to use "language" in this broader sense. This is more compatible with common usage and it coincides both with the term "philosophy of language" (not philosophy of speech or discourse) and with the concern of this project in "theological language" in its most extensive sense, i.e., involving problems of meaning, expression, communication, and confirmation. Thus my provisional definition is : language is a dimensional capacity of the human understanding to be a bearer of meaning, a medium of communication, and a means of access to reality.[3] This definition for language will form the basis for the investigation in later chapters which will involve explication and development of the characteristics of language set forth here.

Ludwig Wittgenstein is one of the pivotal figures in the contemporary debate concerning the philosophy of language. It should be emphasised that the understanding of language revealed in this operating definition and developed in the present work is particularly endebted to philosophers of language, such as Urban, who were influenced by modern idealism. However, this definition is also appreciative of the insights of the later Wittgenstein. My position shares with Wittgenstein a conviction about the interconnection of language and thought. Perhaps more important is our common concern for a dimensional understanding of language and experience. As Jerry Gill notes in his evaluation of Wittgenstein,

---

[1] Urban, *Language and Reality*, p. 67.

[2] Macquarrie, *God-Talk*, p. 67.

[3] The debt to Urban, *Language and Reality*, p. 37, in regard to this definition will be obvious. However, the differences in definition between Urban and myself refer not only to my change in the latter part of the definition from "as a sign or symbol of reality" to "a means of access to reality", but also include my emphasis on the dimensional nature of language. The contrast in our positions will become apparent as the study develops.

"The dominant theme of Wittgenstein's later thought is that language is a multi-functional, 'many splendored' phenomenon which cannot be limited to the confines of logic and science".[1]

In reference to my provisional definition of language, attention must now be given to two additional distinctions that should be maintained within the scope of the wider generic conception of language.

Discourse : The Context of Living Speech — Discourse is the situation in which the human capacity for speech is brought to fruition. It is in the discourse situation, the interchange between persons, that human language comes to its natural fulfillment. This is the context in which linguistic signs are accepted and interpreted and thus made efficacious for communication and enlightenment. Urban directs attention to the imperative nature of this context when he describes it as the notion of "die erlebte Rede", living speech.[2] Articulation, or language in the more confined sense of words and sentences, has reality or comes to mature meaning only in this living speech community. It is language in the narrower sense of vocabulary and syntax which mediates the discourse situation.

John Macquarrie has developed a clear and concise explanation of the discourse situation in his book *God-Talk*, and I will use it here as a guide.[3] He begins by stating that the complex situation in which we say anything is characterized by a triadic relationship consisting of (1) the person who says something, (2) the matter about which something is said, and (3) the person or persons to whom something is said. The major consequence of identifying the discourse situation is to exhibit that a clear understanding of the nature and structure of language, in the sense of articulation (words and sentences) and thus of its meaning, must make reference to the particular discourse situation in which that type of language has arisen. Macquarrie maintains, and I think correctly, that a significant limitation of the logical positivists was their failure to distinguish between language (language in the narrower sense of articulation, words and sentences) and discourse. Thus words and sentences were treated in isolation from living discourse and became an abstraction. This was an abstraction that so limited the meaningful use of language that large portions of human experience were simply

---

[1] Jerry Gill, *The Possibility of Religious Knowledge* (Grand Rapids : William B. Eerdmans, 1971), p. 98.

[2] Urban, *Language and Reality*, p. 135.

[3] Macquarrie, *God-Talk*, pp. 65ff.

ignored or degraded by this analysis. Wittgenstein reacts in a similar way against a notion of language characteristic of his own earlier work, which identified the function of language as that of naming objects and picturing states of affairs. "A main cause of philosophical disease—[is] a one-sided diet : one nourishes one's thinking with only one kind of example".[1] It will be maintained in the course of this discussion that such a limitation is to consider only one dimension of human language as constituting the whole field. In order to make a judgment about meaningfulness or truthfulness, the analysis of words and sentences is dependent on a reference to the discourse situation in which the language arose.[2] I wish to contend that this judgment also depends on the dimension of human language being employed within this context of living speech.[3]

The provisional definition thus reads : Discourse—The context of living speech is the triadic situation in which the capacity for human speech is brought to completion in words and sentences (articulation) and where the linguistic signs are received and interpreted by the speech community. Now it is necessary to focus on articulation itself, which is narrower than discourse and constitutes a special use of the term "language".

Articulation : Vocabulary and Syntax—This definition involves a narrower use of language which refers only to words and sentences. The normal termination of the speech process results in collections of sounds—that is, words—or signs representing those sounds, written words, and the ordering or arrangement of those words. The maturing of the capacity of speech is consummated in a specific vocabulary and an orderly arrangement of that vocabulary : a syntax.[4] This does not refer simply to the more limited concept of grammatical syntax, but to the orderly arrangement of words that results in significant meaning

---

[1] Ludwig Wittgenstein, *Philosophical Investigations* (New York : Macmillan, 1953), p. 155.

[2] Macquarrie, *God-Talk*, p. 67. He qualifies this by stating that some languages, notably scientific language, can manage better than others when abstracted from the discourse situation. As a relative distinction, this is probably true; but it will be maintained here that no particular language, including science, can come to fulfillment apart from the discourse situation.

[3] Macquarrie goes on to distinguish essential elements in discourse : expression, representation, and communication (*ibid.*, pp. 68f). The various aspects of the discourse situation will be considered in detail later.

[4] *Ibid.*, p. 84. Macquarrie indicates that the distinction between vocabulary and syntax follows the procedure of Rudolf Carnap in his work, *The Logical Syntax of Language* (London : K. Paul, Trench, Trubner and Co., Ltd., 1935).

in the discourse situation. Mature meaning is at least partially a function of communication. So the precise meaning of a word in our vocabulary is partially determined by its position in the ordering of other words and by its location in a particular speech context; namely, in discourse. Meaning involves a recognition of linguistic syntax.

There is an apparent terminological problem here. Some previous studies of language and often common usage employ the term "language" to indicate both the wider generic notion as well as specific words and sentences. This is a problem in the critical analysis of language (in the generic sense) only when one fails to specify the area about which he is making an assertion. For example, when one makes a reference to "theological language", is he asserting something only about its vocabulary and syntax? Or about the way in which theological statements are used in discourse? Or about man's capacity for speech and thus the source for theological symbols? In order to maintain some important distinctions I have chosen to employ the term "language" for the generic reference, and when the reference is questionable, to use "articulation", or vocabulary and syntax, as a reference to specific words and sentences within a particular discipline.

The summary of this discussion is the following provisional definition : Articulation—Vocabulary and syntax are the actual words and their orderly arrangement which are the products of the speech process and which find their functional home in the context of human discourse.

This concludes the initial analysis of what could be called the basic classifications within a study of human language. We proceed now to a brief consideration of some additional orienting distinctions. In the critical analysis of any specific vocabulary operating in a definite discourse situation, we say that the words and phrases are, or function as, signs, symbols, signals, metaphors, analogies, myths, similes, and so forth. Obviously it is impossible, short of a full philosophy of language, to identify and relate all these terms. There are, however, certain terms which, due to their importance and frequency of occurrence, require our examination. A distinction upon which many of the basic studies of language have focused (Cassirer, Urban, and Langer, to name just a few) and one which is significant for my own analysis is that between "sign and symbol", or rather, as I will suggest, that between "signal and symbol".

Sign, Symbol, and Signal

Our generation has witnessed an extraordinary rise in the interest in symbolism. This is manifest in such diverse fields as philosophy, psychology, natural science, history, art, and religion.[1] The problem in this expanding concern is that almost every conceivable object and situation has been described at some juncture as being a symbol or as having a symbolic function. As the editor of a work, *Myth and Symbol*, which attempts to demonstrate the breadth and depth of this concern for symbolism, F.W. Dillistone observes that symbolism is too imprecisely used today and that we need to secure and limit its meaning for reasons of intelligibility.

> In such a period it is important to examine the use of these words, not with any desire to be finicky or pedantic, but in order to safeguard a certain precision in language and to prevent these terms from losing all force and meaning. This is perhaps especially the case in the theological realm, for both image and symbol have a long history of use in religious contexts and they may well provide significant links between theology and culture in our contemporary world.[2]

Even a more specific problem is the tendency to assert that all language is symbolic. However, without further qualification that statement becomes meaningless, because it obliterates the distinctive symbolic functions of language.[3] It is the task of this section to define more precisely how the term "symbol" will be employed in this study and specifically what is meant by the symbolic or non-symbolic function of a term or phrase in a particular context.

First it is important to distinguish between the wider and narrower concepts of symbolic. The wider concept of symbolism simply refers to a "representational function". A symbol is that which stands for or represents another thing in a particular situation or under certain specified conditions. This wider reference means that almost everything can

---

[1] E. L. Mascall, *Theology and Image* (London : A. R. Monbray, 1963), pp. 3-4. Mascall gives evidence of this rise by outlining the major works in symbolism in regard to religion from Edwyn Bevan's *Symbolism and Belief* to Mircea Eliade's *Images and Symbols*.

[2] *Myth and Symbol*, F. W. Dillistone (ed.) (London : S.P.C.K., 1966), p. vii.

[3] Urban, *Language and Reality*, p. 411. The author accuses Stebbing, Richards, and Whitehead of contributing to this confusion by referring to all language as symbolic and thus failing to distinguish the different ways in which "symbolic" and "symbol" are employed.

be appropriately designated by a thinking subject as a symbol for something else. Thus almost every word or phrase is capable of becoming symbolic in its wider representational function. This wider concept of the symbolic is serviceable only in distinguishing the symbolic from the literal; i.e., that which lays claim to nothing beyond itself, but rather is actual, complete, and self-evident.

This means that the term "symbol" or "symbolic" refers one to the notion of meaning. A symbol is a "vehicle of meaning". In standing for something else it requires an act of interpretation in order to determine its significance. This may involve in its more elementary form simply discovering that object or situation for which it stands in a straightforward one-to-one relationship. Or it may be a much more complex process of interpretation which involves an expansion of the symbol and an analysis of its designatory and even intuitional references. However, to proceed beyond this initial indication of symbolic as being representative in function and being a vehicle of meaning, we must proceed to the narrower definition of symbolic. Here one must distinguish between the symbolic and non-symbolic and indicate the distinctive characteristics of the symbol in this more limited sense. Thus some discussion about how "sign", "symbol", and "signal" will be used in the context of this study is mandatory.

The pattern in several significant works which refer to the problems of language has been to draw a distinction between "sign" and "symbol". This procedure is used, among others, by Urban,[1] by Langer,[2] and by Tillich.[3] Tillich's use has made these terms virtually standard in contemporary theological discussion. However, as critics have noted, his terminology is somewhat at variance with good English usage and tends often to be confusing in ordinary discussion where sign and symbol are employed interchangeably.[4] It seems to me that this distinction between "sign" and "symbol", or, as I will suggest, between "signal" and "symbol", is valuable insofar as it indicates the divergent functions which various linguistic modes may perform. However, I think it is an oversimplification to think this distinction either is or ought to be exhaustive. "Symbol" has at least two quite distinct and appropriate

---

[1] Urban, *Language and Reality*, pp. 404f.

[2] Susanne Langer, *Philosophy in a New Key* (New York : Mentor, 1951), pp. 37f.

[3] Tillich, *Systematic Theology*, Vol. I, p. 239, and "The Nature of Religious Language", *Theology of Culture*, p. 54 (Chicago : University of Chicago Press, 1951).

[4] For example, John Macquarrie, *Principles of Christian Theology*, p. 123.

applications, both a wider and a narrower one, as will become evident. If "signal" and "symbol" are given a sufficiently limited meaning to be significant, the more focused meanings will not encompass the full range of linguistic expression. In relation to their ordinary usage, the terms often tend to overlap. It appears more helpful to understand "symbol" and "signal" as being two widely divergent points on a continuum of linguistic modes of meaning rather than two distinct or separate realms that completely exhaust the field. The notion of a continuum will be developed in the course of this section as a possible means of dealing with a very complex and confusing assortment of terms. The clarity one would desire is at present beyond reach, but perhaps some progress toward intelligibility is possible.

Consequently, I would prefer to reserve "sign" as a generic term to indicate any vehicle of linguistic meaning, whether it be a signal, symbol, or some other form.[1] "Sign" employed in this way is in a sense comparable to the "wider" utilization of the concept "symbolic". Thus one might prefer, for the sake of precision, a reference like "sign-function" in place or the wider concept of symbolic defined previously. However, such a substitution would be at variance with the way "symbolic" is employed generally and is helpful only as a point of clarification. The nature of linguistic meaning will be considered in detail in a future chapter. However, for the moment let us consider a basic distinction between two types of linguistic signs : signal and symbol. This is done in order to set this study in the context of the contemporary discussion and to emphasize the need for a limited and specialized use of "symbol".

A signal is a linguistic sign that indicates the existence—past, present, or future—of a thing, event, or condition.[2] A signal is a "designatory sign"[3] which simply calls our attention to the thing, event, or condition. A signal or designatory sign itself does not warrant our attention; it simply "announces" the existence of the object to the thinking subject. The signal is something to act upon, whether that response be physical

---

[1] The preference for "sign" as a generic term is based on Langer's "Preface to the Second Edition" of *Philosophy in a New Key*, pp. v-vi. This in turn is based on the usage of Charles Morris in his *Signs, Language and Behavior* (New York : Prentice Hall, 1946).

[2] Langer, *Philosophy in a New Key*, p. 58. Langer's terminology provides a guide in this discussion.

[3] Reference is based on Urban's use of "designative sign," *Language and Reality*, p. 407.

or mental. It is a signal in the sense that it demands our attention, our action, our response, even though the sign itself could not be said to have an explicit meaning beyond this "attention-calling" function. It is, I think, perfectly clear that much of human language is composed of words and is arranged in a syntactical structure that allows for just this kind of function. "Telephone" may be a verbal signal for a particular object which calls my attention to it in the same way the ringing of the bell on the telephone is a non-linguistic signal that calls my attention to the same object. A signal functions in this way because it is an arbitrary or conventional sign which has no special relationship to that to which it refers. It is an operational sign which has been established and accepted in a given speech community over a period of time. The context will, of course, also influence the function of the signal. However, the signal does not express or reveal anything about the person, thing, event, or condition to which it refers. This word or phrase may, at some earlier time, have had a special kinship with that to which it refers which allowed it to actually illuminate or express the object of its reference. However, now the term has only a designatory function.

In contrast to the signal we have the symbol, which in Husserl's terms is a "significative sign".[1] The symbol has an intrinsic relationship to that which it symbolizes. A genuine symbol claims to have special affinity with that to which it refers, or as Tillich expresses it, the symbol "participates in the reality" of that which it symbolizes. Tillich maintains that due to this special relationship, symbols have the capacity to open up certain levels of reality both within and beyond ourselves because of what they allow us to see or even cause us to see.[2] The symbol gives us a special type or knowledge which provides special insight into the nature of its referent. Urban tells us, following Cassirer, that in all genuine symbols —or as he prefers to say, "insight symbols"—an intuitive element is to be found.[3] Urban calls on Kant for support :

> Here we wish merely to emphasize the intuitive character of the genuine symbol and, more particularly, the kind of similarity which exists between the symbol and the thing symbolized, as Kant sees it. It is not similarity as in the case of the "picture". The "sense" of the symbol is not "the common form of representation", as it is in case of the sense of a picture, but similarity in *the way of reflecting on the two things*; a common rule of operation.[4]

[1] Urban, *Language and Reality*, p. 405.
[2] Tillich, "The Nature of Religious Language", *Theology of Culture*, p. 58.
[3] Urban, *Language and Reality*, p. 406.
[4] *Ibid.*, p. 409. References to Immanuel Kant are from *The Critique of Judgment*, J. H. Bernard (trans.) (New York : Hafner, 1914),sec. 59, p. 248.

Urban goes on to assert that "the genuinely symbolic is bound up with the intuitive and cannot be separated from it".[1] He is using "intuitive" here in contrast to the "perceptual", and this notion of intuition particularly involves non-sensuous intuition (*Erlebniss*) of values, qualities of entities, or realities beyond the perceptual sphere. There is an intuitive element in knowledge which is necessarily connected with symbolic language. Urban asserts that perhaps his most important thesis is the "identity of intuition and expression", namely that expression is an constitutive part of the knowing itself.[2]

It is my contention that this intuitive element which is characteristic of the symbolic involves the notion of "awareness". The symbol functions for the subject as a vehicle of meaning that lays claim to an authentic awareness of a person, event, thing, or condition which cannot be directly communicated. Therefore, the intuitive awareness conveyed in the symbol must be expanded and interpreted.

"Awareness" is becoming a pivotal notion in contemporary discussions of epistemology. An illustration of this is found in the recent work of Jerry H. Gill, *The Possibility of Religious Knowledge*. Gill builds on the epistemological work of Michael Polanyi concerning "tacit knowing".[3] Knowledge is understood by Gill to be characterized by "awareness and response". Gill declares that "A sound view of language necessitates interpreting knowledge as a function of contextual, dimensional, and tacit *awareness*. Grasping meaning in language depends upon being tacitly aware of the various dimensions or forces which make up the context of any given statement. Thus knowledge is inextricably bound up with experiential awareness".[4] It is my intention to concentrate on the special capacity of intuitive awareness integral to symbolism.

The symbol is characterized and therefore distinguished from the sign by its special intrinsic relationship to that which it symbolizes. The intuitive awareness which is conveyed by the symbol provides it with the power to supply a particular type of knowledge and, within the symbolic dimension of language in which it operates, significant insight into the nature of that which it symbolizes. It will be the thesis of this study that symbol ought to be understood as an "illuminating", "transformational",

---

[1] Urban, *Language and Reality*, p. 408.

[2] *Ibid.*, p. 347. The problem of the relationship of language to thought and knowledge will be examined further in a following section.

[3] See Michael Polanyi, *Personal Knowledge* (Chicago : University of Chicago Press, 1958) and *The Tacit Dimension* (Garden City : Doubleday, 1966).

[4] Gill, *Possibility of Religious Knowledge*, p. 117.

and "pointing" linguistic sign which, due to its kinship with or participation in the thing symbolized, makes that thing, through an awareness of it, present and manifest to those in a given community who understand and employ the symbol. The symbol is neither identical with the thing symbolized, nor is it an arbitrary representation of it. Rather, due to the very nature of language, the symbol has the capacity to communicate authentic awareness and intuitive insight.

The case is being made here for a specialized and limited use of "symbol" when it is applied in the narrow sense. F.W. Dillistone defends this attempt to limit the scope and therefore accentuate the proper significance of the symbol. In this interest he offers a definition for symbol which parallels and supports the thrust in this study. Symbol is limited to "that which points towards, shares in, and in some way conforms to, a reality which cannot be fully expressed through any descriptive languages or visual forms already available to us".[1]

G.S. Kirk in *Myth : Its Meaning and Functions in Ancient and Other Cultures* makes an important contribution in setting the discussion of symbol, particularly in relation to myth in the context of its historic development and the contemporary debate concerning theories of symbolic and mythical expression. Kirk engages in a critical dialogue about the nature and role of symbol and myth with such figures as Evans-Pritchard, Freud, Cassirer, Levi-Strauss, and Jung. The emphasis in this discussion by Kirk returns to the dialectical and dynamic character of a symbol. "In terms of 'understanding', a symbol is of something —possibly of a complex of ideas and emotions, but not an indefinite and self-contradictory one. Its meanings are conditioned by those of other symbols or subjects with which it is associated; a myth is, after all ... a statement about action".[2] The vital principle of the symbol and the myth it shapes is dynamic and not static. At least the recognition of this dialogue furnishes the background for an understanding of how symbols influence action, how their potential is actualized. Interpretation plays a crucial role in this dynamic process.

The symbol cannot fulfill its capacity or come to its intended fruition of providing this particular knowledge and insight until it is, at least partially, expanded and interpreted. This means that this interpretation must take place in *non-symbolic* language; namely, in conceptual language

---

[1] *Myth and Symbol*, p. 107.

[2] G. S. Kirk, *Myth : Its Meaning and Functions in Ancient and Other Cultures* (London : Cambridge University Press, 1970), p. 267.

which is not primarily characterized by an intuitive element. All poetic, scientific, and religious symbols require interpretation.[1] The problem now arises whether by non-symbolic one must mean just signals or simple designatory signs which have no essential connection with that to which they refer. I think the answer to this is clearly "no". The language of interpretation ought not to be limited simply to arbitrary signs for "attention directing"; we are also concerned with their expressive meaning. For language which we employ for the expansion and interpretation of a symbol ought in many instances to have something more than a purely arbitrary connection with that to which it refers. This form of language has a kinship to its referent as well; the issue is one of degree or dimension of language involved. Thus the types of human articulation or the forms of linguistic signs cannot be limited to what we have called signal and symbol, no matter how important this initial distinction might be. There must be other forms for conveying linguistic meaning and therefore other basic types of linguistic signs. Some forms will be most closely associated with the symbolic in terms of claiming some kinship with the object to which they refer, yet they do not make the claim to authentic awareness or intuitive insight. Non-symbolic is, as Urban suggests, primarily a limiting rather than a definitive term. In the symbolic the intuitive element is primarily operative; in the non-symbolic, which is frequently not diminished to the signal level, the conceptual is operative. This coincides with the notion of a continuum rather than an exhaustive division between signal and symbol. It is the suggestion of this study that one important linguistic form within this conceptual or non-symbolic dimension is the analogical. There exists an analogical form of human articulation that can be distinguished from both the symbolic and the merely signalistic. I will suggest that analogy ought to be understood as a descriptive tool or as a principle of interpretiaton. The analogical function should not be seen as a means of obtaining radically new knowledge, but rather as a descriptive tool for expressing and explicating that which is grasped prior to this in the context of intuitive insight. This intuitive insight is a result of an awareness of reality apprehended via the symbolic dimension of human language. It is this non-symbolic, this conceptual dimension of human language, which enables language to be a medium of communication as it interprets the symbolic.[2]

---

[1] Urban, *Language and Reality*, p. 411.

[2] *Ibid.*, p. 413. "It is important also to emphasize the non-symbolic function of language as medium of communication. It is here, as we shall see later, that the solution

As suggested previously, it seems necessary to me to proceed in the direction of indicating a kind of continuum on which meaning functions could be located. This would constitute an attempt to indicate in a tentative way the dimensions of human language and corresponding to this the dimensions of human thought that are expressed in these forms. In addition the means of verification or confirmation in the various dimensions where judgments of meaning and truth are made would be explicated. However, this actual attempt must be postponed until the nature of language itself has been considered in more detail. In particular, this involves a consideration of the relationship of language to reality, to meaning, and to communication.

of the problem of the interpretation of the symbol is to be found. The notion of the interpretation of the symbol presupposes that there is non-symbolic language in which it may be interpreted".

CHAPTER TWO

LANGUAGE AND REALITY

In the history of philosophy man has been as much concerned with the meaning of "language" as with the meaning of "being". Man's conception of the relationship between "word" and "thing", between language and reality, has been crucial to the development of human understanding and culture. Urban in fact sees man's special preoccupation with the problems of language as marking the critical turning points in the evolution of human culture.[1] The further contention of Urban is that the history of Western thought can be characterized in terms of the struggle between two major evaluations concerning the nature of human language—"high and low evaluations of the word".[2] Our concern is not to trace the history, but rather to concur with Urban about the central importance of this distinction and thus take up a position in regard to the essential struggle concerning the nature of language. Failure to take a stand on this issue is to leave a basic assumption concerning language obscured and thus place in question the results of any investigation on the subject.

This struggle is often described in terms of the classic debate between the "nominalist" and the "realist" of the late Middle Ages. The argument of the nominalist was that references to universals or any abstract terms were merely conveniences of language or necessities of thought but had no realities corresponding to them; these words and terms were mere labels or arbitrary constructions for the purposes of communication.

The realists argued to the contrary that universals refer to objective reality and that words such as "self", "external world", and "God" are not mere labels or empty words. Although distinctions between high and low evaluations of language could be said to be characterized on the side of the high evaluation by a realist and on the side of the low evaluation by a nominalist, this is not the critical focus here. The realist-

---

[1] Ernst Cassirer has also pointed out that the history of the philosophy of language has yet to be written. However, one of the major contributions has been made by Cassirer himself in *Die Philosophie der Symbolischen Formen*, Vol. I (Berlin : Bruno Cassirer, 1923), Chap. I. A more concise account of this history is given by Urban, *Language and Reality*, pp. 22f.

[2] Urban, *Language and Reality*, p. 23.

nominalist debate was embedded in a rather complex structure of metaphysical presuppositions which do not focus precisely on the problem that confronts us today. This debate usually concentrated on particular terms and their relationship to so-called "objective reality" in such a way as to abstract the term or reference, what we have called articulation, from the actual discourse situation. In light of these factors, I prefer to use the terminology of Urban in regard to this distinction; namely, high and low evaluation of language. Also, some of Urban's essential insights serve as a guide in asserting my own presuppositions about the nature of language.

What we have termed the low evaluation of language interprets human articulation as an arbitrary construction of the human mind intended primarily for communication within a given human community. Languaguage becomes in the last analysis merely a method for the adaption to and control of environment which limits its meaningful use to the apprehension and expression of objects within the physical world.[1] There is an essential distrust of human language in regard to its capacity to express anything about the nature and structure of reality. Since language is an arbitrary instrument primarily fashioned by the mutual agreement of a given society, there is no need to go beyond an analysis of the standards by which this conventional instrument is applied; namely, beyond its practical use. There is an essential skepticism about the relation between language and cognition, since language is merely the means of conveying that which has already been perceived by the mind. There is a nominalist tendency here which treats words and phrases as simply labels for particular things, events, or conditions.[2] Urban associates this low evaluation of language with the sophists, medieval nominalism, sensationalistic empiricism, and in the modern period with what he describes as the neo-nominalism of Bergson, Russell, and Whitehead.[3] But the predomi-

---

[1] Urban, *Language and Reality*, p. 31.

[2] It is interesting to note insofar as the low versus high evaluation of language is seen in terms of the conflict between nominalism and realism that both Tillich and Macquarrie condemn extreme nominalism. Tillich, *Systematic Theology*, I, p. 177 : "Radical nominalism is unable to make the process of knowledge understandable". Macquarrie, *God-Talk*, p. 91 : "All I have tried to do so far is to show the inadequacy or even the poverty of a thoroughgoing nominalism". Whereas both criticize realism to some extent, Tillich clearly asserts his preference for realism insofar as it stresses the participation of the knower in the known. "In this respect realism is correct and able to make knowledge understandable". (I, p. 178).

[3] Urban, *Language and Reality*, Chap. I, *passim*. The critique of neo-nominalism is pursued throughout, important references coming on pp. 34f, 50f, 368f, and Appen-

nant issue throughout these various historical manifestations of the low evaluation of language is the denial of the fitness of language itself to be a means of access to reality.

An analytic and critical study of Urban's notion of metaphor by Warren A. Shibles has recently appeared. This excellent study provides important supplementary data for my own interpretation by comparing Urban's views on metaphor and symbol with those of thinkers such as Aristotle, Max Müller, I. A. Richards, Philip Wheelwright, L. Susan Stebbing, Northrop Frye and Max Black. In placing the role of metaphor in the context of philosophical reasoning Shibles summarizes the dual evaluation theory of language in the following way :

> The low evaluation of language is held by nominalists and modern logical positivists and many, if not most, empiricists and sceptics. The general contention of such philosophers is that language distorts reality. ... The main point here is that the low evaluation of language is maintained by many if not all who deny large areas of our experience such as the ethical, religious, metaphysical, etc. It is in contrast with this low evaluation of language that Urban maintained that a theory of language should be broad enough to account for all of the areas of linguistic experience without condemning one or another area of experience as "meaningless".[1]

The high evaluation of language maintains that human articulation ought not to be understood solely as the arbitrary and conventional construction of the human mind for the intended purpose of communication. Human language is, to be sure, a result of the constructive activity of the human mind. But it is not merely this; the priority in the fashioning of human language rests not with man but beyond him in a reality that can be distinguished from man, reality itself. Human language is an instrument of human understanding, but it is neither merely arbitrary nor conventional. Rather, it will be maintained that knowledge and language are inseparable. The particular terms employed and their ordering may provide essential understanding and insight concerning the object referred to. Thus terms like self, external world, and God are not mere labels or empty words, but they embody an intellectual intuition as opposed to a sensuous intuition.[2] The crucial issue for the high evaluation of language, as far as this study is concerned, is the contention that reality can be expressed and that language is the vehicle for this

dix III, p. 741. I personally would have some reservations about describing Whitehead as a neo-nominalist despite his concern to redesign language.

[1] Shibles, Warren A., *Analysis of Metaphor in Light of W. M. Urban's Theories* (The Hague : Mouton, 1971), p. 14.

[2] Urban, *Language and Reality*, p. 26.

expression. Language is intended to be not just a medium of communication, although it is that, too, but rather, a means of access to reality.
I have maintained that language is the distinctive characteristic of man
and it assumes such a significant role precisely because within a particular
dimension language provides this access to reality and thus accounts
for the possibility of man's openness to Being.

Urban goes on to associate this high evaluation of language with Plato,
Aristotle, medieval realism, and most forms of rationalism and idealism.[1]
This high evaluation of language manifests a realist tendency in its trust
in language. This trust forms the condition of valid naming and of the
communication of meaning. Urban stands clearly in the idealist tradition
and thus defends the high evaluation of language as the authentic
approach and even goes so far as to identify it as "the postulate of all
positive cultural epochs" and the low evaluation of language as the
"beginning of scepticism and relativism".[2]

This struggle between the high and low evaluation is based on just
that—an evaluation of the nature of language. It is a foundational presupposition about the way in which language ought to be understood.
I think Urban is correct in defending the high evaluation of language
and in demonstrating in his own work its importance for the positive
development of culture. Many of the important insights about language
upon which this study draws have been achieved by members of the
idealist tradition; e.g., von Humbolt, Cassirer, and Urban. However,
to concur with the insight embodied in what we have termed the high
evaluation of language does not limit one to an idealistic conception
of reality. The most crucial assertion is that language provides an
adequate access to reality. This evaluation spans a wide variety of historical philosophical viewpoints, as Urban himself has indicated. Among
contemporary philosophers of religion, Jerry H. Gill who develops a
functional theory of language indebted to the insights of Ludwig Wittgenstein and J.L. Austin asserts one of his underlying convictions :

> ... the best way to obtain an understanding of the major features of reality and
> experience is to pay close attention to the function and structure of language. ...
> It is my contention that the structure of reality is mediated through experience,
> and that experience itself is mediated through language. Thus the main character-
> istics of both reality and experience are reflected in the various uses and functions
> of language.[3]

[1] Urban, *Language and Reality*, Chap. I, *passim*.
[2] *Ibid.*, p. 24.
[3] Gill, *The Possibility of Religious Knowledge*, pp. 91-92.

Another philosophical perspective is represented in John E. Smith who in his 1971 Presidential Address to the Metaphysical Society of America argues that articulation is integral to Being. "In short if we are determined in our thought by a faithfulness to all that we encounter, embracing man-in-the-world and the world-brought-to-explicit-intelligibility in the language situation, we must conclude that articulation belongs essentially to that complex".[1] This high evaluation would in essence also encompass the thought of Martin Heidegger, particularly in his later writing, who was called into question the metaphysical tradition of the West from Plato on.

It has probably been evident from my remarks so far that I wish to firmly align myself with a high evaluation of language. The central assertion that language is a fit instrument for apprehending and communicating reality must be affirmed. Language and words do not belong entirely to the realm of subjective "opinion" and convention or to natural process, but rather, as Urban maintains, there subsists a deeper connection between the realm of words and the realm of being.[2] However, this study will contend that there are in fact different dimensions of human language and that all human articulation does not function continually or directly to provide access to reality.[3] Language, however, has this capacity within a particular dimension when it is functioning in an "authentic" way. One of the tasks of the following investigation will be to present a proposal which will sketch out and distinguish these dimensions. But it is a particular dimension of language, the dimension of the symbolic, which accounts finally for the "validity of the word" and justifies this evaluation.

Urban has demonstrated the perennial nature and central significance of this presupposition about the nature of language. He has associated

---

[1] John E. Smith, "Being, Immediacy, and Articulation", *The Review of Metaphysics*, Vol. xxiv, No. 4 (June 1971), pp. 604-605. It should be noted that Smith's use of "articulation" is comparable to my definition of "language" in Chap. I. He also criticizes what he calls idealist tendencies to identify Being and articulation so that language *is* the whole of reality.

[2] Urban, *Language and Reality*, p. 37.

[3] It is the proposed dimensional understanding of the nature of human language which allows us to balance the claims for the power and adequacy of language as an access to reality, exemplified in the later Heidegger and the "New Hermeneutic", with the claim for clarity and verifiability in language usage as urged by the "Linguistic Analysis" philosophers. Both claims are legitimate and can be reasonably accounted for on the basis of different dimensions of language and their distinctive natures and functions.

his own view with the high evaluation of language in regard to the basic issue of whether language can be an authentic means of access to reality. In my agreement with Urban, I would take support from his claim for the general dominance of the high evaluation in the history of philosohy in the West. However, I would wish to assert a more radical position on this than does Urban. In my view, language is not just an access to reality but the primary access to reality. It seems to me that in our generation we have had a tendency to underestimate human language in regard to this capacity. We have allowed ourselves to be convinced that language by its nature and function is primarily intended and equipped to talk about the physical world of chairs, trees, and cows. We imply and often state that it is only by "stretching" or "distorting" ordinary language that it can be made fit to talk about the non-physical world, about the spiritual about reality itself. However, it may be that just the opposite is the case. The real power of language and therefore the distinctive characteristic of its nature is exactly the capacity to talk about and provide insight concerning the qualities, experiences, and realities that are non-sensuous. This includes references to love, freedom, Being, and God. Perhaps our talk about ordinary sensuous objects is in fact suitable, but only a secondary use of language. We have established the norm for language at exactly the wrong end of the spectrum or dimensional scale; namely, with the familiar and observable rather than with the significant. In so doing, there has been a forgetfulness of the power and adequacy of language manifested in a particular dimension that constitutes the access to reality.[1] Perhaps only in a foundational dimension of language does man reach his full potential as a human being. Only in the "authentic" use of language does man manifest his authentic existence by demonstrating his radical openness to Being. Just as language itself is the distinguishing mark of man's humanity, thus only this proper use of this language allows his human existence to come to fulfillment. We must examine then the power of language as an instrument of access to reality. In developing this theme I wish to turn to a modern philosopher who has devoted much of his attention to the problem of language and who has been the principal source of my own recognition of this situation. The man

---

[1] Paul Ricœur emphasized this power of a particular level of language in a lecture at Union Theological Seminary in the Fall of 1966 entitled "The Word and the Words —the Levels of Significance in Language and the Relation to Biblical Theology". Ricœur affirmed the transcendent aspect of language which makes it a medium that directs us to reality.

who has made the theme of his own later work "mediation upon language", and who, although he stands in a different philosophical tradition than Urban, asserts with unrestrained enthusiasm his own particular "high evaluation of language". This is, of course, Martin Heidegger.

Language and Being

"Language is the house of Being".[1] This famous and intriguing phrase of Heidegger's found in the letter "Über den Humanismus" indicates why his work has become the focus of concern in recent years for many who are seeking a clue to the nature of language, particularly those who are attempting to reevaluate the relationship of language to the rest of human experience and especially to what we have given the general name reality itself. Heidegger is, however, more of an inspirational prophet than a systematic guide. His statements about language are often terse and difficult to understand, his terminology appears to be in perpetual development, and there is the additional problem of the relation between the so-called "earlier" and "later" Heidegger.[2] Yet in all this there is an excitement and persuasive force about his reflections on language which lead one to suspect that contained here are valuable

[1] "... Die Sprache ist das Haus des Seins ...". Cited from Martin Heidegger, *Platons Lehre von der Wahrheit. Mit einem Brief über den "Humanismus"* (Bern : Francke, 1947), p. 53. The *Brief über den "Humanismus"* comprises pp. 53-119 and will be hereafter cited as *Brief ... Humanismus.* Another edition of the "letter" alone is Frankfurt : Klostermann, 1949.

[2] This *Kehre* [variously translated as "turning" (Macquarrie), "reversal" (Richardson), and "conversion" (Veresny)] in Heidegger's thought has been the focus of much debate among students of Heidegger's work. John Macquarrie in an article "Heidegger's Earlier and Later Work Compared" in the *Anglican Theological Review* (January 1967) describes briefly some of these divergent positions (as indicated above in the different translations of *Kehre*), and gives five points of difference between the earlier and later Heidegger. Macquarrie asserts his preference for seeing the "unity" of the thought of the earlier and later Heidegger. "We must keep the two sides of his philosophy together in a dialectical tension, for neither the earlier nor the later thought can stand in isolation" (p. 15). This position is supported by Heidegger's own comments in a letter to Father W. J. Richardson contained in the preface (xxii-xxiii) to Richardson's book, *Heidegger : Through Phenomenology to Thought* (The Hague : Martinus Nijhoff, 1963). I would agree with the judgment of Macquarrie, but for the purposes of this study the emphasis has been on the later Heidegger because it is here that he developed most clearly his concern for language as the "house of Being" and the stress on foundational or essential thinking. However, I would see these later writings not as superseding but rather as supplementing and completing the existential analysis of language in *Sein und Zeit.*

and illuminating insights about the nature of language. My brief comments fail to do justice to the complexity of Heidegger's thought, but the intent of this abbreviated view of Heidegger's notion of language is to highlight some of his highly suggestive discernments and thus allow him to be an inspirational prophet for us in his own particular "high evaluation" of language.

It has been Heidegger's unwavering quest from the beginning of his philosophical labors to discover the sense or meaning of Being[1] and its truth.[2] This quest has resulted in the intensive scrutiny of "human thought" insofar as it is necessary to "think the Being Process" and a stress upon a special dimension of thinking called "foundational thought" (*das wesentliche Denken*). However, the primary means of thinking Being is to question the meaning of Being. This method of questioning Being resolves itself, particularly in the later Heidegger, in the analysis of language. For it is language — and I would wish to assert language in a particular dimension—which provides man with his special access to Being.[3] Thus the later Heidegger is especially concerned with what we may describe as the relationship between language and Being.

[1] Heinrich Ott, an important interpreter of Heidegger for the theological discipline, has asserted that the term "Being" seldom occurs in the later Heidegger. Ott contends that Heidegger has a concern for a reality that is beyond or deeper than Being and that "the theme of language as history's room, the theme of thinking as historic hermeneutic, is broader than the theme of Being". ("What Is Systematic Theology?" *The Later Heidegger and Theology*, J. M. Robinson and J. B. Cobb, Jr. (eds.) (New-York : Harper & Row, 1963), p. 208). It remains to be seen whether "Being" is in fact surpassed or whether the word "Being" simply tends to be identified with other terms such as "Logos". This issue of whether the notion of "Being" can be successfully by-passed in theology is, I think, still very much open to question. I tend to think that Being cannot and should not be by-passed, because it provides a basis for genuine and universal claims of meaning and truth in theology.

[2] W. J. Richardson, *Heidegger : Through Phenomenology to Thought*, p. 24. I am indebted to Richardson in two ways. First, his investigation of the meaning of "thought" in Heidegger happens to parallel and often overlaps my own concern for "language". He often functions as a guide through the very large and complex corpus of Heidegger's work. Second, I had sought a consistent translator for some of Heidegger's key terms and phrases, such as *das wesentliche Denken*, which is variously rendered by different authors as "essential", "primordial", or "foundational" thinking, depending on the context and translator. Due to the wide range of Richardson's translation of Heidegger, he serves best as the single translator of those passages dealt with in this study. He provides a type of consistency that would be lacking in the use of multiple translators. Thus, unless otherwise noted, Richardson will be the English translator of quoted Heideggerian words and phrases employed in this chapter.

[3] Richardson, *Heidegger* ..., p. 397. "Now how does man fundamentally have access to Being? Here Heidegger speaks for himself : by language".

However, even to get a toehold on our problem we must indicate what Heidegger might mean by Being. It is not possible to define Being in an absolute way, precisely because Being reveals itself historically. But it is perhaps possible to give, as we have previously, a provisional definition. Heidegger understands Being to be the "lighting-up-process" by which beings are illuminated as beings.[1] The closest thing we can point to as a definition came in the letter concerning humanism in 1947, where Heidegger states :

> Being, indeed—what is being? ... Being—it is not God, nor [some] ground of the world. Being is broader than all beings—and yet is nearer to man than all beings. ... Being is what is nearest [to man]. Yet [this] nearness remains farthest removed from him. ...[2]

Being ought to be understood not as an entity but something more akin to a process and thus commentators, including myself, sometimes use phrases such as the "Being-process" or the "lighting-up-process".

Being is, of course, a notoriously difficult concept to define. Yet, there are some striking parallels between Heidegger's understanding and that of other philosophers who are also concerned with the relationship between language and Being. For example John E. Smith in his attempts to interpret the meaning of Being and to find a predicate for Being which is less inadequate than others and which provides a fruitful basis for further analysis concentrates on the notion of "process" and the predicate of "power". As Smith asserts, "the process view does not entail the severe restrictions that go with the setting apart of knowing as a privileged context within which to characterize Being".[3] Smith declares that "Being is Power", and he interprets this in terms of three correlative concepts: insistence, persistence, and expression. "That is to say, it belongs to the nature of power to insist or assert itself and thus to exclude both the indeterminate nothingness and the determinate other; to persist or extend itself beyond compression into an instant; and finally to express

[1] Richardson, *Heidegger* ..., p. 6.

[2] Heidegger, *Brief,* ... *Humanismus*, p. 76. "Doch das Sein—was ist das Sein? ... Das 'Sein'—das ist nicht Gott und nicht ein Weltgrund. Das Sein ist weiter denn alles Seiende und ist gleichwohl dem Menschen näher als jedes Seiende. ... Das Sein ist das Nächste. Doch die Nähe bleibt dem Menschen am weitesten ...". It may be that Heidegger's specific denial of the identity of Being and God may depend on the idea of God that Heidegger understands to be normative in the tradition of Western Christianity. Another conception of God may mean that Being and God are much more closely related than is recognized by Heidegger.

[3] Smith, "Being, Immediacy, and Articulation", p. 596.

itself in manifold modes of relationship with others which serve as the basis of intelligibility".[1] It is the focus on Being's expression and relation to others, a concern Smith and Heidegger share, which propells one toward the problem of articulation or language.

According to Heidegger Being reveals itself within and to the beings. Being ought not to be understood as "a being", but rather as that power or that process which makes man what he is, which simply "lets him be".[2] It is that which is the nearest to man by virtue of the fact that it not only lets him be, i.e., supplies the power of being, but it also enables him to enter into relationship with other beings and especially with other men. It is this nearness to man, this power to "let be", which allows me to identify Being for the purposes of this study with that which I have been describing prior to this in general terms as "reality itself". So as I proceed to analyze the role of thought and language as an access to Being, one may interpret this in terms of the sphere of the high evaluation of language—the fitness of language to serve as an access to reality itself.

Yet Being is also described as farthest from man. It is ironic that its distance is in fact a product of its nearness. Being appears to be hidden from man precisely because it is not "a being" and thus is not assimilable by man's ordinary structures of understanding. Just because it is the power that lets man be and thus is so intimately bound up with his existence, it can be overlooked or forgotten. So Being as the lighting-up-process not only reveals itself, but can be said in this very revealing process also to hide itself. W.J. Richardson calls this the "positivity" and "negativity" of Being and understands them to be complementary movements of a single force.[3] Having noted this process of affirmation and negation in Being's revealing of itself, I will give it further attention later. But I move now to an examination of the positivity. What is the sense or truth of Being and how is that made manifest?

Heidegger begins early to manifest his interest in language and to indulge in etymological studies. He constantly reminds us that the literal meaning of $\dot{a}$-$\lambda\eta\theta\epsilon\iota a$, truth, is "unhiddenness"[4] or "non-concealment"

---

[1] Smith, "Being, Immediacy, and Articulation", p. 596.

[2] The notion of "letting-be" or "to let be" has its source for me in the thought of John Macquarrie (see *Principles* ..., p. 99 and *passim*), but it has its roots in Heideggerian terminology.

[3] Richardson, *Heidegger* ..., pp. 8-9.

[4] Martin Heidegger, *Sein und Zeit*, 6th ed. (Tübingen : Niemeyer, 1949), p. 33, n. 1, pp. 219ff. See English translation by J. Macquarrie and E. Robinson, *Being and Time* (New York : Harper & Row, 1962), p. 57, n. 1. pp. 261ff.

(*Unverborgenheit*). The truth of Being is in fact its non-concealment. Being's revealing of itself, its non-concealment, in both its positive and negative aspects, is that which enables the beings to become non-concealed.[1] Being constitutes this power of letting-be which enables man to be what he is. It is the revealing of Being and man's capacity to receive that revelation that allows man to move in the direction of authentic existence.

Now we must ask where this non-concealment, this lighting-up-process takes place. According to Heidegger, it takes place in "Dasein", in "Therebeing", in man himself. The relationship between Being and *Dasein*, between Being and man, is exceedingly complex and will not detain us here except to say that the relationship is characterized by what was initially described as an "ontological difference"[2] between Being and *Dasein* and what is described in the later Heidegger simply as "the difference".[3] Thus we must operate in terms of the relationship or correlation between these two distinct realms, Being and *Dasein*. Being discloses itself *to* and *in* man. According to the later Heidegger, Being certainly holds the primacy, but in order for Being to reveal itself, in order for non-concealment of Being to occur, *Dasein* (man) is necessary. Man is understood as being characterized primarily by his relationship, his openness to Being; man is an "ek-sistence". So Being needs its There (man) in order to be itself, just as man needs the revealing of Being in order to reach his own fulfillment. This is a mutual relationship, but one in which Being always maintains the primacy.

The place in which Being discloses itself is man. Now we must inquire about the method or means of Being's disclosure. The answer to the relationship between Being and man, lies in the analysis of thought.[4] The answer to the meaning or truth of Being lies in the attempt to "think Being". It must be stated immediately that what Heidegger has in mind here is a special kind of thought process, "*das wesentliche Denken*". It is a special type of thought that transcends the subject-object polarity in order to think Being. This "foundational thought", rather than dominating Being with its own objectifying structures, simply lets

---

[1] Richardson, *Heidegger* ..., p. 9.

[2] Martin Heidegger, *Vom Wesen des Grundes*, 3rd ed. (Frankfurt : Klostermann, 1949), p. 15.

[3] Heidegger, *Unterwegs zur Sprache* (Pfullingen : Neske, 1959), p. 24.

[4] Much of the discussion concerning "thought" is indebted to the thesis of Richardson as developed in the introduction to his book and thus will not be footnoted in every detail.

things be. This type of thought is the fulfillment of the relationship between Being and man. Foundational thought tries to meditate on Being as the process of non-concealment. Being maintains its primacy and thus this type of thought is called upon to acquiesce to Being. Being can be understood as sending itself into *Dasein* as a "mittence" (*Geschick*), in fact in the form of a plurality of "mittences" or "intermittence" (*Ge-schick-te*) which constitutes a history.[1] So foundational thought must think Being-as-History. Thus the relationship between Being and *Dasein* has also a gift-like character about it. The disclosure of Being is a revelation that operates according to the primacy of Being but not without the existence of foundational thought, and finally, not even without the language of man. It is required of foundational thought that it be "docile" to or attend to Being; namely, that it responds to the "mittence" of Being by letting Being be itself. Docility means the proper response on the part of foundational thought to the primacy of Being, of reality itself. But this response, this "attending to Being", is possible only because the nature of man is constituted by his radical openness to Being. Man has a privileged access to Being that is the basis of his unique mark of humanity. A neglect of foundational thought involves for Heidegger the neglect or even forgetfulness of authentic thought itself. He recognizes other forms of thought, particularly "calculative" or "presentative" thought as it is associated with logic, but these appear not to be considered really "authentic".

It is my contention that what is clearly implied here, if not explicitly worked out, is the need to distinguish between various dimensions of human thought. There is for Heidegger at least one particular dimension, foundational thought, which can make claim to a specific access to Being, to reality itself. This dimension of thought has a special relationship to its object —one might almost say a participation in it—which gives it the power to make that object, through an awareness of it, manifest. This occurs only insofar as thought is docile or attends to Being's disclosure, one might say, to Being's self-revelation. There is for Heidegger, as we have noted, another form of thought which does not function in this way. What is more significant for our concern is what is missing here : an attempt to clarify and distinguish the particular levels of thought and to indicate their relationship to one another. To call one dimension of thought authentic ought not to impugn the other dimensions, as I

---

[1] Richardson, *Heidegger* ..., pp. 20-21. The terms "mittence" and "intermittence" are formulated by Richardson.

think it does in Heidegger, but ought to be a means of distinguishing its unique function and perhaps the priority of that function. This name should not imply that all other levels are somehow inauthentic and therefore unnecessary. We should be reminded also of the finitude of man's response and of the positive and negative aspect even of this special dimension of foundational thought. Being not only reveals itself but also hides itself in this lighting-up-process.

Now what does all this have to do with language? The primary means of thinking Being is the analysis of language, and thus the particular concentration of the later Heidegger concerns a meditation on language, as is evidenced in *Unterwegs zur Sprache*. To question the meaning of Being via foundational thought is integrally bound up with the origin and nature of language itself. To interrogate Being, i.e., to question the meaning of Being, results in an attempt "to bring Being into word".[1] The conclusion is that man's primary access to Being is by language. It is not by thought alone that Being is disclosed, but rather it is "through thought that Being comes to language".[2] Being is always on the way to language. This leads to some quite extraordinary claims about the origin and nature of language.

First, Heidegger affirms that the primacy in language, at least in authentic language, lies not with *Dasein* (man) but rather with Being. For it is in the naming process, in the rise of language, that Being is formed into a word.[3] It is even suggested that if Being had no meaning and if man had no way of comprehending this meaning, there would be no language at all, and certainly no authentic language. In *Sein und Zeit* Heidegger talks about the relationship of man's capacity for speech and the $\Lambda \acute{o} \gamma o \varsigma$.[4] In the later Heidegger, Logos gets defined as aboriginal utterance and Logos tends to be identified with Being.[5] Thus Logos

---

[1] Martin Heidegger, *Einführung in die Metaphysik* (Tübingen : Niemeyer, 1953), p. 100.

[2] Heidegger, *Brief ... Humanismus*, p. 53. "... dass im Denken das Sein zur Sprache kommt ...".

[3] Heidegger, *Einführung in die Metaphysik*, p. 131.

[4] Heidegger, *Sein und Zeit*, pp. 32ff.

[5] Cf. Macquarrie, *God-Talk*, p. 166. "But in his later work, Heidegger comes near to identifying Being and language, and many of the things he earlier said about Being now get said about language". However, Logos or aboriginal utterance is not to be simply equated with human articulation. Therefore, I do not think this move in the later writings leads to the conclusion that Being and language are identical. Being is a process, but also a power that comes to word. Being discloses itself in and to man via language. Authentic language allows Being to be revealed in its truth

(Being) in its disclosure is a coming-into-the-open so far as it comes into language. The question is : why does one not recognize that language has its origin in Being? The reason for this can be attributed to the finitude of language; the power of Being's primacy in language is concealed in its very disclosure in *Dasein*. This finitude will make language appear to be at the disposition of man when actually the opposite is true. Man seems to have invented language and employed it with a kind of arbitrary autonomy, when the fact is that man has discovered himself only in and through language insofar as Being comes to word.[1] Being maintains its primacy in language.Every man has the capacity for authentic language and thus the possibility of developing this privileged access to Being. However, there are some men, according to Heidegger, who are endowed with a special gift for language; e.g., the poets[2] and the thinkers.

But, looking first at every man's capacity, we must ask how Being can come to word, how can the relationship between Being and man be fulfilled within language. In regard to man's role in this disclosure of Being, the emphasis is first not on speaking but rather on listening, not on speech but on silence. The claim is made that man can speak authentically only when he has first been addressed.[3] This means that there must be some way in which the speech of everyday living can come to the truth that is proper to it. This means that man in his use of language must first be silent and listen for the authentic utterance of Being. Man must "attend" to Logos (Being) as the aboriginal utterance, in much the same way it was necessary for foundational thought to attend to Being. Heidegger distinguishes between "mere listening" (*blossen Hören*) and real "attending" (*Hören*).[4] Real attending means that language must be docile to Logos. There must be a prior attending to Being and a disclosure on the part of Being before our words may be authentic. Thus, talking and listening must be oriented toward the Logos, because it is in this docility toward Logos that authentic language is grounded. All human language is, of course, affected by finitude and thus is fragmen-

---

and therefore allows beings to be manifest for what they are. Being is disclosed in language so that Being's self-disclosure and language are inseparable, but Being and human language are not identical.

[1] Richardson, *Heidegger* ..., p. 293.

[2] Martin Heidegger, *Holzwege* (Frankfurt : Klostermann, 1950), p. 274.

[3] Cf. Macquarrie, *God-Talk*, p. 163.

[4] Heidegger, *Einführung in die Metaphysik*, pp. 99ff. *Hören* could be translated in the second phrase as "listening". However, translating it as "attending" makes the contrast with "mere listening" more evident.

tary and only partially achieves an authentic status. The standard for this docility to language and thus the authentic use of the word rests, according to Heidegger, with the masters of the word—poets and thinkers.[1] It seems to me that one need not make the range of the authentic use of language as exclusive as Heidegger does, and that it may stretch farther into the capacity of every man than Heidegger seems willing to allow. But the significant point for our investigation is the indication by Heidegger of a special dimension of human language by which man has a special access to Being, to reality itself. This special dimension of language is characterized by a power of transmission and by a pointing beyond itself to a docility toward Being that allows Being to manifest itself, even if only in a concealed way, within human language itself. Heidegger does not refer to dimensions of thought and language, but I think his insights can bear that development.

How is man then specifically related to this language which is a product of his attendance in thought and speech to Being? Heidegger wants to break through an interpretation of man centered on the essence-existence dichotomy. "He interprets man purely out of his relationship to Being —as transcendence, as ek-sistence".[2] A crucial factor in this interpretation of the nature of man is "language". Language provides that access to Being and thus it is language which is unique and characteristic of man. As Heidegger notes, even man's body is different because it is geared toward that which is unique in him, the uttering of language.[3]

Man uses language, then, not merely as an instrument of communication, although it may be that as well; but the central thrust of authentic language is "to bring beings as such for the first time into the open ...".[4] Language allows beings to be manifest as what they are. Only via language does man come to fulfillment. For if the utterance is authentic, it projects a light. The lighting-up-process, the non-concealment of Being, takes place in language. Being must be conceived as aboriginal Logos, so "language is the house of Being".[5] This famous phrase appears to mean that Being somehow dwells in words, in human discourse. We have noted that the primacy of Being as emphasized in the later Heidegger dominates all beings. However, Being is so near to man that this domination is

---

[1] Heidegger, *Einführung in die Metaphysik*, pp. 131, 141.

[2] Richardson, *Heidegger ...*, p. 390.

[3] *Ibid.*, pp. 389-390.

[4] Heidegger, *Holzwege*, p. 60. "... die Sprache bringt das Seiende als ein Seiendes allererst ins Offene ...".

[5] Heidegger, *Brief ... Humanismus*, p. 53.

not evident. Man may and usually does simply forget or ignore the presence and nearness of Being. However, it is precisely in language and by language that this nearness is manifest. Language may be described as the "house of Being" because "language is the illuminating-concealing arrival of Being itself".[1] Heidegger's philosophy gives to language a fundamental role in the coming to fulfillment of man himself. But this language is not simply an instrument at man's disposal. "Hence language is an event that has Being as its ultimate origin, a house that is arranged according to a pattern inscribed as Being and prescribed by it. ... 'Being is always underway toward [language] ...' ".[2] Being is to be understood as Logos. Therefore one cannot think Being without doing so in language, thus bringing Being into word. This results in the conclusion : "the thinking of Being must go the way of language".[3]

If language is the house of Being, then it follows that man, according to his nature as a linguistic being, one with the capacity for language, must "be a lodger in this house".[4] Man can be seen insofar as he is docile to Being and thus seeks after authentic language to be the guardian of Being in its truth, or the shepherd of Being. But the primacy of Being in thought or in language is not to be forgotten. So it is not the task of the lodger to fabricate the house, but rather to bring it to completion.[5] It will be the task of this study to carry this suggestion farther through an attempt to clarify the respective roles of Being and man in fashioning human language. Thus foundational thought plays a crucial role in supplying the words and sentences, the articulation, for Being's self-disclosure, while "Being diffuses its light on and through these words".[6] It may be as Heidegger suggests, that if man is going to restore to language its authentic status and recover again some of the potential power of language, then this may mean remaining silent and speaking seldom in order to combat the idle talkativeness of normal discourse. Heidegger's emphasis on the authentic nature of language concludes that, if language seems banal today, this is a result of the fact that the relationship between Being and man is not adequately understood and brought to completion.[7]

---

[1] Heidegger, *Brief ... Humanismus*, p. 70. "... Sprache ist lichtend-verbergende Ankunft des Seins selbst".

[2] Richardson, *Heidegger* ..., p. 535. Included quote is from *Brief ... Humanismus*, p. 79. "... Es ist stats unterwegs zu ihr ...".

[3] *Ibid.*

[4] *Ibid.*, p. 540.

[5] *Ibid.*, p. 543.

[6] *Ibid.*, p. 541.

[7] *Ibid.*, p. 541.

How are we to differentiate between "authentic" language and that which we call banal or which has succumbed to the lure of "everyday-ness"? Authentic language, as well as foundational thought, is considered by Heidegger to be a response to Being. We are told in a lecture on language, now included in *Unterwegs zur Sprache*, that human language is man's hailing response to the original hail of Logos (Being) in aboriginal language, "utterance".[1] It is man that is summoned by aboriginal language. It is this primal action of Being in its self-disclosure which makes authentic human language possible. But man comes to realize this only at the end and usually attributes to human language a "low evaluation" that sees language as an instrument of communication fully at his disposal. "Authenticity in the use of language is achieved in the moment of man's free response to the hail [of Being] addressed to him...".[2] Man's task is to respond to the hail of Being in his use of thought and language. This becomes possible as a result of man attending to Being, his docility toward Logos. But this docility should not be equated with passivity. Man first listens. He attempts to attend to Being, but he must also respond. He not only listens, but he also speaks. He is acquiescent, but he also questions. The later Heidegger moved in the direction of the primacy of Being over the beings and in his view of hermeneutics from questioning to listening. But the earlier position was never abandoned in favor of a totally passive stance. So "advancing with reticence characterizes the manner in which mortal man responds to [the hail of $\Lambda \acute{o} \gamma o \varsigma$ as] Scission. In this fashion mortal man dwells authentically in aboriginal Language".[3] It is also necessary to take cognizance of the fact that authentic language takes place only insofar as man achieves his own authenticity, only insofar as the relationship between Being and man is brought to fruition by man's attending to Being and thus comprehending its self-disclosure.

What is meant, then, by banal or inauthentic language? Heidegger asserts that man is very susceptible to the lure of everydayness in language. This means the use of words as merely "conventional signs" or "sounds filled with meaning to be used as the instruments of daily living ...".[4] In what I would describe as the "low evaluation" of language, man misses the presence and dominance of Being. In so doing man is led away from

---

[1] Heidegger, *Unterwegs zur Sprache*, p. 30.

[2] Richardson, *Heidegger ...*, p. 580.

[3] Heidegger, *Unterwegs zur Sprache*, p. 32. "Das Zuvorkommen in der Zurückhalt-ung bestimmt die Wiese, nach der die Sterblichen dem Unterschied entsprechen. Auf diese Weise wohnen die Sterblichen im Sprechen der Sprache".

[4] Richardson, *Heidegger ...*, p. 610.

what Heidegger describes as authentic language. Banal language is inauthentic precisely because it focuses merely on the signal character or contextual meaning of human language and thus on its use primarily as an instrument of communication. Banal language ignores and obscures "the essence of language [which] is Being's self-expression to us in language".[1] It fails to realize that "language is the house of Being".

Despite Heidegger's major contribution in regard to the analysis of language—his high evaluation of language as the means by which Being discloses itself and thus man is provided with an access to Being—the question must be raised whether he is not both too demanding and too exclusive in his interpretation of what constitutes authentic language. The implication appears to be that there are only two modes of language, authentic and banal or inauthentic. Heidegger implies that the goal of all language is to be authentic. But the issue is whether all human language, at all times, either can or ought to be "authentic" in Heidegger's sense of the term. Is it really conceivable that all modes of human language can have as their intent this docility to Logos which allows for the self-disclosure of Being? Would it not be more comprehensible and more feasible to distinguish dimensions of human language? One particular dimension, the symbolic, should be recognized as having the capacity and responsibility to embody Being's self-expression to us. In this dimension and through the power of foundational thought, language can become the "illuminating-concealing arrival of Being itself". But does it not obscure the disclosure, the revelation, of Being if all language operates in the same dimension or on an equalitarian level? For example, the poet and thinker (philosopher) do not speak "as a poet" or "as a thinker" in all instances of expression. There must be other dimensions of language to interpret the original disclosure, and these other dimensions of language are not necessarily "inauthentic" in the sense of being unnecessary; they simply have other functions. It may be that one work or one section of a work by a poet or thinker may be more capable of providing an access to Being, and thus be more "authentic" than another. It does not make the other works or parts of the work unnecessary, since they may provide the required introduction or the indispensable interpretation or unpacking of the crucial section.

Sometimes words are used as "conventional signs" or as mere instruments of communication without a transcendent dimension even by the poet and thinker. The significant point is to recognize that language

[1] Macquarrie, *God-Talk*, p. 166.

has this capacity to disclose Being and thus to restore to words part of their precious and even mysterious quality. But it is both unrealistic and tends to obscure Heidegger's essential insight concerning the power of language to demand that all human language function in this dimension or else be classified as banal. "Authentic" may be considered too demanding a term to be applied to a particular dimension of language unless one realizes that it indicates an evaluation of a special function of language which today is often ignored or denied. Banal is certainly too derogatory to be applied to all other dimensions of language. The attempt to distinguish between these various dimensions is a task that still lies before us.

I have suggested that Heidegger's scheme is not only too demanding in its analysis of "authentic language" but also too exclusive. This raises the question as to whether it is appropriate to restrict the exclusive use of authentic language to the thinkers and the poets or even to imply this kind of restriction.[1] It may be the case that some poets and thinkers have a special gift for language which allows them the propensity for attending to Being and thus achieving authentic language more frequently than other men. In this sense they may be guides or standards for the employment of the power of human language and thus we can see them as "guardians" of the house of Being. Yet if we claim that all men have the capacity for authentic language, and that in some measure man's fulfillment as *Dasein* (man) depends on his response to the hail of Being in thought and language, then it appears to me too exclusive to restrict this to poets, thinkers, and conceivably a few others. Rather, it seems necessary to recognize not only the capacity of all men for this unique dimension of language but even their fragmentary fulfillment of this capacity, even when they are not explicitly conscious of having done so on the basis of their prior docility to Being. For even some of the philosophers and poets included in Heidegger's study were evidently not explicitly aware of their attendance to Being.

---

[1] The question is raised in Richardson's conclusion as to how we can differentiate between the poet and the thinker (p. 635), or who it is that really thinks : individual man, all men, humanity, or essence of man (p. 634). This critique points to the fact that further clarification is needed in regard to who actually participates in foundational thinking or utters "authentic" language.

Summary

How, then, can we summarize Heidegger's role in this investigation as an inspirational prophet concerning the nature and function of language? First, Heidegger has developed a "high evaluation" of language which understands human language to provide man with the access to Being, to reality itself. Second, Heidegger maintains the primacy of Being over man in the origin and development of human language, especially in regard to the authentic dimension of language. Thus man most be addressed before he can speak; he must attend to, be docile toward Logos (Being). Third, Heidegger asserts that language is characteristic of man; it is that about him which is unique and defines his nature by allowing him to be open to Being. Fourth, there are positive and negative aspects to human language which must be taken into consideration. The positive aspect is a result of Being's self-disclosure, the negative aspect a result of language's finitude. Fifth, there is an inseparable bond between thought and language because it is through thought that Being comes to language. Sixth, it appears to be not only warranted but necessary to speak of dimensions of thought and of language in order that sufficient significance can be attributed to "foundational thought" and "authentic language" as contrasted with other dimensions of these human capacities. Heidegger's claim that language is the house of Being appears to be not only justifiable but also exciting and illuminating. What is required now is a more specific explication of the dimensions of human thought and language in order that the implications of this insight might become more intelligible.

It is necessary now to turn to our provisional definition of language within the context of this high evaluation of language and see what is meant by saying that language is the "bearer of meaning" and "a medium of communication".

CHAPTER THREE

LANGUAGE AS THE BEARER OF MEANING
AND A MEDIUM OF COMMUNICATION

Language is the distinctive and characteristic feature of man. Language has the power to provide man with his unique access to reality. Yet this access should be made intelligible, and the demand for intelligibility requires an examination of the nature of language in more detail in order to understand how this characteristic instrument of man functions and on what basis it can be described as a "bearer of meaning" and a "medium of communication".

Language as a Bearer of Meaning

The ground for this stress on language as the bearer of meaning is the conviction that the essence of language is found in meaning. Cassirer describes this thesis as the principle of *Primat des Sinnes*. The consequence of this affirmation means that in the study of the philosophy of language, and this appears also to be true for modern linguistics, one is not concerned with the sound or with the motor processes and tactual sensations that account for sound.[1] But rather, these sounds, motor processes, and tactual sensations are significant only insofar as they are the bearers of what language really is; namely, meaning. Language is a kind of "*Urphenomen*, neither reducible to or explainable in terms of non-linguistic fact".[2] This results in the denial of the adequacy of physical, physiological, or even psychological approaches to language. Language should be studied with a view toward its unique structure and function. Language cannot adequately be comprehended when it is understood as an element of nature or a highly developed form of animal cries. Human language is understood as being not reducible to any form of pre-human behavior, but rather, it can be summarized as "non-instinctive, voluntary ... human activity".[3] This view of language has rather firmly

---

[1] Urban, *Language and Reality*, p. 63.

[2] *Ibid.*, p. 62.

[3] Urban, *Language and Reality*, pp. 92-93. This remark is to distinguish language from pre-human behavior, but does not have reference to its relationship to Being.

fixed itself within modern linguistic science. Historical perspective in support of this thesis is supplied by Cassirer when he traces a movement in regard to language from *Geist* to *Natur*, illustrated in the movement from Hegel and Von Humbolt to Darwin. Yet this has now been retraced to an emphasis not on Nature but on Spirit. So language is seen today not so much as a part of nature but rather as an embodiment of Spirit. It is not simply a mechanical development but a creative activity of the human mind.[1] So I would wish to reject, as do Urban and Heidegger, the positivistic and naturalistic interpretations of language in favor of a view consistent with a high evaluation of language which proclaims "the primacy of meaning".[2]

However, this emphasis on the primacy of meaning should not suggest a return to a "picture theory of meaning" as developed by Bertrand Russell and the early Wittgenstein.[3] Their theories focused on a definitive meaning for propositions which demanded empirical verification for assertions of meaningfulness and truth. It is now generally accepted among philosophers of language that there are multi meanings and uses for language that defy the kind of categorization demanded by the picture theory of meaning. Therefore "meaning" is qualified by "use". The context of language points toward a location for a specific meaning along a continuum of meaning functions. As the later Wittgenstein declared after having rejected his own early position, "One cannot guess how a word functions. One has to look at its use and learn from that".[4] A crucial element in the meaning of a word or sentence is an awareness of its context and use.

In a previous discussion of sign, symbol, and signal I indicated that a verbal sign in its widest sense was a "vehicle or concentrate of meaning". Now I must turn to a more specific analysis of linguistic meaning. It seems to me that Urban is essentially correct when he focuses on the relationship between the verbal sign and the thing signified as the central source of the notion of meaning. "The essence of language is the repre-

---

[1] Urban, *Language and Reality*, pp. 93-94.

[2] The concern here is to reject specifically the implied metaphysics of positivism and naturalism in reference to the relation of language and reality. The contribution of the positivist in the area of logic has made a significant contribution to the analysis of language, and the value of this logical technique is not disparaged here.

[3] Bertrand Russell in "Philosophy of Logical Atomism", *The Monist*, V (Oct. 1918-July 1919) and Ludwig Wittgenstein in *Tractatus Logico-Philosophicus*, trans. Pears and McGuinness (London : Routledge, 1961).

[4] Ludwig Wittgenstein, *Philosophical Investigations*, p. 109.

sentation, *Darstellung*, of one element of experience through another—
the bi-polar relation between the sign or symbol and the thing signified
or symbolized, and the consciousness of that relation".[1] However, meaning is not solely a function of representation; it is also a function of use.
The relation between the sign and the thing signified may take on various
forms or different meaning functions. One of the tasks of clarifying
linguistic meaning is to identify and differentiate these various types
of meaning. The various forms that this relation between sign and thing
signified may assume are dependent on the nature of the verbal sign
itself and on the interpretation given to the verbal sign by either the
speaker or the hearer in the context of its use.

However, it becomes obvious, as soon as one introduces phrases
such as "the consciousness of that relation" or "the interpretation given
to the verbal sign", that one is involved with more than just the two
components of the speaker, who intends some meaning by the use of
the verbal sign(s), and the hearer, who interprets the verbal sign to
mean something. Words, if they are said to have meaning, must have
that meaning for someone and to someone. This brings me to another
important point made by Urban, that "language and linguistic meaning
exist only in the speech community. In other words, part of the notion
of meaning in the linguistic sense is communication and communicability".[2] It is not feasible to analyze the verbal sign in abstraction from
living speech, from the discourse situation. Rather, one must look on
meaning as that which comes into being, as an expressed and understood
relation between sign and thing signified within a given speech community
and in the sphere of a given universe of discourse. Meaning is not simply
something which first exists and may then be communicated. Rather,
linguistic meaning comes to maturity only by the act of communication.

In the discourse situation the human capacity for speech is consummated in articulation itself, the actual words and sentences. The verbal
signs, which are concentrates of meaning, are in the discourse situation
vehicles of expression which must be interpreted or understood. These
verbal signs are unpacked and given a functional meaning by being located in regard to a given speech community, a universe of discourse, and
a particular meaning function. It was previously noted that the discourse
situation is constituted by a triadic relationship between the thing
signified, the speaker, and the hearer. The verbal sign is the mediating
agent which makes the discourse situation possible. It is the complex

[1] Urban, *Language and Reality*, p. 66.
[2] *Ibid.*, p. 67.

nature of the relationship between these component parts that partially constitutes the notion of linguistic meaning. The emphasis I wish to make here is that the notion of meaning includes the idea of interpretation or understanding.[1] There is no self-evident, causal meaning of a verbal sign.[2] It comes to have maturity of meaning only when it embodies an intention; namely, when it expresses something, and when that expression is received and understood by another person.

Turning to the discourse situation, focus first on the speaker, who employs the verbal sign(s), who uses words and sentences to express something. There is intentionality involved in his use of a verbal sign. This verbal expression presupposes communication, either overt or latent.[3] The speaker intends that what he says will be, or at least is capable of being, understood by someone else. The intentionality in his expression will vary from speech occasion to speech occasion. He may wish to organize his verbal signs so as to describe a concrete situation, arouse a certain type of emotional response, convey intuitive insight, or perhaps do all three. However, the various meaning functions of his language can be analyzed and distinguished. So in regard to the bi-polar relation between sign and thing signified, the speaker attempts to structure that relationship by the use of his language so as to bring his intentionality to expression. (The speaker cannot always bring his intention to complete expression in the discourse situation. This is due to the nature of the verbal sign itself and its inability to perfectly fulfill the linguistic function). Therefore, one element in the discourse situation which determines the meaning function is that of *expression*, which is conditioned by the intentionality of the speaker.

The second component in the discourse situation which reacts to the bi-polar relationship between sign and the thing signified is the hearer. It may be a person, a group of people, or even a reader if the language is in written form. What the hearer in the triadic discourse situation must do if linguistic meaning is to come to fruition is to "understand" or "interpret" what is stated. To understand in the linguistic sense means first to apprehend the meaning of words as expressive verbal signs.[4]

---

[1] Urban, *Language and Reality*, p. 107.

[2] This requires some qualification which will be considered later in this section, because there is a sense in which a sort of meaning is given in the self-disclosure of Being. But linguistic meaning in the full sense only comes to maturity in the discourse situation.

[3] Urban, *op. cit.*, p. 115.

[4] *Ibid.*, p. 120.

It is true, I think, to say with Urban that in the strict sense we do not understand things, but only expressions. Therefore, only language can be said to be understood. Of course, we talk about understanding things or events. But what we really mean is that we recognize things or understand an event insofar as it is an expression of meaning.[1]

I have been employing the term "verbal sign" so far in this section in a very general way. It has not been indicated whether we are referring to a verbal sign utilized as a "signal" or a "symbol" or some other form, nor has it been precisely noted whether we are referring to an individual verbal sign or to a collection of signs with a definite syntax. However, to attain maturity in linguistic meaning usually requires that we have a specific group of verbal signs with an intelligible structure; namely, a sentence or a situational context for a word or phrase which may only be implied.[2] It ought to be indicated that in careful usage we do not really understand individual words, but only sentences or terms in a situational context. Words can be recognized in the sense that we can know that to which they refer, but this is not really understanding.[3] Understanding involves the apprehension of the intentionality embodied in the verbal expression. It requires a pattern of words or a syntax before mature linguistic meaning can be said to exist. I have spoken of terms as vehicles of meaning. However, for maturity of meaning to occur, these linguistic signs must be set in a situational context. The sentence, either expressed or implied is one component in that context. Non-verbal aspects such as discourse situation, gestures, and facial expressions also contribute to the context. The word or term may be the key to meaning, but for understanding and maturity of meaning to occur, the role played by the situational context must be considered.

Husserl notes that the two conditions for linguistic meaning are "*Gestalt*" and "intention".[4] The *Gestalt* is the pattern of words which allows them to be understood, which gives them meaning. This is evident when we encounter a sentence in which the words have been rearranged or even an essay where sentences or paragraphs are not in the proper

[1] Urban, *Language and Reality*, p. 121.

[2] It should be recognized that such a thing as a sentence-word exists which simply allows the other words to be understood. For example, when a child simply says "Cold" he can be understood to mean "I am cold" or "The snow is cold". Cf. *ibid.*, p. 123.

[3] In this regard, Macquarrie (*God-Talk*, p. 85) cites the distinction held by some philosophers between the kind of meaning that belongs to single words, "signification" (*Bedeutung*), and that which belongs to sentences, "meaning" (*Sinn*).

[4] Cf. Urban, *op. cit.*, p. 123.

order. We can say that the result lacks meaning because it lacks an intelligible pattern appropriate for this context. This is particularly obvious in the translation of a foreign language where one may recognize all the individual words from a dictionary, but unless he knows their proper arrangement or syntax, the precise meaning eludes him. The second aspect, that of intention, is more significant for our study. If understanding is to occur, the hearer must apprehend and acknowledge the intentionality embodied in the verbal expression.[1] This means that the hearer must do much more than simply recognize the words and their syntactical pattern. He must also grasp the intention of the speaker embodied in this verbal expression. This involves two aspects. First, the speaker and the hearer must be members of the same speech community; namely, there must be a common recognition of words and their syntax. Second, there must be a recognition of a common universe of discourse. The hearer must apprehend and acknowledge the presuppositions of the speaker in regard to the matter about which he has made a verbal expression. A "universe of discourse" in this sense is partly determined by the mutual acknowledgment of intentions and values on the part of the speaker and hearer.[2] This is the means by which understanding develops. It does not mean that the speaker and hearer must agree about the correctness or appropriateness of the expressed intentions and values. However, it does mean that one must recognize that these intentions and values do exist and that they are informing the verbal expression of the speaker.

The discourse situation then involves a kind of polarity between expression and understanding. Only when the relation between the verbal sign and the thing signified is located within a common speech community, is interpreted within a common universe of discourse, and is characterized by verbal expression and the understanding of that expression can linguistic meaning in a mature sense be said to occur. However, as we noted before, there are various types or modes of linguistic meaning which must be identified in order that the intention of the speaker may be more precisely defined and in order that the basic condition for understanding may reach a more satisfactory level.

To attempt to give *the* definition of linguistic meaning in the midst of the present debate on the nature of language would be both pretentious and misleading. In contrast to an earlier period when C.K. Ogden and

---

[1] Urban, *Language and Reality*, p. 125.
[2] *Ibid.*, cf. pp. 126-127.

I.A. Richards could write a book entitled *The Meaning of Meaning*,[1] which sought to establish a normative position on this matter, there is today a general recognition of the diversity of meaning. "There are many different ways of conceiving meaning, and what is true of a meaning in one conception is often false in another".[2]

J.L. Austin has been particularly helpful in demonstrating that words have a variety of uses and therefore a variety of meanings. Austin also rejects any assumption that statements have only one function or meaning at a time. Rather, speech is an activity in which a variety of "forces" are operating simultaneously. A philosophical analysis may identify particular kinds of speech-acts as Austin himself attempts to do, but this is an abstraction from the speech activity. The contribution of Austin's philosophical analysis is to identify and describe the "performative" function of language. The title of his major work announces the thesis, *How To Do Things With Words*.[3] In an earlier work Austin describes the "I do" of a marriage, ceremony, the "I apologize" situation, and the christening of a ship. He concludes, "In all these cases it would be absurd to regard the thing I say as a report of the performance of the action which is undoubtedly done—the action of ... christening, or apologizing. We should say rather that, in saying what I do, I actually perform that action".[4] It is this recognition of the performative power of language which leads Austin to distinguish between kinds of speech-acts and their associated meanings within the variety of functions of language. In a similar way I feel it is necessary to indicate my understanding of the general structure of linguistic meaning in order to ascertain what is meant when I claim that language is the "bearer of meaning".

Despite the risk of oversimplification, I must give some indication of what the various modes of linguistic meaning might be, or perhaps more accurately stated, what basic types of meaning functions can be distinguished. Chapter IV will be devoted to a more specific consideration of what is meant by a speech community and a universe of discourse.

The speaker uses either a verbal sign or more specifically a collection

---

[1] C. K. Ogden, I. A. Richards, *The Meaning of Meaning*, 1st ed. (New York : Harcourt, Brace and Co., Inc., 1923).

[2] L. J. Cohen, *The Diversity of Meaning* (New York : Herder and Herder, 1963), p. 169. Quoted from Macquarries, *God-Talk*, p. 114.

[3] J. L. Austin, *How To Do Things With Words* (Cambridge : Harvard University Press, 1962).

[4] J. L. Austin, *Philosophical Papers* (London : Oxford University Press, 1961), p. 222.

of verbal signs to express his intentionality. He wishes to convey, express, or demonstrate something about an aspect of reality. It may be very trivial or it may have tremendous import, but in either case there are certain types of expression, or meaning functions, which allow him to express his intentionality more adequately. Also, if that intentionality is going to be understood, if one wants to assert that he knows what a statement means, then he must be able to distinguish what type or types of meaning functions are being employed. Also, the range of legitimate types of meaning one is willing to recognize determines what capacity or power he is willing to grant language. Urban claims that a threefold conception of meaning functions is generally accepted, although these types of meaning or expression are often described by different terms.[1]

These types of meaning can be designated as : the indicative, the emotive, and the intuitive.[2] The first two types of meaning are, I think, quite clear and generally accepted. A speaker employs his verbal signs or words with an indicative meaning when he wishes to denote or to refer to a particular object, activity, attitude, quality, person, etc. Whether he does this directly or indirectly, he wishes to point out or draw attention to a particular state of affairs in order that a hearer may take note of this situation and understand what is referred to. The indicative meaning function could also be characterized as informative, descriptive, or conceptual. The second meaning function is that of the emotive. This is utilized when the speaker wishes to employ his verbal signs in order to evoke or elicit emotion on the part of the hearer. His intentionality is brought to completion in speech if his words arouse a certain emotion; e.g., joy, despair, fear, hate, etc. The third meaning function, which I have termed the intuitive or the symbolic, is the most difficult to characterize and also the most controversial. In the intuitive meaning function, the verbal signs employed by the speaker do not simply indicate or inform the hearer about the objects[3] indicated. Neither do they simply evoke a certain emotive reaction to the object or situation. Rather,

---

[1] Urban, *Language and Reality*, p. 136.

[2] This follows the terminology suggested by Urban with the exception of the third type of expression which he calls "representative" rather than "intuitive" in this initial classification. J. L. Austin's notion of a "performative" function which falls in the category of a "perlocutionary act" deals with the effects of saying certain words and therefore could be the result of any of the types of meaning I have cited here, but is most frequently linked with the "intuitive".

[3] "Object" is used here as an element in the triadic discourse situation and has the widest general reference to physical object, person, situation, concept, etc.

the words actually make possible an authentic awareness of that object itself. They conjure up or make us alive to the object.[1] This is possible because the verbal symbol (here I use the specific term "symbol" rather than the more generic term "sign") actually participates in the reality of the thing symbolized. It has an affinity to its object which allows it to have this capacity or power. Urban describes this capacity of the verbal sign for intuitive meaning by asserting that it has a kind of "intrinsic expressiveness"[2] which allows the words to make the object actually present to the human understanding to a more or less adequate degree.[3]

It is obvious that in any given expression of intentionality on the part of the speaker, no one meaning function can be said to operate exclusively of the others. When one describes a situation with primarily an indicative function in mind, it would rarely be exclusive of all emotive meaning and often closer scrutiny might disclose a degree of intuitive meaning as well. Likewise with the emotive, with the exception of an expressive sign or grunt which could hardly be described as language in terms of our definition, there also occur elements of the indicative; the nature of the response may actually be evoked by a partially hidden intuitive element as well. The intuitive is taken by me to be one type of meaning function, although it has a more specialized meaning for me than it does for Urban.[4] However, when one can identify or make a claim for an intuitive meaning function, this would always be in conjunction with an indicative element and normally an emotive element. The major issue is that when a speaker expresses his intentionality, one meaning function normally has the priority and in order for meaning to come to fruition by its consummation in understanding, the hearer must be sensitive to the meaning function intended by the speaker or else his intentionality is not adequately expressed and one cannot really say that he understands what is meant. Confusion exists and communication ceases to occur on a particular topic when there is no common agreement between speaker and hearer on the type of meaning function operating, or when

---

[1] Note the defense and development by Urban of the "intuitive type "of meaning upon which much of my thought is based. See Urban, *Language and Reality*, pp. 143ff.

[2] Urban, *Language and Reality*, p. 141.

[3] There are obviously limitations to the manner in which this happens since we are dealing with a symbol and not the object itself. However, the emphasis here is on the capacity and power of this intuitive meaning function.

[4] Urban, for example, extends the intuitive element until it is present in all the major parts of speech : nouns, verbs. etc, (*Language and Reality*, pp. 150ff).

the hearer denies the legitimate range of meaning functions claimed by the speaker, particularly if he should deny the capacity of language to have intuitive meaning. I will return to the range problem in a moment, but will first give a brief example of these various meaning functions. In light of the emphasis on the "diversity of meaning" this schema for meaning functions purports to give only a general structure; the divisions between the meaning functions are somewhat fluid and tend to overlap.

Imagine my conversation with a college acquaintance in which we are discussing a mutual friend who, upon the completion of his theological training, took a position as the pastor of a church in a suburban area. The church he serves has been caught up in the racial crisis and violence of that city. At one point in our conversation I make the statement : "The Church is destroyed". We can already assume here a common speech community and a common universe of discourse. However, this statement may have a different consequence partially depending on the meaning function which is employed in my statement. It may be intended as an indicative, descriptive statement in the sense that it is the prelude to informing my acquaintance that the physical building occupied by the congregation and described as the Church has actually been destroyed by fire as a reaction to the activities of the pastor and some of the church members in the community. This would not be free of an emotive meaning and perhaps not of intuitive meaning, but the primary thrust is the indicative which subsequently can be clarified by the use of other sentences such as a description of the time and place of the destruction. However, utilizing yet another type of meaning function, namely the emotive, it may be my intention to evoke the sympathy and compassion of my acquaintance for the situation of our mutual friend, which in intention is irrelevant to whether the Church in indicative terms has been actually burnt to the ground or simply fragmented by internal divisions so as to destroy its effective ministry as a Church. Here the emotive function is primarily at work but it may contain indicative and intuitive meaning as well. In any case the emotive meaning function embedded in my intention may be clarified by further interpretation. Finally, it may be the case that my primary intention in the use of my words is to conjure up or make alive in the experience of my acquaintance the reality designated by the word "Church". "Church" is employed here not just as an indicative or emotive verbal sign, but as a dynamic "symbol" that conveys meaning beyond that which can be accounted for by indicative reference to a sociological entity or an evocation of emotion about a historically defined community. Rather, the verbal symbol through its intuitive meaning has capacity to supply awareness of its object. The meaning content of the verbal symbol "Church" employed in its intuitive dimension opens up an aspect of reality for the hearer. It is not just a particular sociological organization in a particular geographical area that is threatened, but one of the structures of meaningfulness in the life of a believer. Thus the intuitive meaning function gives my statement a whole new dimension. To understand my statement only on an indicative or emotive level, while ignoring or denying the intuitive element, would be to fail to understand my intention, and thus linguistic meaning in this case would not be fulfilled.[1]

As this example suggests, there is a danger in denying the intuitive meaning function of language for this restricts the range of genuine communication. This limitation is the result of reducing language to a dual theory of linguistic meaning.[2] The intuitive statement tends to be identified with the emotive and thus no issue is raised about its truth or falsity because it is denied any cognitive status. This means that a large number of our expressive statements, particularly in universes of discourse such as religion, ethics, and the arts, are viewed as being merely emotive and without cognitive value. This view, however, stems from a particular view concerning the nature of language, which we have called into question previously under the name of the "low evaluation" of language. This presupposition about the dual function of language fails to make sense out of too wide a range of human discourse and is the result of faulty phenomenological analysis. It is the claim of those supporting a third type of meaning function in language that this theory more adequately accounts for the way human language actually operates. The intuitive cannot be reduced merely to the subjective or emotive because it has a quality of communicability. Many with whom we communicate can both recognize and respond to the power of the verbal symbol as an access to reality. The answer to the question of how one confirms or authenticates the statements which claim to have an intuitive meaning function lies in the area of communication. The

[1] The traditional distinction between the "literal" as referring to the indicative and the "figurative" as referring to the intuitive and the emotive might be used, but it is inadequate for this study. The new conceptuality is employed to emphasize the distinctiveness of an intuitive meaning function apart from the emotive.

[2] Urban, *Language and Reality*, p. 137. Macquarrie also warns against what he calls "A simple-minded division of language into informative and emotive". *God-Talk*, p. 90.

assertion of an intuitive meaning function in language is based on the conviction "that language is so related to reality that it can conjure up that reality, make us live through the characters and qualities of things themselves".[1]

Language is the bearer of meaning. However, the notion of meaning includes expression and understanding. Linguistic meaning cannot come to maturity and thus cannot be properly understood apart from the discourse situation. To declare prior to the discourse situation what can be "meaningful" and what is "meaningless" is a result of a normative presupposition about the nature of language which is, I think, a distortion of linguistic meaning. For it appears that any statement which comes to expression and is in fact understood by another person, or is capable of being intelligibly apprehended, cannot be described as "meaningless". The speaker employs the verbal signs to express his intentionallity. It is the location of the speaker's statement within a particular speech community, in relation to a universe of discourse, and as utilizing a certain meaning function which makes it understandable to another. It is this confirmation or acceptance within a living speech community which constitutes the maturation of linguistic meaning.

This does not imply, however, that linguistic meaning is only a functional matter which is the result of a rather complex mutual agreement within a given community. Nor is linguistic meaning merely something which is created by man in order to make human communication possible. The recognition of an "intuitive" meaning function tends to point beyond the human speech community. I have maintained that it is precisely in the intuitive meaning function of language that the capacity or power of language to provide an access to reality is evidenced. As I contended previously, agreeing with Heidegger, Being discloses itself in language. Man, by being attentive to this disclosure, this non-concealment, comes to fulfillment as man. The primacy in language rests not with man but with Being. This indicates that some kind of "meaning" must be inherent in the nature of language itself insofar as man is open to this disclosure of Being in language. However, I would wish to deny either that meaning is solely a "given" of language and thus the work of Being, or that meaning is solely a creation of man for the purpose of human communication. To single out either aspect is, I think, to distort the nature of language.

But how then can one account for the respective roles of Being and

[1] Urban, *Language and Reality*, p. 149.

man in fashioning human language?[1] It is my contention that one must attempt to distinguish dimensions of human language. It is in what I shall term the symbolic dimension of human language—the area in which the transformational and pointing symbol operates, the capacity of language that is manifest in the intuitive meaning function—that the encounter between Being and man is focused. It is in the symbolic dimension of human language that one experiences Being's self-disclosure. It is in this dimension that one can understand what is meant for language to be the "house of Being". Man is confronted here with the "mystery" of language, but this must be distinguished from any alleged "magical" power of language. In emphasizing what has normally been the under-rated capacity of language to provide an access to Being, I do not wish to support an interpretation of a supra-historical language that is some-how "given" to man and which he receives gratefully and passively. To the contrary, man is an active participant in the creation of language and of meaning, as I have attempted to demonstrate in this section.

How is this mutual creation by Being and man of language as the bearer of meaning to be conceived? I have declared that the basic mater-ial for thought and language is supplied by man in the cultural process of the creation of a linguistic sign, a vehicle or a concentrate of meaning. However, this verbal sign is yet to be developed or extended and its meaning certainly has not come to maturity. Now man, the potential speaker, has certain verbal signs[2] at his disposal which form the found-ation for his thinking and speaking. Most of these verbal signs will go through a process of development before they come to maturity in the discourse situation or in the act of communication. It is in this process of development of the verbal signs that man may encounter Being in language.

Being has the primacy in language to the degree that it can be said of man that he is not able to speak authentically until he has been spoken to. He must listen to or be attentive to Being prior to this use of language. The meaning or truth of Being is in its non-concealment, in its power of "letting-be" that enables man to be what he is. But this surely cannot mean that man is unable to speak at all or that he is unable

---

[1] Being is spoken of here almost as an "agency". This is the problem of a proper language about Being. Being is a power or process that is conceived or spoken of by us symbolically as an agency. Being is an ontological reality but not "a being" or "an entity". One speaks of Being in anthropomorphic terms only symbolically.

[2] It should be recalled that sign is being employed here in the generic sense.

to express his intentionality in any way without first becoming docile toward Being. What this implies for me is that man cannot speak "authentically" apart from his reception of Being's self-disclosure in language. The essence of language is this capacity or power to provide an access to reality. It is in this encounter that man is able to come to a new self-understanding through that which is revealed to him in authentic language. It is my contention that the point in language where this occurs is in the symbolic dimension, in the recognition and acceptance of transformational and pointing symbols. We said previously that it was *through* thought that Being comes to language. This occurs when the verbal sign is developed via thought, namely, by means of the dimension of thought we have described as foundational thinking, and is transformed into a symbol. The nature of this verbal sign which has become a symbol is such that it now participates in the being of that which it symbolizes. The symbol has the capacity to convey authentic awareness and thus insight concerning that which it symbolizes. This is a result of the symbol's development in foundational thinking. When the whole man meditates in this way, he is indeed attentive to Being.

The meaning of Being, its truth or non-concealment, comes into language, I think, by disclosing itself in certain transformational symbols; i.e., in the symbolic dimension of human language. The symbol, as a result of its encounter with Being, is able to function in the discourse situation in such a way as to open up a new aspect of reality to the speaker and hearer alike. Symbol ought not to be understood here merely as a single verbal sign or word that through its development has acquired this symbolic capacity. The symbol may be a single word in a certain context, but it is often a collection of verbal signs, a phrase, sentence, or paragraph, that together constitute a symbolic entity because of its capacity to open up an aspect of reality, to convey authentic awareness; in short, to embody the meaning of Being's self-disclosure. Thus we can say that "language speaks". It embodies a meaning of such magnitude that a man can claim he does not speak authentically until he has been addressed. This means until his form of meditation on that subject matter is such that it is capable of transforming or developing his own language so that it is an appropriate response to that which he has discovered through the disclosure of Being in language. An element of significant meaning is then in a sense really given in language. Something is revealed that is not of man's creation. Being then in maintaining its primacy can be called the source and origin of authentic language.

However, if the development or source of meaning can be said to rest with Being, the maturation or consummation of meaning rests with man. For regardless of the capacity of the symbol or symbolic dimension of language, the symbol must actually assume a symbolic function in the discourse situation. The symbol must be received and confirmed as an authentic symbol. The capacity of a symbol to provide an access to reality must be recognized by the speaker and utilized not only for his own insight but for the expression of his intentionality. Even beyond this, before meaning can be said to come to maturity, before understanding can complement expression, the symbolic power of the symbol must be apprehended by the hearer. Only then can authentic meaning come to fruition so that one can grasp the full significance of the claim that language is the bearer of meaning. Meaning is the mutual creation of Being and man, what one might describe as the result of a dialogue between the Logos of Being and the Logos of man, or the language of Being and the language of man.

But we cannot stop here. Not only is Being disclosed in language, it is also concealed in language. The symbolic dimension of language has a power that should not be underestimated. It must be recognized, however, that the symbol is not identical with that which it symbolizes.

The symbol or the symbolic dimension of language must be interpreted by the nonsymbolic dimensions of language; in order that the symbol may be received and recognized for what it is; in order that its proper function may be accorded it so that it can convey the awareness of which it is the bearer; and in order that the symbol may be commended to those who do not understand it. For all these reasons we must have the interpretation of the symbol and we must have some means of verifying or authenticating the statements made in the symbolic dimension as well as the other dimensions of human language. The symbolic must be related in a dialectical way to the other dimensions of language.

However, before turning directly to the various dimensions of language and to the question of authentication, I must consider the third part of the provisional definition given for human language.

Language as a Medium of Communication

In the study of language some philosophers have assumed that language is primarily or even solely a medium of communication between man and man. Language is construed as a kind of arbitrary mechanism invented by man in order to convey information or ideas from one individual to another. I have already raised objections to this "low evaluation" of language, but I think it will become clear from an analysis of the nature of what Urban describes as "intelligible communication"[1] that this view of language is inadequate to account for what happens in the act of linguistic communication.

It was asserted that linguistic meaning and therefore language, insofar as it is a bearer of meaning, comes to maturity or fulfillment only in the discourse situation, in the context of living speech, in the act of communication. It is correct, I believe, to say with Urban that language has no reality apart from the speech community.[2] The focus of language both as an access to reality and as a bearer of meaning becomes apparent in the context of communication. In fact, real communication is dependent on both these capacities of language. However, I must now define communication in the context of this study.

Urban makes a useful distinction between "behavioral "and "intelligible" or "real" communication. "Behavioral" communication is limited to the here and now and is primarily a "cue to behavior".[3] It is particularly characteristic of animal communication which, because of its merely signalistic nature, cannot be classified as language in the proper sense. But man also employs behavioral means of communication when he conveys something with gestures, pantomime, or movements of the eyes. "Intelligible communication", on the other hand, is not limited to the here and now because it always entails understanding. This understanding involves a complex process of interpretation. We indicated before that in a proper sense only language is understood. Thus intelligible communication *ultimately* involves a linguistic transaction even when—and this is quite often true—this linguistic act of communication is based on an interpretation of what "is said" in another medium of communication.[4]

---

[1] Urban, *Language and Reality*, pp. 228ff.

[2] *Ibid.*

[3] *Ibid.*, pp. 229f.

[4] There are non-linguistic means of communication. However, if a judgment is going to be made about the meaning and truth of that which is communicated, so as to place it in the range of intelligibility, then ultimately language is employed. As Urban illustrates, both artistic and mathematical forms do communicate. The issue is whether they are the final and adequate means of communication. He contends, "It is much more reasonable to say that both say something, but what it is that they really say can be ultimately expressed only in terms of language" (p. 267). This theory of the primacy of linguistic communication is developed in *Language and Reality*, pp. 264-267.

We can define intelligible communication as a linguistic transaction in which verbal signs are understood by the hearer in all relevant respects in a similar way to that intended by the speaker.[1] In order for meaning to come to maturity, in order for intelligible or real communication to exist, "understanding" is necessary as the correlate to expression. Communication then is not the transfer of ideas but a "sharing" between speaker and hearer. It is the sharing of a mutual understanding about some aspect of reality. Our language provides access or lights up a certain aspect of reality that is now available to both speaker and hearer through the medium of language.[2] But what is it that makes possible the understanding which constitutes the basis for this sharing? What are the necessary conditions for communication?

The conditions necessary for communication have been outlined before in relation to the notion of meaning. They are : (1) A common speech community; (2) a common universe of discourse; and (3) a recognition of a common meaning function. The latter condition was developed in the section on language as a bearer of meaning and will be considered again specifically in a section devoted to the dimensions of human language in which these functions have their roots. The focus here is on the first two conditions.

The first condition of communication is fairly obvious. If understanding is to occur, the speaker and hearer must have a common speech community; namely, they must have an understanding of the language in which the linguistic transaction is being carried on. A problem arises in regard to translation from one speech community to another — whether that translation is from French to English or from a language of a primitive tribe to a contemporary cultural language. Anyone who has attempted to translate a complicated work into another language, particularly a literary or philosophical document, is aware of that element in the work which is untranslatable, that element in the original document which cannot be adequately conveyed in the medium of a different language. It seems to me necessary to make some distinction between layers of translatable meaning, as has been suggested by such students as E. Sapir and K. Vossler. The "outer layer" (Vossler's term) is that which contains our "intuitive record of experience" (Sapir's phrase); namely, that which has been disclosed in language and is therefore capable of being universally understood. The "inner layer" contains

---

[1] This follows the pattern of Urban's definition, *Language and Reality*, p. 233.

[2] A similar position is taken by Macquarrie in *God-Talk*, p. 74.

the specific way in which this disclosure has been grasped by a particular language and this is not readily accessible to those outside this particular speech community. The outer layer is translatable and contains in most instances that which is essential for understanding and communication. The inner layer is not translatable and, although it certainly adds to the adequacy of understanding, is not usually essential for communication. These layers are not always clearly distinguishable, and it is true that a work may be dominated by one layer rather than another. A novel by Hemingway may be more readily translatable than is a poem by E.E. Cummings.

There are limits to translation, and it is a much more complicated process than often is realized. However, a theory such as that of the dual layers helps to make the translation process more intelligible and to make us sensitive to the limits of translation. The central point is that things do get translated, even the works of Kant and Heidegger, from one speech community to another with amazing adequacy. Thus for communication to occur, there must exist a common speech community either naturally or as a consequence of translation.

The second condition of communication is a common universe of discourse. When one is unable to communicate with another, that is, to convey his intentionality adequately, he is likely to say that the other person "speaks another language". This does not actually mean that he speaks French and his companion speaks English, but rather, that the context in which he conveys the statements is radically different from that in which it is interpreted. Since verbal signs have multiple references, a verbal sign must be located in a particular linguistic context in order to establish meaning. This linguistic context is what we mean when we refer to a "universe of discourse".[1] We have mantained that linguistic meaning does not come to maturity until it is recognized as existing within a particular universe of discourse. What is asserted here is that a contextual theory is crucial to the nature of meaning. This theory contends that meaning cannot be determined in isolation from discourse, which we described in our provisional definition as the context of living speech. Meaning necessarily involves reference to a universe of discourse

---

[1] The phrase "universe of discourse", which is so important to this study, is traced by Urban from its origin in logic to its present emphasis on a "*limited* universe" which makes meaning as a determinate reference possible and on a "universe of *discourse*" where context is determined by communication. See *Language and Reality*, pp. 198-199.

which becomes a condition for comunication. But a "universe of discourse" may not be identified or reduced to environment. Rather, the universe of discourse is constituted by the recognition of the same presuppositions and values on the part of the speaker and hearer. It is a sharing of a linguistic context. "Such a universe of discourse is both created and maintained by the mutual acknowledgment, on the part of communicating subjects, of certain presuppositions without which the universe in question has no being, and the particular references within it no meaning".[1]

Our definition of intelligible communication is dependent on the hearer's understanding, in all relevant respects, of the verbal signs in a similar way to that intended by the speaker. One of those relevant respects is a similar or common universe of discourse. In order for the importance of this to be grasped, we must remind ourselves of what Urban terms the "elliptical" nature of language whereby much more is understood in language than is expressed.[2] There is what one can refer to as the mysterious element in communication. Communication cannot be conceived of as the transfer of ideas from one mind to another, but rather, of a shared understanding which implies that much which is not expressed is simply "understood". This is achieved partially on the basis of a mutually recognized and acknowledged universe of discourse. Urban provides an apt illustration when he notes that the word "marriage" may mean different things as expressed by a jurist, a priest, and an anthropologist.[3] In each case, a different universe of discourse may be involved; respectively, a legal, a theological, and a anthropological. Each universe of discourse has its own idioms or "types of intelligibility". Thus, when two priests talk about marriage as a sacrament, there is a great deal which simply is "understood" because there is a sharing of a type of intelligibility, a common foundation of presuppositions. Thus intelligible communication is possible partially as a result of a common universe of discourse. This does not mean that communication cannot take place between the jurist, priest, and anthropologist on the subject of marriage. There is, of course, translation between one universe of discourse and another, just as there is between one speech community and another. What is involved in this process of translation is that a sharing of presuppositions and values occurs that

---

[1] Urban, *Language and Reality*, p. 199.

[2] *Ibid.*, p. 234.

[3] *Ibid.*, p. 240.

determines the meaning. This may be done imaginatively, which means, for instance, that the jurist recognizes and acknowledges the existence of the presuppositions and values expressed by the priest as the describes marriage as a sacrament. The jurist may not in fact believe that marriage is a sacrament, but he must imaginatively share this universe of discourse if communication is to take place. Sharing in a universe of discourse is a matter of gradation. One can share part of another universe, but rarely all of it. The emphasis is on a common universe, not as a sufficient guarantee, but rather as a necessary condition for meaning, understanding, and therefore communication.

We can identify, then, in language multiple "universes of discourse" or contexts for linguistic meaning. These are the foundation for a mutual sharing between a speaker and a hearer which results in understanding. The totality of discourse can be understood as divided into various contexts in a variety of ways, depending on what is mutually acknowledged by speaker and hearer as they reside in a particular speech community. One accepted way of making the division for purposes of the analysis of language is between various "languages" or universes of discourse which are employed by certain disciplines or fields of study. Thus, as does Urban, we can speak of large universes of discourse such as the scientific, the poetic, the religious, and the metaphysical.[1] Cassirer has a similar division in his concept of different "symbolic forms" which constitute or characterize certain linguistic contexts. However, it seems to me that the concept of a universe of discourse can also be employed in a narrower way to indicate any context in which a type of intelligibility is embodied in a systematic way which provides the condition for understanding. Thus one can speak of a Christian, or a Judaic, or a Buddhist universe of discourse within the wider universe of religion. Similar divisions could be made in philosophy, art, science, etc. These divisions tend to overlap as do speech communities and types of meaning functions. The important issue is the recognition and acknowledgment of a "type of intelligibility".

It seems to me that this stress on the various universes of discourse has a good deal in common with the emphasis in recent linguistic analysis philosophy on the "use" of words as they are employed in various forms of discourse. This emphasis is opposed to the earlier stress by the logical positivists on a prior definition of "meaning" in terms of

---

[1] Urban, *Language and Reality*, p. 1.

tautological or empirical validation.[1] Also, the now-famous notion of
Ludwig Wittgenstein in *Philosophical Investigations* of "language
games", in which certain rules operate, seems to embody just this concept
of types of intelligibility. The problem is that either the notion of a
"universe of discourse" or a "language game" can ultimately be insignificant if it is regarded as based merely on mutual recognition and acknowledgment of certain presuppositions and values or certain rules. For then
people can tell you to go live in your universe of discourse or play your
language game and they will operate in theirs. Wittgenstein appears
to avoid this critique by grounding his notion of language-game in the
use of words and therefore in the fabric of life itself. He declares,
"... the term 'language-game' is meant to bring into prominence the
fact that the *speaking* of language is part of an activity, or of a form of
life".[2] This notion of a universe of discourse or a language-game will
be finally significant only if it makes a claim for the truth or authenticity
of one universe or game over against another, particularly when they are
in conflict. One must indicate how the various universes or games are
related, whether there is any order of priority, and how one is to translate between one universe or game and another, since we obviously
live in more than one universe or play more than one game at a time.
The notion of a "context", despite the multiple ways it is precisely
developed, is crucial for the accurate assessment of the nature of language.
Yet context alone is not sufficient if one wishes to claim that language
is an access to reality and that it can enable us to make judgments about
the truth, falsity, or authenticity of what we encounter in experience.
One must go beyond context to ask the question of what makes this
intelligible communication possible. What accounts for this "mutuality
of mind",[3] this common understanding between speaker and hearer?
How can the mysterious element in the amazing adequacy of communication be made intelligible?

  In order to speak to these questions I turn first to the third condition
for communication : a recognition of a common type of meaning function. This concept was treated in detail in the former section, but it is
important to note that it comes to fulfillment only in communication.

---

  [1] A good exposition of this movement plus the important distinction between "use"
and "usage" is given by J. A. Martin, Jr., *The New Dialogue Between Philosophy and
Theology* (New York : Seabury Press, 1966), pp. 116-118.
  [2] Wittgenstein, *Philosophical Investigations*, p. 11.
  [3] Urban, *Language and Reality*, p. 233.

For this sharing between the speaker and hearer, this "mutuality of mind", comes about not only when a common speech community and a common universe of discourse are established, but also when it is recognized and acknowledged which general type of meaning function has the primacy in the given speech event; namely, whether the speaker's intentionality and the hearer's understanding coincide in that the verbal signs are seen as having primarily an indicative, emotive, or intuitive meaning function. This does not always depend on one explicitly choosing one function over another. In a good essay the three functions tend to interpenetrate. Only when a problem in communication arises, when the speaker or writer is not understood, is it necessary to analyze the primary meaning function that is operative in a given assertion. However, the full range of meaning functions must be recognized in order to account for intelligible communication in human discourse.

When all three conditions (common speech community, universe of discourse, and meaning function) are met, then understanding takes place, meaning comes to maturity, and communication occurs. It can be seen now that communication is an exceedingly complex process, and when it is properly understood, it is amazing that as much communication takes place as actually does. Indeed, the question is raised as to how one accounts for this mutuality of mind, this sharing process? If there is to be a mutual recognition and acknowledgment of presuppositions and values, and if these are to be apprehended, they must in a sense be *there*, they must transcend the communicating minds.[1] In order for intelligible communication to occur, there must be a "given" in language, a common experience or aspect of reality that is capable of being illuminated. It is maintained, therefore, that there exists a basis beyond man for these presuppositions and values that make understanding, meaning, and communication possible.[2]

---

[1] Urban, *Language and Reality*, p. 239.

[2] Urban goes on to refute a naturalistic or behavioristic theory of communication on the basis that it merely assumes this mutuality of mind without accounting for it. He proceeds to support a transcendental theory of an underlying unity, either an "all-embracing mind" or an "over-individual society of minds" (p. 155), which accounts for this sharing and thus for real communication. (See *Language and Reality*, pp. 243-250). Metaphysics in the "idealistic tradition" of Urban is not well received in some philosophical circles today. However, I am convinced that the metaphysical or, as I have described it, metempirical questions are unavoidable either for theology or philosophy. There is an indication that even some analytically oriented philosophers such as Peter Strawson in *Individuals : An Essay in Descriptive Metaphysics* (New

It is the position of this study that Being discloses itself in language and establishes a "given" of language which accounts for this mutuality of mind. In some mysterious way, an aspect of reality is illuminated for us in the speech event itself. The speaker and hearer come to a mutual recognition and acknowledgment, to a sharing, of that which has been opened up to both of them in the discourse situation. But this process depends on what we have called a capacity or power of language to provide an access to reality, on a "high evaluation" of language. This is why it can be said that man cannot speak authentically until he has been addressed. He must be attentive to that which is disclosed in language. For one aspect of meaning involves that which is revealed as a result of the development of certain verbal signs in an encounter of man with Being. Here is the creation of transformational symbols which provide an authentic awareness and cognitive insight into the nature of reality itself. It is this power of language as manifest in its symbolic dimension that ultimately accounts for intelligible communication, for the mutuality of minds. There is a sense, therefore, in which not only foundational thinking and "authentic" language but also intelligible communication are dependent on man's being attentive to Being in its self-disclosure in language. For without this, a crucial aspect of meaning is abandoned and communication is reduced to the arbitrary or conventional agreement of a given speech community. But this explanation fails to make intelligible the "understood" element which is a vital factor in communication as we experience it. Also, it fails to make intelligible how there can be a translation from one universe of discourse to another. What is the common element which cuts across the various universes of discourse and makes possible translation and communication between them? It is my contention that there are certain dimensions of language which operate in all universes of discourse. In one of these dimensions, namely, in the symbolic, we find the disclosure of Being focused. This symbol must then be expanded and interpreted in another dimension of language. However, it is this universal dimensional character of language that operates in every speech community and in every universe of discourse that is the foundation for the maturity of linguistic meaning,

York : Doubleday Anchor Books, 1965) are raising again the metaphysical questions. In any case, I think Urban is right in pointing toward the necessity of some reality beyond man that accounts for this mutuality of the mind. Strawson clearly rejects a "revisionary" metaphysics represented by Urban, but he is willing to accept "descriptive" metaphysics which at least cracks the door to a reconsideration of metaphysical questions.

the consummation of communication, and the fulfillment of authentic language. For it is in this dimensional analysis of human language that we can begin to understand how Being discloses itself in language (that is, in transformational symbols), how these symbols are interpreted, and finally, how one can proceed to authenticate these symbols and to employ them as the ultimate foundation for intelligible communication.

CHAPTER FOUR

DIMENSIONS OF LANGUAGE

It has been a thesis of this study that a key to proper understanding of the nature of human language can be discovered in the recognition and identification of certain divisions : dimensions, levels, or strata of language. A recognition of the nature, function, and relationship of these dimensions provides one with an insight into the essential power of language. It is the operation of these distinguishable dimensions and their interdependence which enables language to be a genuine access to reality where Being discloses itself in language and thus lights up the human situation. It is also this dimensional structure which allows language to be a bearer of meaning insofar as linguistic meaning comes to maturity in human discourse. It is the dimensional understanding of language as an access to reality and a bearer of meaning which accounts for the realization of intelligible communication and thus completes the notion of language as a medium of communication. So I turn to an examination of this dimensional structure of human language, being fully aware that some terms and explications may be imprecise and inadequate because this is an exploratory study. However, I am convinced that some recognition of the dimensional structure of human language is crucial to an adequate understanding of the nature and function of language.

Concern for distinguishing various divisions in the structure of language has precedence in the work of other authors focusing on the nature of language who also have at least some interest in its function in regard to religion. I could name as illustrations those who have been significant in my own research. Urban makes distinctions both between types of meaning in language and universes of discourse. Cassirer and Langer have divisions akin to universes of discourse that utilize various symbolic forms. John A. Hutchison talks about strata of language,[1] and Heinrich Ott speaks often of levels of thinking and speaking, distinguishing particularly between objectifying and non-objectifying levels.[2]

---

[1] Hutchison, *Language and Faith*, p. 58.

[2] Heinrich Ott, "Non-Objectifying Thinking and Speaking in Theology", *Distinctive Protestant and Catholic Themes Reconsidered*, Robert W. Funk (ed.) (Harper & Row, 1967), pp. 112ff.

Finally, Paul Ricœur stresses "levels of significance" in language,[1] which has been a catalytic idea in my own thought. However, many of these divisions, with the exception of Urban's types of meaning, Ott's still undefined levels, and Ricœur's suggestions about a "hierarchy of language", tend to break down along lines which, if allowed to stand alone, are insufficient. The primary divisions, and frequently the only divisions which have been established in recent studies on the nature of language, fall into what we might call discipline categories. Thus one claims to have a language division peculiar to philosophy, art, natural science, psychology, history, etc. On the basis of these discipline categories the effort is then made to develop the characteristic thought pattern (on occasion referred to as the logic) of certain disciplines. It seems to me that the natural division between disciplines is justifiable within limits as an initial and necessary step. This study draws a similar distinction between various universes of discourse which have types of intelligibility which are the result of mutual recognition and acceptance of common presuppositions. However, the difficulty with this type of division, necessary as it is at an initial stage, is that it leads to an isolation of various disciplines in regard to intelligibility, translation, and communication. Religious language may claim a distinctive thought pattern, as may psychology or certain art forms. But unless there exist other structures of language which cut across this disciplinary division, a particular universe of discourse may become essentially isolated and thus unintelligible and incommunicable. Judgments about the truth or authenticity of statements made in one discipline, to say nothing of the possibility of actually understanding what is meant by a certain statement, become endangered without further structures of language to mitigate this schema of disciplinary isolation. It is my contention that such additional structures do exist and in fact are an essential aspect of the nature of language itself. Thus, in addition to the vertical divisions between the various disciplines or, as I would prefer to say, universes of discourse, there exist also horizontal divisions which cut across or through every universe of discourse.[2] These horizontal divisions are what I have described as dimensions of human language.

Before I proceed to an indication of what I conceive as the nature of

---

[1] Ricœur, "The Word and Words ...". (Address at Union Theological Seminary).

[2] The vertical and horizontal terms supply a spacial illustration for the purpose of grasping the proposal, but all linguistic analysis is a step back from the actual operation of the speech community and this illustration ought not to be pushed too far.

this dimensional structure of human language, a word ought to be said about the term "dimension" itself. Dimension is preferred over "level", "stratum", or "layer", as each of these terms tends to represent permanence, independence, and separation. I believe "dimension" better conveys the idea of flexibility, of interconnectedness, and of essential unity.[1] The dimensions of language, as outlined here, are flexible in the sense that there is no absolute line of demarcation which distinguishes one dimension from another in every situation. They are overlapping and tend to blend together so that in borderline cases it is not always possible to say with certainty what dimension of language is operating in a given case. There is a universality about a dimension which makes it present to some degree in all speaking. These dimensions are also interconnected in the sense that one dimension of language requires another in order to complete its own function. These are dimensions of the whole language structure in the sense that they cannot function in isolation from one another. Finally, dimension manifests the sense of essential unity where no contradiction between dimensions is possible if they are rightly understood, because they converge at the point of their source and each has a distinctive purpose. Conflicts in language can certainly occur, even within a dimensional understanding, but the unity of language is apprehended and emphasized over the conflicts.

The notion of "dimensions" as applied to language is an attempt to avoid the categorization of reality and experience into compartments or realms. Jerry H. Gill, sets what he describes as a "dimension-model" over against a "realm-model" in his discussion of experience as dimensional.

> What does taking the dimension-model seriously involve? The primary point in using a dimensional approach to interpret experience is to emphasize the "simultaneity" of human existence. That is, rather than conceive of reality and experience as divided into separate realms, it is more helpful and more faithful to experience to conceive of them as having simultaneously interpenetrating dimensions.[2]

It is a dimension-model which I have applied to the nature of language.

This chapter will be an attempt to identify and characterize the two basic dimensions of human language. Within the limitations of this

---

[1] The term "dimension" and the reasons for its use follow Paul Tillich's distinction in regard to "dimensions of life", *Systematic Theology* (Chicago : University of Chicago Press, 1963), Vol. III, pp. 12ff.

[2] Gill, *Possibility of Religious Knowledge*, p. 119.

study, I will attempt to indicate the nature and function of each dimension and also to indicate the way in which they are interconnected on the basis of a dialectic relationship. The two dimensions are the Symbolic and the Conceptual.

The Symbolic Dimension

I have maintained that language constitutes man's primary access to reality. It is in language that Being discloses itself. Language is the arrival of Being itself, both clearing and concealing. Yet, even though this high evaluation of language conceives of the word as the unique access to the nature of reality, it is not a perfect means of access because the very nature of language itself also places limitations on this medium. Not only does Being reveal itself in language, but it also conceals itself there. There is an element of mystery, of transcendence, about Being which defies comprehension and assimilation by human language, human thought, or human emotions, regardless of their quality or intensity. Language at any dimension is incapable of completely manifesting how Being is in itself. Essential mystery must and should persist. There is that about the nature of reality which is inexpressible and incomprehensible. Ian Ramsey, in his book *Models and Mystery*, argues that there is a mystery which confronts every discipline from natural science and theology to psychology and the social sciences.[1] Models,[2] Ramsey claims, provide disclosures about the mystery of the universe to the natural scientist or the theologian about which he must be articulate.[3] There is, however, mystery and uncertainty in each of these cases. Michael Foster, in his critique of linguistic analysis philosophy, maintains there is a mystery at the foundation of all philosophy and the demand for absolute clarity leads only to a reduction in the sphere of reality.[4] The element of mystery, of the inexpressible, is quite generally recognized. The recognition of this limitation in language, due to this element of the inexpressible, protects the notion of the transcendence of Being, but it does not condemn language as entirely inadequate.

[1] Ian T. Ramsey, *Models and Mystery* (New York : Oxford University Press, 1964), pp. 1, 22ff.

[2] Models with appropriate qualifiers appear to function in some ways similar to what I have described as symbols.

[3] Ramsey, *op. cit.*, p. 20.

[4] Michael Foster, "Contemporary British Philosophy and Christian Belief", *Christian Scholar* (Fall 1960).

Rather, just the opposite is the case. In spite of the element of mystery, it is precisely the *adequacy* of language that is affirmed and emphasized by such philosophers of language as Martin Heidegger and those who have been influenced by him. Gerhard Ebeling and Ernst Fuchs, who have utilized Heidegger's insights in theology, both affirm the essential adequacy and power of language. Ebeling decries what he calls "the devaluation of words in general".[1] These authors wish to call attention to the adequacy of language by referring to what they call a "word-event" (*Wortgeschehen*—Ebeling) or "language-event" (*Sprachereignis*—Fuchs). Here language brings something about, it has an effect. As Fuchs asserts, language "lets being 'be' temporarily, makes it an event".[2] Another theologian who has been influenced by the work of the later Heidegger is Heinrich Ott. Although his position can be distinguished from that of Ebeling and Fuchs, he too stresses the adequacy of language and the idea that it effects something. Ott claims that "speech does not simply 'denote' "; we must "become free to ask what it actually does".[3] Ott's answer is that man is led by the word into a "way" —a way that leads man before himself and "before reality itself as something veiled".[4] Man is brought by language before mystery.

However, what is sometimes implied by those wishing to affirm the adequacy and power of language is that *all* speaking has this capacity to bring man before reality itself, to disclose Being to him, to have this "eventful" character. Ebeling in an interview in December 1967 exemplified this for me by saying that even the simplest event, such as a mother calling a daughter to her, has this eventful character. It is sometimes claimed that language is fulfilling its proper function as language *only* when a kind of dramatic disclosure occurs. Other uses of language are demeaned as being banal or idle talk. However, I would maintain that this type of claim, which is an over-extension or exaggeration of a correct insight about the nature of language and its essential power, makes the disclosure of Being in language unintelligible. In fact, this view ultimately prohibits language from exercising its innate power because it has no way to come to consummation; i.e., to have this disclosure interpreted.

---

[1] Gerhard Ebeling, *God and Word*, James W. Leitch (trans.) (Philadelphia : Fortress Press, 1967), p. 4.

[2] Cited from *The New Hermeneutic*, James M. Robinson and John B. Cobb, Jr. (eds.) (New York : Harper & Row, 1964), p. 58.

[3] Ott, "Non-Objectifying Thinking ...", *Distinctive Protestant and Catholic Themes* ..., p. 114.

[4] *Ibid.*, p. 120.

This is a consequence of the failure to realize that language has distinctive dimensions and that we must recognize and acknowledge these in order to do justice to the full range of language's capacity.

It is not in every event of speaking, not in every dimension of language, but rather, it is in the symbolic dimension of language, operating in potentially every discipline, that Being discloses itself, that language constitutes an access to reality. It is in the realm of this symbolic dimension of language that both the self-disclosure and the mystery of Being are balanced and thus protected. This is an amazing claim to make about language, and specifically about a particular dimension of language. But I am convinced that it is just such a radical understanding of the dimensional structure of language which accounts for those experiences when we are confronted by a spoken or written passage that seems to convey such insight or new understanding that a new dimension of reality, a new realm of experience, and a new level of self-understanding are opened up for us. This is the power of a verbal sign when it becomes an "illuminating" and "transforming" symbol. This is the self-disclosure of Being.

However, the genuine symbol does more than this; it becomes not only an illuminating and transformational symbol but also a pointing symbol. Precisely because it is a symbol, having an intrinsic relationship to that to which it symbolizes but yet not identical with it, it points beyond itself to an experiential encounter with the thing symbolized which can never be directly or adequately apprehended by any form of language. This is the mystery of Being.

How is it possible to make the nature and function of a symbolic dimension of language intelligible on the basis of the understanding of language developed in the previous sections of this study? First, it has already become clear that the type or form of verbal sign which functions here and makes the symbolic dimension of language possible is the "symbol" in the narrower sense of symbolic as set forth in the section on provisional definitions. The essential characteristic of the nature of the symbol is that it has a special intrinsic relationship to that which it symbolizes, It can be said, in Tillich's terminology, to participate in the reality of that which it symbolizes. It is in the symbolic dimension of language that the intuitive meaning function is predominant. But what can this mean? I asserted previously that the point at which one could say that Being discloses itself in language is the development of the verbal sign into a symbol. This is the point at which man is attentive to Being. Man opens himself in his meditative processes to Being's speaking. At this point the subject-object split is overcome or moved beyond in the form of non-objectifying thinking. I affirmed previously that it is through thought that Being comes to word. This clearing occurs by means of a particular dimension of thought which we have described as foundational or essential. It is here, then, that the verbal sign is transformed into a symbol which now, by the act of Being's self-disclosure in language and the structure of language thus constituted, is capable of conveying an authentic awareness and cognitive insight concerning that which it symbolizes. What we have called the "transformational symbol" is a way of making that which it symbolizes present and manifest for the person or group which meaningfully employs the symbol. This is how we can claim that Being has the primacy in human language and that human language provides the access to reality itself. But it must be recalled that at this juncture the symbol has only this capacity which has not yet been realized. Realization entails confirmation and acceptance of the symbol via interpretation.

I also asserted that Being and man are mutual creators of language as a bearer of meaning. Meaning is in some measure a result of the creation of this transformational symbol. At this point something is given in language. New insight into some aspect of reality is conveyed by the symbol. Here one can talk about that which is revealed, that mystery surrounding some aspect of experience which is illuminated.[1] It is this objective "given", this non-concealment of Being, which establishes the foundation for meaning. It is a meaning which could not come about without man's contribution of the initial verbal sign and which cannot come to maturity apart from the discourse situation. However, the primacy of Being in the symbolic dimension of language forms the foundation for language as a bearer of meaning.

It has been established previously that intelligible communication is a complex affair. For the hearer to understand in a similar way the way the verbal signs employed by the speaker depends on a common speech community, a common universe of discourse, and a recognition of a common meaning function. "Understanding" presupposes a "mutuality of the mind" which makes intelligible communication possible. In turn, this mutuality of the mind depends on the existence of some objective meaning and the fact that it can be embodied in human language. The dimensional structure of language makes this intelligible. It is in the

---

[1] This development of a verbal sign into a symbol will be the point at which I will speak about revelation in the chapters on theological language.

symbolic dimension that Being discloses itself and therefore provides an insight into the mystery of some aspect of reality. Being via this disclosure creates in conjunction with man a transformational symbol which becomes the bearer of this (objective) given. This given establishes the basis for the mutuality of mind which makes it possible for us to account for intelligible communication. Thus, a grasp of the nature and function of the symbolic dimension of language enables us to determine how language can be a medium of communication.

However, the symbolic dimension of language employs verbal signs not only as illuminating and transformational symbols; they are also simultaneously pointing symbols. These symbols have the capacity to convey significant content in the form of authentic awareness and cognitive insight. Yet this is still non-univocal predication, an indirect way of speaking. The very nature of that which is symbolized defies univocal predication or a direct way of speaking about it. The power of the symbolic dimension if properly understood, is that it conveys a form of knowledge yet escapes the prohibitive and restrictive consequences of literal predication. Thus, as a pointing symbol the developed verbal sign points beyond itself to an existential encounter with the thing signified. It points to a time and place where man must be attentive and listen to the speaking of Logos. It points to the area where the subject-object split is overcome in non-objectifying thinking and speaking. It points to the place where man responds to the "hail" of Being.

Just as the verbal sign as an illuminating and transformational symbol manifests that being discloses itself in language, so the verbal sign as pointing symbol declares that Being also conceals itself in language. The transcendence of Being is not violated. The ontological difference between Being and the beings is not ignored. The mystery of Being is not eliminated. The inexpressibility of Being is not dissolved. Rather, both the mystery and the inexpressibility are preserved by means of the symbolic dimension of language. This means that the symbol employed in this dimension of language has both an affirmative and negative aspect.[1] The affirmative aspect is the significant content a symbol carries. The negative aspect is the degree to which a symbol negates itself in order to point beyond itself. It must negate its literal reference

---

[1] The idea of the affirmation and negation of symbols is based on a view of Tillich's stated in *Systematic Theology*, Vol. I, p. 239, as well as in numerous articles on symbolism. This notion is also developed by Urban in *Language and Reality*, p. 427. This dialectic of affirmation and negation will be considered in this study in connection with the religious symbol.

in order to maintain its power to convey authentic awareness. Without negation there is the threat that the symbol might become distorted and thus be identified with that which it symbolizes. The constant danger is that of confusing the symbolic with the literal. Also, the negative aspect reminds us of the limitations and inadequacy of any verbal form pertaining to the disclosure of Being. So a necessary aspect of the symbolic dimension of language is a dialectic of affirmation and negation in regard to specific symbols.

It was noted previously that the disclosure of Being in language has a historical aspect. Being becomes non-concealed or uncovered at one historical period in a different way than in another. If this disclosure occurs in the symbolic dimension of language, then one must take into account the rise and decline of key symbols. Tillich refers to this as the birth and death of symbols.[1] Just as no one symbol alone is adequate to represent an aspect of reality but must be supplemented by others to account for the negative element inherent in the symbol, so a symbol can be born and it may die. A symbol's birth begins when a sign is developed into a genuine symbol by its encounter with Being's self-disclosure in regard to some aspect of reality. However, before it can become a transformational and pointing symbol in a full sense with creative power, it must be interpreted and accepted as a symbol. This process of interpretation and acceptance is cultural and historical. Also, when a symbol fails to provide authentic awareness and cognitive insight into that which is symbolized, it can be said to decline or die. One must recognize the continual process of specific symbols operating within the symbolic dimension of language. This rise and decline is evident with all types of symbols, but can be analyzed in detail only within a particular universe of discourse.

My primary concern has been to maintain that dimensions of human language do exist and that the symbolic dimension is crucial for the adequate understanding of linguistic meaning, communication, and even the relationship between language and reality. It should also be noted that an analysis could be made of various general types of symbols that operate in such a way that they form what might be called sub-dimensions of the symbolic. A comprehensive analysis of the sub-dimensions of the symbolic is beyond the scope of this study since this would ultimately involve analysis of symbolic forms in each universe of discourse. How-

[1] Tillich, "The Meaning and Justification of Religious Symbols", *Religious Experience and Truth*, p. 4.

ever, one basic distinction might be made between "primary", "insight",[1] or "integrative" symbols and "secondary", "explanatory", or "corroborating"[2] symbols. We have insisted that the symbolic dimension spans all universes of discourse and that the characteristic feature of the authentic symbol is that it has a special, intrinsic relationship to that which it symbolizes. Yet in each universe of discourse there are at any given historical time certain primary or key symbols that provide the pivotal insights. The awareness or understanding carried by these symbols are foundational for the entire universe of discourse because they tend to integrate the knowledge in a particular area. Without these insight or integrative symbols, the universe of discourse ultimately lacks consistency and coherence. In addition to insight symbols there is a larger group of symbols which yield not only awareness of their objects but also lead to the apprehension of the insight symbols. They function as explanatory or corroborating symbols. The important fact is that they are still in the symbolic dimension and not in the conceptual or descriptive dimension of language where symbols are interpreted by means of expansion and evaluation.

Some philosophers of language have been concerned not only with the absence of the symbolic or intuitive element from language, but particularly with the loss of key or insight symbols which provide an orientation for the direction of human life itself. Susanne Langer describes these as our "life-symbols", the symbols of our *Lebensanschauung*.[3] It is the hope that our consideration of the nature of language and particularly its capacity in virtue of its symbolic dimension may help us to recover, or at least to consider seriously again, the value of certain integrative symbols for life orientation. But this becomes possible only if we revitalize our understanding of symbols in order to realize the power as an access to reality inherent in the symbolic dimension of language.

We have attempted to indicate the nature of the symbolic dimension of language which is characterized by the development of a verbal sign into a symbol. The symbol referred to here is an illuminating and transformational symbol in that it provides authentic awareness of that reality which it symbolizes and thus makes that reality present and mani-

---

[1] The term "insight symbol" is used by Urban; e.g., p. 414. However, it is employed here in a somewhat more specialized way.

[2] The use of "corroborating symbol" here is indebted to Tillich, in "Existential Analysis and Religious Symbols", *Four Existentialist Theologians*, Will Herberg (ed.) (Garden City, New York : Doubleday Anchor Books, 1958).

[3] Langer, *Philosophy in a New Key*, p. 242.

fest to those who employ the symbol meaningfully. The symbol characteristic of this dimension is also a pointing symbol in that it points beyond
itself as a symbol to an existential encounter with the thing symbolized.
This involves a dialectic of affirmation and negation. The function of
the symbolic dimension is to provide the structure for the disclosure
of Being in language, to supply an essential "given" for linguistic meaning, and to establish the necessary foundation for intelligible communication.

At this point the relationship of the symbolic dimension to another
basic dimension of language must be considered. The question of the
interdependence and the transition from one dimension to another is
central for an understanding of the nature of human language. It is the
thesis of this study that the symbolic dimension can neither manifest
its nature, as so described, nor fulfill its function in separation from the
non-symbolic dimension of language. Every symbol demands interpretation. Only then is it capable of being understood and only then can
we make an adequate judgment about its truth or authenticity as a symbol.
The symbol, in order to allow that term any significant meaning, must
be interpreted by linguistic signs operating within the non-symbolic
dimension of language. The non-symbolic provides more precise information, is necessary in order to facilitate understanding and intelligible
communication, allows linguistic meaning to come to maturity, is subject
to verification, and even provides a means of recommending certain
symbols by establishing their depth and reasonableness. The dimension
of language in which this interpretation takes place is the conceptual.

The Conceptual Dimension

The conceptual dimension of human language requires less explication
than does the symbolic precisely because this is the region in which
we usually assume our language primarily operates. In fact, the conceptual has gained an almost authoritative status. The danger here is that
sometimes we assume language is doing its proper job when it is conveying
information or functioning in a descriptive way. The conceptual dimension is not an indirect but rather, a direct way of speaking. The nature
of this dimension is such that the verbal signs employed are intended
to give objective knowledge. The conceptual meaning produced by these
verbal signs is intended to be clear and precise. The assertions made in
the conceptual dimension are subject to the standards of formal logic

and are capable of being verified. This is the realm in which technical thinking as opposed to foundational thinking is manifest.[1]

It is in the conceptual dimension of language that the indicative meaning function predominates. This dimension is present in every universe of discourse from natural science to philosophy and theology. Here one is dealing with clear and distinct concepts which claim to convey objective information and therefore are subject to the standards of formal logic, to empirical verification, or to a form of verification characteristic of the universe of discourse in which these statements operate. It is clear that a very large proportion of our normal discourse operates in just this conceptual or descriptive realm. Problems arise, however, which lead to a distortion in the understanding of the full scope of human language either when it is asserted that all language is restricted to the conceptual dimension of language, or when the conceptual dimension is claimed to be banal or lacking in significance and thus its imperative contribution is not recognized and appreciated.

The first position is represented by those defending what I have described as a low evaluation of language or a nominalist position. The demands of this position were most clearly made and its influences most in evidence in the case of a movement in philosophy known as logical positivism, which took the language of natural science (and, I would contend, only a particular aspect of that) as providing the sole criterion for meaningful language. The key issue for the logical positivist is that the meaning of a statement is determined by the way in which it is verified. However, verification is conceived here in a rather narrow sense since the "verification principle" for the positivist rests on the assertion of the priority of sense data and logical form in the means of verification. It is generally conceded today that there are few logical positivists operating under the assumption of this earlier position. However, even in the wider forms of linguistic analysis philosophy, which have their roots here, the element of nominalism still prevails.[2] The intuitive element of language is questioned, if not denied (with some exceptions, such as in the work of Strawson). The emphasis has admittedly moved from "meaning" to "use", but language is still analyzed primarily as a product of a given cultural community. The function of language as an access to reality, which I see as crucial to the adequate understanding of the nature of language, is denied or seen as beyond the scope of philosophy. Language

---

[1] The dimensions of thought, only introduced here, are explicated in Chapter V.

[2] Martin, *The New Dialogue Between Philosophy and Theology*, p. 184.

is thus restricted to the conceptual dimension or relegated to the realm of emotive utterance that lacks a cognitive element.

The second view is assumed by those who are so concerned with the essential power of language as an access to reality that the predominant dimension of language becomes the symbolic rather than the conceptual. The disclosure of Being in language and the resulting eventful character of human articulation are so stressed as to make any other dimension of language somehow inappropriate or insignificant. Thus human language which does not manifest this disclosure character is described as inauthentic, idle, or banal. This tendency is represented in theology by a group which can loosely be designated as those concerned with the "New Hermeneutic",[1] most notably Ebeling and Fuchs. The focus of this movement, influenced by Heidegger, is on Word as address that demands obedient response on the part of man and not on word as interpretation and understanding. What is underestimated, if not ignored, is the cultural factor in language which is at least partially responsible for language's meaning and use.[2]

It appears to me that the solution to this tendency toward bifurcation, and thus the distortion of the proper understanding of language by the exaggerated claims of positions whose basic insight is essentially correct, is the recognition of the dimensional nature of language. This allows language to have its own authentic function and purpose within a given dimension. But more important is the notion that it is the very interconnectedness of the dimensions that allows them to function

---

[1] An analysis of "The New Hermeneutic" as a movement is given in J. W. Robinson and J. B. Cobb, Jr., *The New Hermeneutic*, and in Robert W. Funk, *Language, Hermeneutic, and Word of God* (New York : Harper & Row, 1966), Part I, Chapter 3 particularly.

[2] Note the critique of Amos Wilder, pp. 198ff., and John B. Cobb, Jr., p. 219, in *The New Hermeneutic*. It is also interesting to mark Wilder's comment in relation to this critique that : "It seems curious to me [Wilder] that he [Fuchs] does not appeal more often to such secular investigations as those of Cassirer, Langer, van der Leeuw, Eliade, and Pettazoni. From my point of view the apologetic advantages of such a frank hospitality to social science would be great. It would mean, however, that the widely recognized cognitive element in speech, gesture, and language would have to be taken seriously. The birth of language and mythical speech in their primary context involve social and cosmic orientation and life-meaning. It would mean that the whole discussion of the word God and its hearing among men would have to submit to the relativities of cultural, semantic, and psychological observation. It is this kind of development which I find missing at many points in the new hermeneutic. As a result, it has too much the character of an inner-theological pursuit" (p. 216). This study has attempted to take seriously some of these secular investigations.

properly at all. Let me attempt to illustrate this by indicating the way in which the transformational and pointing symbols operating in the symbolic dimension of language require interpretation within the conceptual dimension.

As I maintained before, to bring meaning to maturity and thus for intelligible communication to occur, interpretation is required. Before that authentic awareness or understanding provided by the symbol can be said to have a "sense" or "meaning" (that is, can be said to be understood), and before one can make a judgment about the truth or the "meaning" of the symbol, that symbol must be interpreted. However, as Urban correctly remarks, "The notion of the interpretation of the symbol presupposes that there is non-symbolic language in which it may be interpreted".[1] The non-symbolic language is to be found in what was described as the conceptual dimension of language. This is sometimes described as "literal language", but I think this tends to be misleading. "Non-symbolic language" is only a limiting notion, since the dimensions of language cannot be absolutely separated. Non-symbolic language indicates language which is direct, precise, and which is capable of verification.

The particular pattern of interpretation is governed by the universe of discourse in which the symbol is employed, but one can examine the process of symbolic interpretation in general in order to indicate what is involved in the interconnection of dimensions of language. Interpretation is the "exploration and elucidation of meaning",[2] or the bringing of meaning to maturity. This forms the foundation for intelligible communication. Urban has a valuable suggestion when he refers to two aspects of interpretation : Expansion and Evaluation.[3]

The illuminating, transformational, and pointing symbol is a contraction or condensation of meaning. The symbol points beyond itself to that which it symbolizes and conveys an authentic awareness of that reality. Interpretation as expansion involves in the first instance expanding the unexpressed reference of the symbol. Expansion attempts to elucidate precisely what the reality is to which the symbol refers. It does this in

[1] Urban, *Language and Reality*, p. 413. There is a sense in which corroborating symbols could be said to interpret key symbols. However, what is really involved is not interpretation but supplementation or balance. Finally, one must turn to non-symbolic interpretation.

[2] Macquarrie, *God-Talk*, p. 147.

[3] Urban, *op. cit.*, pp. 428ff. Urban's basic distinction is employed here, but I have used slightly different terminology.

terms which are conceptual and therefore more generally comprehensible. However, I would maintain that this is not merely the substitution of non-symbolic for symbolic sentences. Interpretation which involves substitution tends to conceal the value of symbol as symbol. The symbol expresses something which cannot be expressed in any other way. Thus, expansion must be understood in terms of interpretation and not substitution. The expansion must be done in order that the symbol may be understood, but it should be done in such a way that the meaning of the symbol is enriched and not dissolved.[1] The symbolic element can never be eliminated because its intuitive character establishes its value as a symbol. The expansion of the unexpressed references of the symbolic into the non-symbolic clarifies the fact that the verbal sign is to be understood as a "symbol"and not as a literal reference. The first step in the interpretation of the symbol is, then, expansion.

The second aspect of interpretation is what I have called evaluation of the symbol.[2] The evaluation of the symbol is the determination of its existential and ontological import, its knowledge value. The expansion of the symbol permits it to be understood, appreciated, and even enjoyed, but does not necessarily raise the issue of its truth or authenticity, of its existential and ontological import. Thus, the symbol must not only be expanded but also evaluated. As I have noted previously, the crucial characteristic of the symbol lies in the relationship between the symbol and the thing symbolized. Thus, the symbol is said to be true or authentic when it is adequate to convey the awareness or understanding of that which it symbolizes. In our use of symbol, this is an adequacy of insight or penetration. The presupposition is that symbols do have meaning and via interpretation they do communicate a type of knowledge. This communication is facilitated by conceptual interpretation. There is a type of symbolic consciousness which is a unique form of cognitive consciousness. As a result of this consciousness we have what could be described as symbolic truth; namely, adequacy of insight or understanding.

The process of interpretation, then, first involves expansion in which the adequacy of a symbol is determined by a process of expansion into non-symbolic terms which are then subject to verification. "Symbolic

---

[1] Urban, *Language and Reality*, p. 435.

[2] *Ibid.*, p. 428. What is here described as "evaluation" is simply called "interpretation" for Urban. I have used "interpretation" as a general term to cover "expansion" and "evalution".

truth", on the other hand, involves the adequacy of symbol as symbol, the adequacy to represent that which one actually experiences. This is adequacy for a symbolic type of consciousness. In the latter case one can speak of an "authentic" symbol or sometimes simply a "good" symbol, meaning that it has the capacity to supply the insight or authentic awareness that cannot be expressed in any other form. Thus I speak of the verification of the interpretation of the symbol in the conceptual dimension of language and of the authentication of a symbol in regard to "symbolic truth". I have revised and elaborated an example employed by Urban to illustrate these two aspects of interpretation.[1] The statement that the state is a living body or an organism is obviously absurd if it is taken in the literal sense of biological functions. However, if the statement is seen as symbolic and is expanded into non-symbolic statements about how the state functions as an organism, it can be significant. These non-symbolic statements might, for example, include concrete illustrations of the interdependence of various branches of government or the event involved in the birth or death of a particular government or nation. These non-symbolic statements may be verified in the attempt to evaluate the organic theory of the state. Here we are dealing with the expansion of a symbol of the state in order to see more clearly that to which the symbol refers. This is done in the conceptual dimension of language. This occurs in all universes of discourse where the symbolic dimension operates, in the scientific, aesthetic, and religious.

However, there is another issue involved. So far I have discussed only the verification of the non-symbolic expansion of the symbol. The further question deals with symbolic truth, with the adequacy of the symbol to provide insight. This cannot be verified in the sense mentioned previously because symbolic truth is not subject to this type of direct verification. However, there is what I have described as the authentication of a symbol. This involves the judgment that the symbol is adequate to express authentic awareness and essential insight into that which is symbolized. The symbol of the state as an organism may provide this type of insight which is not simply reducible to verification of its expanded statements. There is a sense in which this authentication only comes about in discourse itself, in intelligible communication where—in the midst of a given speech community, a common universe of discourse,

---

[1] Urban, *Language and Reality*, p. 443. This illustration has its basis in Kant's use of two symbolic representations of the State, the mechanical and the organic, in *The Critique of Judgment*, pp. 248-249.

and an agreement on the dominant meaning function of the statement—
the symbol is received as supplying awareness and understanding to our
symbolic consciousness. The symbol is then evaluated as being authenticated. But the conceptual dimension of language plays a significant
role even in relation to symbolic truth. For the conceptual or non-symbolic interpretation of the symbol functions to recommend our consideration of certain symbols as more likely to be authentic than others.
If the expansion and interpretation of the symbol in a particular universe
of discourse results in declarations which are coherent and consistent
with the views that one holds concerning other aspects of his existence
in the modern world, as expressed in other universes of discourse, then
this symbol is recommended for further consideration, exploration,
and elucidation. If, however, the expansion or interpretation results in
conclusions which stand in contradiction or violent contrast with other
views one holds about the nature of his existence, then the authenticity
of the symbol or its interpretation are placed in question. This means
that the symbolic dimension is not completely consigned to foundational
thought, but the critical function of technical thought and the judgments
of standard logic and verification are applicable insofar as they recommend or discourage the consideration of the authenticity of specific
symbols. This is to maintain not a rationalistic but a reasonable approach
to the symbolic dimension of human language.

     In the discussion of the symbolic dimension of human language,
I indicated that there was only one particular type of verbal sign which
was employed because of its essential power and the unique function
of the symbolic dimension. This verbal form was obviously the symbol
used, not in the wider sense of merely representative, but rather, in its
narrower sense of an illuminating, transformational, and pointing symbol.
It is, of course, quite a different matter when one considers the types of
verbal signs which are operative within the conceptual dimension of
human language. Here is not one verbal form but many. All the types
of verbal signs which are capable of providing conceptual information
are applicable. Thus, ways of speaking which are direct rather than indirect and which provide objective knowledge because they are precise
in their method of expression are to be included here. When both the
intention and result of the employment of a verbal sign is to supply
conceptual information, descriptive definition and illustration, or direct
denotation, then one is involved with the conceptual dimension of
human language. The types of verbal signs employed in the conceptual
dimension run the gamut from analogy to direct declarative statements

to signals. Obviously, all these verbal forms neither can nor need be considered in detail in this study. However, I do wish to suggest one verbal form for more extensive analysis : analogy.

The concern for analogy is due to the theological interest and the role analogy has played in the development of systematic theology. However, beyond this immediate consideration is the fact that analogy is not usually classified as being in the descriptive realm. Analogy is not normally understood as a means of providing objective knowledge which is subject to the standards of formal logic and to appropriate verification. Rather, analogy often is interpreted as that means of moving from the known to the totally unknown. It often is understood as the medium by which language and thinking incorporate new knowledge. Analogy frequently is utilized as the method of stretching language in order to encompass the unknown. This latter view leads to the result that symbol and analogy often are used interchangeably or synonymously. Even one who agrees with my thesis about dimensions of language might tend to locate analogy in the intuitive or symbolic dimension rather than in the conceptual dimension.

However, it is the suggestion of this study that analogy ought to be understood as a "descriptive tool" or as a "principle of interpretation" which is operative in the conceptual dimension of language. Analogy should not be seen as a means of obtaining new knowledge, but rather, as a conceptual tool for expressing, expanding, interpreting, and illustrating a new cognitive understanding gained prior to this in an existential encounter constituted by authentic awareness and essential insight; namely, via symbol. Symbol illuminates; analogy illustrates. Symbol and analogy as understood here are neither synonymous nor contradictory. Rather, they are complementary and strategically interconnected insofar as they fulfill their respective and appropriate functions. The nature and function of symbol and analogy are determined by the dimensions of language in which they operate. This integral and complementary relation is a result of the nature of human language itself. This constitutes, then, a tentative proposal concerning the relationship between symbol and analogy. Such an understanding of the nature, function, and relation of symbol to analogy is more intelligible than their frequent identification or their contradiction. This proposal is reinforced by being congruent with a dimensional understanding of the structure of human language.

I would agree with Niels C. Nielsen that "Analogy is not so much a method for gaining new knowledge as a means of making clear what is already implicit in a particular context".[1] It is just this clarifying or descriptive function of analogy which makes it a reliable methodological instrument not only for theology and philosophy but for all disciplines of inquiry. Analogy, considered as a linguistic form, may be a way of relating two expressions, both functioning within the conceptual dimension of language. It may also be a way of expanding and interpreting a statement made in the symbolic dimension by relating it to a statement made in the conceptual or non-symbolic dimension. In both cases there are held to be certain points of similarity and certain points of dissimilarity which are illustrated by the use of analogy. Analogy provides clarification and therefore valuable knowledge by means of the comparison, but this is knowledge by means of clarification of that which is already implicit in the context and not by a leap of insight or the disclosure of a new understanding. The latter is supplied not by analogy, an instrument of explanation, but by symbol, an instrument of insight. In each case the use of analogy asserts a particular kind of relationship, a similarity, between the statements, entities, conditions, etc., that are involved.

It was part of my intent in the use of analogy as a descriptive tool to make the nature of the analogical relationship clear. There is also a further step—the process of identifying the positive and negative aspects of the analogy; namely, those aspects which are in fact similar and provide objective knowledge and those aspects which are dissimilar and tend to mislead. But analogy is a methodological tool and the statements which are made positively or negatively are subject to the laws of formal logic and to appropriate forms of verification. Only if the latter is possible can these statements provide the basis of intelligible communication, because here there exists a means of laying claim to the reasonableness of our statements. The symbol operating in the symbolic dimension points beyond itself to direct encounter or participation, claims only authentication, and is not verifiable in this way. However, the interpretation of the symbols in the conceptual dimension employs linguistic forms that speak directly and must be subject to verification. It becomes obvious that they are interconnected, one requires the other. The symbol requires the analogy (or some other verbal form in the conceptual

---

[1] Niels C. Nielsen, Jr., "Analogy as a Principle of Theological Method Historically Considered", *The Heritage of Christian Thought*, R. E. Cushman and E. Grislis (eds.) (New York : Harper & Row, 1965), p. 198. Nielsen's article initiated much of my thought about the relationship of symbol to analogy, but he would probably not draw the same conclusions from his insights as I do.

dimension) to expand and interpret it if it is to reach mature meaning and thus facilitate intelligible communication. The analogy requires the symbol to provide insight, new understanding, and at some ultimate point an access to reality itself.

One should be reminded that just as symbols are characteristic of particular universes of discourse, so are analogies (or other types of verbal signs which are employed in the conceptual dimension of language). For instance, the theories which account for the form of the analogy and those things which may count toward its verification or non-verification are determined by the universe of discourse in which it operates. Also, one should note that just as there are various forms of symbols and no one form is adequate in all cases, so there are various forms of analogies and no one interpretation exhausts its potential interpretative power within a specific universe of discourse.[1]

I have focused briefly on analogy in my consideration of the conceptual dimension of language because of its importance in the contemporary discussion and its confusing and sometimes controversial relation to symbol. But the relationship of symbol and analogy is only one way to illustrate the dimensional structure of language and the interconnectedness of these two initial dimensions.[2] There are other forms of the conceptual dimension which must be left for development at some future date.

---

[1] Nielsen, *The Heritage of Christian Thought*, pp. 200, 219. Nielsen also maintains the need for a variety of types of analogy.

[2] At one point in my research I seriously considered specifying an emotive dimension of language as well. However, as a result of dialogue with Professor Tom F. Driver, I came to the conclusion that this would be an error. As Professor Driver maintained, the emotive element in discourse is not a separate dimension but rather a function of the two basic dimensions of language, the symbolic and the conceptual. Emotion is not true or false but proper or improper to a specific situation. Emotion based on a false conceptuality is an irrational emotion, and a strong emotion evoked by an inauthentic symbol is absurd. One really requires the symbolic and the conceptual dimensions to be able to pursue any analysis of the emotive. Because upon analysis emotion dissolves into a conceptual or symbolic awareness. There are some occasions on which emotion is more properly directed than on others. However, since one cannot evaluate or identify emotion without reference to the conceptual or symbolic, then the emotive is best regarded as a function—a subjective function in a hearer or speaker—and not as a distinctive dimension of language.

Summary

In brief summary, it has been the conclusion of this section that a dimensional understanding of human language is not only consistent with a high evaluation of language, but it is necessary in order to make intelligible how language can function as an access to reality, a bearer of meaning, and a medium of communication. An exploratory schema was proposed which identified two dimensions of language which operate in every universe of discourse. The symbolic is the location of the disclosure of Being and provides authentic awareness and cognitive insight, and the conceptual is the realm of non-symbolic interpretation and provides conceptual information and objective knowledge. It is my contention that it is possible to intelligibly account for the fact that Being does arrive at non-concealment, that linguistic meaning does come to maturity, and that intelligible communication can occur only when the nature and function of each dimension is recognized and acknowledged and the dimensions are seen in their interdependence and dialectic relation. The symbol requires interpretation by the conceptual. The conceptual requires symbolic insight. The "illuminating", "transformational", and "pointing" symbol is the verbal sign which characterizes the adequacy and power of the symbolic dimension. The analogy, interpreted as a "descriptive tool" or "principle of interpretation", is seen as an illustrative verbal sign of the conceptual dimension.

The basic outline for a theory of the dimensional structure of language has been developed. It is now necessary to examine the dimensions of thought which parallel the proposed dimensions of language in order to make a case for a comprehensive theory of language upon which an intelligible understanding of symbolism might be based.

CHAPTER FIVE

DIMENSIONS OF THOUGHT

It is "through thought that Being comes to language".[1] This assertion by Heidegger raises the central issue of this chapter. What is the relationship between thought and word? How can one conceive of the relation between our thoughts, the words and sentences that embody these thoughts, and that to which they refer? The problem which confronts us is that of language and cognition.

A dimensional structure of language, as has been maintained, is necessary in order to have an adequate comprehension of the nature of language and to make intelligible the notions of meaning and communication, as they have been developed here. If Being comes to language through thought and certain forms of thought empower specific forms of language, then not only is a dimensional understanding of language required but also a dimensional conception of thouhgt or reason as well. It was suggested previously that the philosophy of the later Heidegger implies a dimensional structure of thought in the distinction between "foundational" and "calculative" or "technical" thought.[2] However, an attempt to clarify and distinguish the particular levels of thought and specifically their relationship to various dimensions of language is only embryonic.

The task of this section will be to set forth in outline form such a dimensional structure of thought which coincides with and is entailed by a dimensional structure of language as developed in the previous chapter. It will be suggested that the symbolic dimension of language is empowered by "foundational" thought or reason and is characterized by "receiving" knowledge. The conceptual dimension of language, on the other hand, is associated with "technical" thought or reason and is characterized by "controlling" knowledge. These two dimensions of thought are dialectically related in a complementary way; they are inter-

---

[1] Heidegger, *Brief ... Humanismus*, p. 53.

[2] "Technical thought" will be used to refer to the kind of thinking that is connected with technicity (*Technik*) and is sometimes called "calculation" (*Rechnung*) or "calculative thinking" (*Verrechnen*).

dependent, each requiring the other to fulfill its proper function. Just as it was noted with the dimensions of language, it is also true with the dimensions of thought that the foundational and technical must be in harmony with one another if understanding and communication are going to occur and result in significant knowledge.

The emphasis of this chapter is upon a dialectical relation between technical and foundational or ontological reasoning. It is well to note that this dialectical emphasis will be a characteristic concern of this study. The basic assumption of this analysis of language, thought, and knowledge is on the dynamic character of our experience and access to reality. The process of change, historical and psychological, points to and accounts for the dialectical nature of the dimensional understanding proposed here. Even Being's disclosure in language is seen not as a static condition but as a dynamic historical process. The "disclosure" of Being has a temporal aspect, in that the encounter with Being in language may be grasped or recognized at a given moment. This disclosure also has a dynamic element where Being's self-disclosure is manifest through a process or a "being present" to those who are attentive to this disclosure in language. These brief remarks are intended to set the context for the discussion which follows.

Relation of Language and Cognition

As a basis for analysis of the proposed dimensions of thought, it is imperative to consider the prior question of the relation between language and cognition. Does cognition operate somehow independently of language and thus supply a form of knowledge that is the result of direct acquaintance with sense data or of a "direct awareness" of the object? Is this form of direct knowledge then embodied in language only as a secondary or additional movement in order to bring about communication? This would mean that the process of cognition, the notion of intuition either sensuous or non-sensuous, is independent of, prior to, and thus separable from expression and from language. On the other hand, can it be maintained that there is no cognition in any significant sense that does not involve language? Is the very act of cognition not already constituted by language in such a way that there is no notion of knowledge possible without linguistic forms, at least implicitly? This would mean that the process of cognition is dependent on language, that there is an identity of intuition and expression, and that thought and knowledge are finally inseparable from language. It is part of the thesis of this study that the latter view is the case and that language and cognition are inseparable. Thought and word are inextricably bound together so that the crucial question will finally become one of the relationship between the expression and that which is expressed, between language and reality. But let us now consider the relationship between thought and word that leads to the assertion of the inseparability of language and cognition.

Reflect upon what process evolves when one thinks about a particular experience; for example, a meeting and conversation with a new acquaintance. As soon as one begins to think about the experience, which involves focusing mental attention on the experience so that it becomes more than a vague awareness, he then makes judgments about it. The meeting was "interesting" or "dull", "pleasurable" or "irritating". The person was "straightforward" or "deceptive", "responsive" or "withdrawn". No matter what one thinks about the experience, certain judgments are made, whether they be trivial or important. These judgments, in order to have any content, namely, to move beyond a vague awareness, must be given a form which allows them to be related to one another. The form which is given to the content of this judgment is a linguistic one, at least implicitly. The form must be expressed in order to have meaning. Or perhaps, since the linguistic form is required only implicitly, one could say that only "expressibility" is necessary, In other words, the verbal expression itself is part of the thought process. As I contended earlier, it is inconceivable to have thoughts without words, at least in a latent form. Thought involves judgment, judgment involves expression, and expression involves language. As Urban states it, "Any experience which is more than a mere vague awareness is already constituted and categorized by language".[1] This is a result of what I would describe as the "process of articulation" and what Urban refers to as the "natural speech construction". These linguistic entities, verbal signs, become the subjects of discourse and the possible objects of knowledge. Language is a result of man's encounter with reality. However, language is also constitutive of that encounter. Thought and language are inseparable.

The inseparability of language and knowledge has also been affirmed. This is a more complex problem because it depends on what one means

---

[1] Urban, *Language and Reality*, p. 332. Urban's thesis concerning the inseparability of language and cognition underlies much of the argument in this section. For a more detailed development of the points made here, see especially Chapter VIII, "Language and Cognition".

by knowledge. Urban has cited two basic notions of knowing.[1] (1) The narrower view of knowledge identifies it with limited and direct reference and finally coincides with empirical verifications. (2) The wider view of knowledge (described as the humane) allows the term to be applied to values or experiences that are not reducible to an empirical level, such as knowledge of "love" or values like "honesty" or "goodness". I would agree with Urban that knowledge must be employed in the wider or humane sense if we are not to eliminate from the field of knowledge a large part of human experience and human discourse. Urban then goes on to explicate, following Josiah Royce, a triadic theory of knowing which distinguishes between (1) knowledge by direct acquaintance or perception, (2) knowledge by description or conception, and (3) knowledge by interpretation.[2] The space is not available to follow through in detail Urban's intricate argument for the inseparability of language and cognition, but several conclusions are important for my own case. It is noted that the elementary form of knowledge is judgment. However, this is a form of judgment that can be determined to be either true or false. Since it has been maintained previously that only assertions are true or false, then knowledge must involve expression and ultimately language. "There is no cognition in any significant sense which does not involve communication and some sort of language".[3] As a corollary, Urban maintains that there is no such thing as knowledge by mere acquaintance. Even acquiring perceptual knowledge (sensuous intuition) is not simply a matter of having the sense data, but if one is to claim knowledge, the sense data must be interpreted by judgment and that judgment must in turn be expressed. The same is true of what can be described as non-sensuous intuition of values or qualities. As soon as knowing moves beyond the area of simply "that is that" and takes on the form of a judgment which makes a claim to knowledge, then that judgment must be expressed. Expression involves language. This can be illustrated, I think, by adapting as Urban does an example from H. Bergson.[4] Let us suppose that language fell into disuse and all communication was dissolved. What then would be left? Certainly nothing meriting the name of knowledge. There would be, perhaps, a vague awareness or an implicit affirmation, "that is that", but without language the con-

---

[1] Urban, *Language and Reality*, p. 337.
[2] *Ibid.*, pp. 339ff.
[3] *Ibid.*, p. 343.
[4] *Ibid.*, p. 341.

tent of the judgment which constitutes knowledge could not come to expression. The conclusion is that expression is not only representative of intuition but also is constitutive of intuition itself (both sensuous and non-sensuous). Here expression and intuition are one, because the verbal expression itself is part of the apprehending or knowing. This means that words are crucial to showing forth the nature of reality. "Knowing in any significant sense of the word is inseparable from language …".[1] The classic expression of this relationship of knowing to language comes in the thesis of Benedetto Croce concerning the "identity of intuition and expression".[2] The contention is that cognition is not separable from language. "One does not first possess an object in knowing and then express the nature of that object in terms of arbitrary and conventional signs [language], but the expression is a constitutive part of the knowing itself".[3] The inseparability of knowing and language is based on the principle already discussed of the inseparability of thought and language.

The notion of the inseparability of language and thought requires at this point a word of qualification. The idea taken from Croce asserting the "identity of intuition and expression" could be misconstrued in reference to my own interpretation to suggest that thought and language are vitrually identical in every regard. I would not wish to stretch the concept this far. The important insight contained in this notion is the emphasis in my study on the issue of inseparability in the sense that language is a necessary part of the thought process. There are probably forms of thought in the sense of general impressions that are prior to language, and perhaps some forms of mystical thought that claim to be beyond language, and perhaps even some thought which does not get adequately formed in actual linguistic articulation. Yet thought which comes to have an intelligible form, which claims to be knowledge and which is capable of communication, is not possible apart from language. Language must be seen as constitutive (in the sense of a necessary cause) of the cognitive process. It is the crucial role of language in regard of thought and knowledge which is stressed in this notion of inseparability. There is a sense in which one must allow for a semi-independence of knowledge from language which would account for the effect new exper-

---

[1] Urban, *Language and Reality*, p. 347.

[2] *Ibid.* The idea is developed in regard to Croce's aesthetics in Benedetto Croce, *Aesthetic as Science of Expression and General Linguistic*, Douglas Ainslie (trans.) (New York : Noonday Press, 1960).

[3] *Ibid.*, p. 347.

iences have on our language. We seek alternative forms of language until we can say "Yes, that expresses what I mean". Yet this is only a semi-independence which fits into the wider context of the inseparability of language and cognition.

It can be concluded that thought and knowledge are bound up with expression. However, on the basis of our previous assertions in the sections on meaning and communication, we are driven to a further conclusion. This is that expression in language always involves intentionality and that "there is no expression without the correlative, understanding".[1] In other words, communicability is not an irrelevant or secondary factor in knowing, but in fact constitutes the very basis of our claim to knowledge. Knowledge involves judgment, judgment requires expression, and expression entails communication. "All knowledge involves communication, either latent or overt".[2] Knowledge must be capable of communication if it asserts a claim to truth. Truth involves verifiability, and I will maintain in the section which follows that verifiability and communication are closely associated.[3] But for the moment, it is enough to see the interrelationship of knowledge, expression, and communication.

If there is no knowing without expression, then whenever we have knowledge there is an element of representation present. There is what Urban describes as a "bi-polar relationship between the expression and the expressed".[4] Language is the form of this representation so that the question of knowledge and truth focuses on the adequacy of the representation or on the adequacy of linguistic expression.

It is the form of representation that provides us with knowledge. How is the expression related to that which is expressed? There appear to be at least two fundamental ways in which the expression represents that which is expressed, in which language may represent reality. The form of representation may be a conceptual one in which a logical structure is provided in the form of a proposition. A judgment is set forth in a conceptual way with the precision of logical order and this proposition is subject to public verification. However, the form of representation may also be a symbolic one in which the picture of reality provided

---

[1] Urban, *Language and Reality*, p. 348.

[2] *Ibid.*, p. 350.

[3] Verifiability here is used in the widest sense of "capable of being affirmed as true or false". The following chapter will deal with a detailed consideration of verification and truth.

[4] Urban, *op. cit.*, p. 347.

is not a conceptual one with the same degree of precision and logical order(although it is not illogical) but rather an indirect form of representation which provides insight and thus knowledge for a form of symbolic consciousness. The result is that there are two different types of knowledge as well as two different forms of representation. One can be described as conceptual or controlling knowledge and the other as symbolic or receiving knowledge. However, the point I wish to emphasize here is that there is no knowledge without an element of interpretation. The form of representation, whether it is conceptual description or symbolic formulation, must be interpreted in order to grasp its sense, in order to see what its explicit or implicit assertion or claim is and thus to verify or authenticate that assertion. This interpretation takes place ultimately in language, so the problems of knowledge and the problems of language are inseparable.

Another important corollary of the principle of the identity of intuition and expression is that the "categories of knowledge are ultimately, and in the last analysis, categories of language in the philosophical sense of language".[1] This means that the way in which one can "determine being or reality is in those forms in which statements about it are possible".[2] Being discloses itself in language. Here one must guard against the tendency to see the verbal in isolation from the non-verbal. Language becomes what it is only in the context of the non-verbal. Language has no existence outside of the discourse situation, and the discourse situation depends on the many non-verbal aspects of that particular existential circumstance. The stress here is on the primacy of language as an access to reality and this is confirmed in the recognition of the linguistic character of the categories of knowledge which results from the connection of language and cognition. "Since knowledge involves both expression and interpretation, the categories of knowledge must ... be those forms in which statements about reality are possible".[3] This leads Urban to agree in principle with the statement by Wittgenstein in the *Tractatus* that "the limits of my language are the limits of my world". However, one must certainly be warned against making those limits too narrow and thus restricting one's world in an illegitimate way. Language must be understood in its full dimensional range, just as the corresponding dimensions of thought and knowledge must be equally broad in scope.

---

[1] Urban, *Language and Reality*, p. 350.
[2] *Ibid.*
[3] *Ibid.*, p. 351.

The scope of language and thought has been a particular concern both in this chapter and the former one. I have described a "symbolic dimension" of language and also maintained the need to recognize a "foundational dimension" of thought. A problem arises here because one appears to have knowledge of "metempirical objects".[1] These are "non-observable" entities about which one seems to have meaningful knowledge. These entities include "objects"[2] such as "spirit" or "God" and qualities such as "freedom" or "will". But according to Kant this is not authentic knowledge nor the product of genuine reasoning, but only *transcendentaler Schein*. The problem is that either a good deal which appears to be knowledge and is consequently meaningful is not knowledge at all, or there is a need for a wider concept of knowledge and of thought and reason. Also, in regard to language there are many assertions such as "the good is love" or "God is a spirit" that, although they are intelligible within discourse and particularly within a given universe of discourse, have no empirical object to which they refer. This means that either a good deal of discourse which seems intelligible is in fact unintelligible or that we need a broader understanding of what constitutes intelligible discourse.[3] The questions raised about the limits of knowledge, reason, and intelligible discourse ought to place Kant's whole critique of reason—and, as it now appears, his implied critique of language as well—in question. As John E. Smith states in *Reason and God* :

> Did Kant really treat reason in its full scope and capacities ...? A peculiar fact about Kant's entire first *Critique* is that nowhere does it have any place within itself for the type of knowledge it purports to be ... [and it] shows powers for reason which the official conclusions of that work rule out. The whole question of the nature and scope of reason must be reopened. ...[4]

Urban notes that "Kant himself never denied the meaningfulness of metaphysical propositions but merely their empirical verifiability".[5] If one is going to escape the dilemma of a limited scope for knowledge, reason, and language, he must recognize an additional form of knowledge, or rather, a dimensional understanding of thought and know-

---

[1] Urban, *Language and Reality*, p. 362.

[2] The term "objects" is employed here not in the sense of a "thing" which is objectifiable, but rather in the sense that it becomes the theme or focus of our thought and language and thus can be described as an "object" in the logical sense.

[3] Urban, *op. cit.*, p. 362.

[4] John E. Smith, *Reason and God* (New Haven : Yale University Press, 1961), p. 19.

[5] Urban, *op. cit.*, p. 365.

ledge. In addition, one must recognize another means of verification, or rather, a distinction between verification and authentication. It will be the aim of this chapter and the following one to indicate possible lines of approach to this problem.

In our initial examination of the relationship between language and cognition, the assertion of the inseparability of thought and language, the affirmation of the bond between knowledge, expression, and communication, and the declaration of the representative element in all knowledge have pointed to the underlying issue in all these questions; namely, the relationship of language to reality. If language is inseparable from knowledge and language is our primary means of access to reality, then the issue is whether language adequately represents reality, whether it is the mold[1] in which reality is disclosed, or whether language distorts reality and is a barrier rather than a bridge. This results in a basic assumption about the philosophy of language which involves the dispute of a high evaluation of language versus a low evaluation, or of realism versus nominalism.

The topic was first introduced in Chapter II, where I affirmed the necessity for a high evaluation of language, including what I described as a realist tendency. In light of my discussion of the inseparability of language and cognition, the reasons for this affirmation have become more apparent. The low evaluation of language or the nominalist position in its various forms denies that language is an adequate access to reality. It asserts that names and words are sounds or signs that stand for objects and entities only in a conventional or arbitrary way. The high evaluation of language or the realist position, on the other hand, maintains that language is in some way "constitutive of the real".[2] Here language is seen not only as an adequate access to reality but in fact as ultimately becoming an essential part of any means of apprehending and thus having significant knowledge of the real. A grasp of the most elementary form of experience is already partially determined by language. This description of language, thought, and knowledge has led me to maintain that language and reality are so closely related that a valid and adequate interpretation of language gives us reality.

John Dewey maintains that, "nominalism makes nonsense of our meanings". This is so particularly in regard to metempirical objects as well as references to values and qualities. The nominalist view regards

[1] Urban, *Language and Reality*, p. 375.
[2] *Ibid.*, p. 366.

as nonsense much of human discourse and what claims to be human
knowledge particularly in reference to the most significant aspects of
human experience such as what constitutes knowledge, truth, or value.
None of these factors can be determined on a nominalistic basis. There
is, however, no real answer to the nominalist position. It is a presupposition about the nature of language and finally about the nature of reality.
One can only point out the way in which this low evaluation of language
leads to a paralysis of intelligible speech, a stultification of discourse,
and finally, a stultification of knowledge as well. This criticism of the
low evaluation of language is applicable if I am correct in following
Croce and Urban in the assertion of the identity of intuition and expression and the consequent bond between knowledge and communication. This chapter and the following one involve not so much argu-
mentation as they do a description. I have employed the insights of
Urban and Heidegger to adopt a position with respect to language,
thought, and knowledge. This problem involves, as I have just noted,
accepting certain presuppositions about the nature of language. One must
then ask, in view of these presuppositions, if this interpretation of language, thought, and knowledge coincides with one's own experience.
In light of my experience, I would claim that an understanding which
includes a high evaluation of language is necessary in order to give sufficient scope and thus adequate interpretation of the way one employs
discourse in intelligible and meaningful ways and the claims one usually
makes for knowledge on the basis of this interpretation.

   I have agreed with Urban that language is, in the last analysis, inseparable from thought and knowledge, and that language is the primary
access to reality or the mold in which reality, as "significant", is given.
However, it is here that I would wish to move beyond Urban in order
to assert the source or basis for this close relationship between language
and reality. Language has the capacity to be this adequate access to
reality because Being discloses itself in language.[1] It is in fact the linguistic
capacity of man's nature that provides him with this privileged access
to Being. Being discloses itself to and in man. However, this disclosure
occurs in language and through thought. Language is the "house of
Being", the illuminating and concealing arrival of Being itself, and it is
through thought that Being comes to language. But this disclosure of

---

[1] Heidegger's view of language provides a guide for supplementing the insights
of Urban. The background for these assertions and the principally Heideggerian
terminology involved were explicated previously in Chapter II.

Being to and in man depends on man's radical openness to Being. It depends on man's "attending" to Being both in regard to language and thought. This requires a particularly receptive element in the nature of language, thought, and knowledge. This can be accounted for by a dimensional understanding of the nature of language and thought. It has been the thesis of this study that Being discloses itself in a particular dimension of language and through a particular dimension of thought which are characterized by a particular type of knowledge. The symbolic dimension of language and the foundational dimension of thought, as characterized by receiving knowledge, are a response to the disclosure or revelation of Being. The previous chapter was an attempt to elucidate the dimensional structure of language. A consideration of the dimensional structure of thought or reason follows.[1]

Dimensions of Thought or Reason

It has been maintained that thought and knowledge are inseparable from language and that language is characterized by distinguishable dimensions. It follows, then, that thought ought to have distinguishable dimensions that are parallel and congruous with the proposed dimensions of language. I suggested earlier that Heidegger's understanding of thought at least implied a dimensional structure that was present in an embryonic form in that contrast between "foundational" (*Das wesenliche Denken*) and "technical" thought.

The two primary characteristics of foundational thought[2] are its *receptive* nature and its *experiential* quality. In foundational thought the thinker is open to the subject matter of his thought. He does not try to control the subject matter, or the "object" if one prefers this term,

---

[1] In this chapter, the terms "thought" and "reason" have been used to a degree interchangeably. This is justified, I believe, on the basis of a general definition and by the manner in which the terms are employed here. Webster's *New World Dictionary of the American Language* (New York : World Publishing Co., 1957) defines "thought" as "the power of reasoning" (p. 1517) and "reason" as "the ability to think [or] form judgments" (p. 1200). Also, in subsequent discussion the way in which Heidegger uses "thought", particularly in regard to foundational and technical thought, is comparable to the way in which Tillich uses "reason" in regard to ontological and technical reason.

[2] For the central discussion of the nature of foundational (essential) thinking, see Martin Heidegger, *Was ist Metaphysik?* 7th ed. (Frankfurt : Klostermann, 1955), pp. 46-51. English translation, *Existence and Being*, Werner Brock (ed.) (Chicago : Regnery, 1965), pp. 357-361.

by imposing the structures of his own thought patterns. Rather, the thinker attempts to be open to the insight or unveiling which comes from the side of the subject matter and occurs in the thinking encounter with it. The tendency of foundational thought is not to dominate the objects of thought; foundational thinking will simply let things be. In this sense it is non- or pre-subjective and non- or pre-logical.[1] This foundational thinking comes to the thinker, in a way, from the subject matter. This "receptive structure" of thought has its basis in a man's nature as "ek-sistence". For Heinrich Ott this receptive structure is a crucial insight in Heidegger's notion of thinking.[2] The receptive nature of foundational thinking is a result of its experiential quality, as it is lodged in an event or occurrence. Ott asserts that "[foundational] thinking is not man's disposing of the subject matter from a position of distance, but rather grows out of an occurrence that happens to him. ... It is not establishing of facts from a distance but rather is experience, encounter".[3] It is through foundational thought that Being discloses itself in and to man. Ott indicates both the receptive and experiential character of foundational thought and its connection with Being in this summary statement about Heidegger's conception of foundational think-ing, or as it is referred to here, "essential thinking", or simply "thinking" :

> ... here it must become clear what "thinking" really means. ... For Heidegger, truth is not agreement of the intellect with the subject matter, but rather *a-letheia* is interpreted as unhiddenness. It is an unveiling, an occurrence. Only by means of unveiling is thinking possible. Thinking takes place insofar as what is to be thought unveils itself. This occurrence of unveiling is the truth of being.[4]

In contrast to foundational thought is what Heidegger refers to as "calculation" (*Rechnung*), here described as "technical thinking". Rather than being receptive, technical thought is possessive. It attempts to dominate or control the object of its thought. Rather than being expe-riential, technical thought is experimental. It isolates and analyzes its subject matter. Rather than being involved with the object of thought in terms of an encounter or occurrence, technical thought is detached and formal as it applies certain logical standards in order to gain the control and the standardization which it seeks. Heidegger associates

---

[1] Richardson, *Heidegger* ..., pp. 19-20.
[2] Heinrich Ott, *Denken und Sein* (Zürich : EZV-Verlag, 1959), p. 164.
[3] Ott, "What is Systematic Theology?" *The Later Heidegger and Theology*, p. 108.
[4] *Ibid.*

technical thought with the thinking of mathematical calculation and he sometimes refers to it as "calculative thought" (*Verrechnen*).[1] Technical thought is seen as being characteristic of the work of natural science, certain types of metaphysical philosophy, logic, and mathematics. In each case Heidegger sees a kind of subjectivistic[2] and objectifying thinking which is in contrast to the existential and non-objectifying thinking of foundational thought.[3]

Reference to the terms "objectifying" and "non-objectifying", used both here and at other junctures in this study, requires some explanation even if it takes the form of an extended "aside" for the purpose of clarification. The use of the terms "objectifying" and "non-objectifying" in reference to thinking and speaking has become increasingly confusing in recent years and a topic of considerable controversy particularly in theological circles. No adequate statement can be made in the few lines available here, but some comment is demanded. It would be generally agreed, I think, that all our thinking and speaking has a reference, a subject, a theme, an object. Thus, in a logical sense, all thinking and speaking is objectifying in the sense of having a referent or theme. It seems to me it would be helpful to call this something like the "thematizing" character of all thinking and speaking and allow "objectifying" and "non-objectifying" to designate the nature of the relationship between the thinking and speaking subject and his subject matter. Some thinking and speaking is objectifying in a sense that it seeks to control its subject matter by forcing it to conform to established patterns of thought and speech and so turns a dynamic relationship into a static one. The subject matter is isolated, analyzed, possessed, and thus made into an object. It is objectified. The relationship is an objectifying one. The aim of this objectifying process is one of control for the sake of standardization, preciseness of expression, and final evaluation. This strictly objectifying relationship has its legitimate function in much of our thought and discourse.

Non-objectifying thinking and speaking is characterized by a different

---

[1] Heidegger, *Was ist Metaphysic?* pp. 49-50.

[2] The term is employed in reference to the control or management of the object by the subject, which causes the subject to completely determine the form of thought. Hence it is "subjectivistic".

[3] The dimensional understanding of thought developed here would agree with Heidegger's recognition of the foundational and technical forms of thought but reject his separation of them. I would emphasize their interdependence and dialectical relation due to this dimensional understanding.

relationship between the thinking and speaking subject and his subject matter. Here the aim is not for possession and control but liberation and reception. Some entities are non-objectifiable, or at least they lose their significance when they are objectified, so there is an element of thinking and speaking which attempts to be open to the subject matter in order to gain insight, to have established patterns of thought and speech transformed, and to maintain a dynamic character in the thought and speech process. This element defies standardization, preciseness of expression, and final evaluation. The subject matter is not objectified. The relationship is non-objectifying. The stress is on the distinctive distinctive character of the relationship. It involves an element of encounter, participation, and union between the human subject and the reality which is the referent of his thinking and speaking. The possibility of actualizing this relationship depends on what power or capacities can be appropriately attributed to various aspects of human thought and language.

The terminological difficulties in this controversy can be illustrated by a continuing debate between Fritz Buri and Heinrich Ott, both professors of theology at the University of Basel.[1] Buri has insisted on the objectifying character of all thinking and speaking, while Ott has stressed the need for non-objectifying thinking and speaking, particularly for theology. However, in their personal discussions, they have reached some basic agreement.[2] This consists in recognizing the necessity of all thinking and speaking to be objectifying in the sense of "thematizing". Yet Buri and Ott both admit that on some occasions there exists a kind of relationship between the thinking and speaking subject and the object of his thought and speech where he does not seek to possess the object in such a way as to make it a "thing" liable to ones scrutiny and control. There are some realities which are non-objectifiable in the sense of possession and control. Yet one thinks and speaks of these objects in a

---

[1] This debate is compactly illustrated for the English reader in *Distinctive Protestant and Catholic Themes Reconsidered*, Robert W. Funk (ed.) (New York : Harper & Row, 1967). Heinrich Ott : "The Problem of Non-Objectifying Thinking and Speaking in Theology", pp. 112-135. Fritz Buri : "The Problem of Non-Objectifying Thinking and Speaking in Contemporary Theology", pp. 136-151.

[2] Specific reference is made here to an English Colloquium, "The Language Problem in Contemporary Theology", conducted jointly by Buri and Ott in the summer semester, 1968, University of Basel. They reached the conclusion that they were in general agreement in the seminar session on June 5. This appeared to be a surprise to both of them.

supposedly intelligible and meaningful way. The special relationship which is reflected in our speaking and implies a corresponding structure of thought is described by Ott as "non-objectifying" (*nicht-objektivierend*) or in his revised terminology as "not strictly objectifying" (*nicht streng[1] objektivierend*). Buri also recognizes that this relationship exists and is reflected in language but prefers to designate it as "symbolically objectifying" (*symbolisch-objektivierend*) or simply as "symbolizing" language.[2] The key factor in both cases, objectifying and symbolizing language, is the nature of the relationship and the element of encounter with or participation in the subject matter about which the human subject is concerned.

The point here is that we need to be clear about what is meant by reference to "objectifying" and "non-objectifying" thinking and speaking in order to resolve terminological difficulties and then concentrate on the question of the nature of the relationship referred to by these terms and the capacities of thought and language implied. It is my own judgment that we not only have but require *both* objectifying and non-objectifying thinking and speaking to account for the full scope of human experience. However, they are dependent on one another and are dialectically related .The best way to demonstrate this interdependence is with a dimensional structure of thought and language. We return now from what, hopefully, has been a clarifying "aside" to the matter of Heidegger's view of tecnical thinking.

As stated, a dimensional structure of thought is only implied in Heidegger's philosophy, and I think a development of such a dimensional notion would strengthen his claims for foundational thought. However, Heidegger works against such a dimensional notion by asserting that technical thought is not real thinking at all. Real thinking restricts itself to the unveiling of Being. This means that science is not involved with thinking but only a kind of calculation. It is here that "logic", meaning "formal logic" or its modern successor "logistics", holds sway.[3] Heidegger wishes to reject this logical, calculative, and objectifying type of reason as not being authentic thinking. This, of course, depends on a special definition of thinking. However, what seems evident is that,

---

[1] An alternative translation for *streng* could be "rigorously". The important factor is the manner (*Art*) of the objectification or the nature of the relationship between subject and object indicated.

[2] This position is particularly well developed in an unpublished article by Fritz Buri entitled "Symbol and Analogy".

[3] Heidegger, *Existence and Being*, p. 227.

regardless of what you call it, this technical mode of thought and reason remains. It is not only indispensable in the investigation of certain levels of reality, but it is also necessary to foundational thought itself in terms of interpreting, describing, and communicating at least part of what is apprehended via foundational thinking. I employed the translation "foundational" for this receptive dimension of thought because the term implies just this—a form upon which other dimensions of thought are built and are dependent. Technical thought is finally dependent on foundational thought, but foundational thought requires technical thought to fulfill itself in formulating and communicating what is involved in the disclosure of Being.

Heidegger's insights have been important for my own proposal concerning the dimensional structure of thought and language for several reasons : first, because of his recognition of and attempt to delineate a type of thinking which has the capacity to be open to the disclosure of Being; second, because of his description of this foundational type of thinking as being characterized by a receptive nature and an existential quality; and third, because of his emphasis on the intrinsic relationship between this foundational thinking and language. The limitations of Heidegger's approach for use in the present study are : first, his unwillingness to recognize technical thinking as a necessary and legitimate form of thought; second, his failure to recognize the status of technical thought and the dimensional structure of thinking which makes the dialectical interdependence of foundational and technical thought imperative; and third, his attitude toward theology as being at best ambiguous so that no explicit support can be claimed on the basis of his own position for a parallel between foundational thinking and a certain aspect or dimension of theological thinking.

I would also like to indicate the contributions of another thinker, Paul Tillich, who recognizes the capacity of a certain form of reason or thinking to be open to the disclosure of Being, and who also affirms distinguishable concepts of reason (dimensions in my terminology). In addition he notes the need for these types of reason to be in harmony with one another if the cognitive act of understanding is to be brought to completion. Tillich gives a systematic and detailed explanation of these various concepts of reason and has, of course, a definite and positive concern to relate his insights on thinking to the theological realm. Thus Tillich is appealed to here as an additional resource and authority for my development of the dimensions of thought and reason, as one who counteracts some of the limitations for my proposal inherent in Heidegger's view.[1]

Tillich makes a distinction between "ecstatic" reason and "technical" reason in relation to his discussion of the rational character of systematic theology.[2] Tillich also makes a more general distinction between "ontological" reason and "technical" reason in regard to the structure of reason itself.[3] I would consider ecstatic reason, "the organ with which we receive the contents of faith",[4] to be a special form of ontological reason. This ecstatic reason has both the receptive nature and experiential quality which we previously found associated with foundational thought or reason. There is a kind of cognition implied here which is to be distinguished from technical cognition. Ecstatic reason has a "completely existential, self-determining, and self-surrendering character. ... Ecstatic reason is reason grasped by an ultimate concern".[5]

Although Tillich distinguishes between technical and ecstatic reason, emphasizing the receptive nature of the latter, he affirms clearly their interdependence, their dialectical relationship, and the need for these two dimensions of reason to be in harmony with one another. The cognitive act is never simply one of reception; rather, the apprehending affects what is received. There is a receiving element in the act of cognition, but it is always accompanied by a giving, forming, or shaping element. "Content and form, giving and receiving, have a more dialectical relationship than the words seem to connote... . It [faith in this case] is simultaneously received by ecstatic reason and conceived through technical

---

[1] It would, of course, be a mistake to imply that Tillich's conception of "ontological" and "technical" reason is identical with what Heidegger means by "foundational" and "calculative" thinking. However, I think there are certain parallels in terms of the characteristics attributed to each type of thought. Despite Heidegger's more specialized use of "foundational" thinking and his denial of the necessity of a bond with "technical" thinking, there is a definite parallel in the emphasis on the receptive and experiential elements in "foundational" thought and "ontological" reason. There is also a parallel in the controlling and experimental element in "calculative" thinking and "technical" reason. In discovering and developing the characteristics and qualities of the proposed dimensions of thought, these two thinkers make significant and comparable contributions. In regard to this study they tend to supplement one another as sources of insight and authority.

[2] Tillich, *Systematic Theology*, Vol. I, p. 53.

[3] *Ibid.*, p. 72.

[4] *Ibid.*, p. 53.

[5] *Ibid.*

reason".[1] The danger of misunderstanding the rational process arises when ecstatic and technical reason are isolated from one another, or when they are conceived as being in basic conflict. Tillich states that "complete harmony"[2] between ecstatic and technical reason is not possible under the conditions of life and existence, but this goal of dialectical harmony is the aim of the rational character of systematic theology.

In a more comprehensive analysis of the structure of reason,[3] Tillich makes a distinction between "ontological" and "technical" reason. Ontological reason is identified with the classical notion of reason as logos. "Ontological reason can be defined as the structure of the mind which enables it to grasp and to shape reality".[4] There is a rational or logos structure of the mind, called subjective reason, and a rational or logos structure of reality, designated as objective reason, which the mind can grasp.[5] The receptive element is again accentuated in this notion of ontological reason. "Grasping" and "forming" in the above definition refer to the receiving and reacting functions of the mind in relation to reality. The "grasping" aspect of ontological reason is a "receiving reasonably" that allows the mind to penetrate to the depth or essential nature of a thing. This is a result of its openness and its involvement with the object of its thought. The "shaping", on the other hand, is a "reacting reasonably" to that which is received. The grasping and shaping elements are interdependent.[6] Thus in ontological reason as in foundational thinking the receptive and experiential elements, which open man up to the disclosure of Being, are crucial.

There is an aspect of ontological reason that points beyond itself to that which is manifest in reason. This is described by Tillich as the "depth of reason".[7] It is this "depth of reason" which indicates the potential power of reason as a medium for the self-disclosure of Being. It becomes the expression of " 'being-itself' which is manifest in the *logos* of being".[8] The depth of reason is its quality to point to truth-itself, beauty-itself, justice-itself, etc. Tillich suggests that this depth

[1] Tillich, *Systematic Theology*, Vol. I, p. 54.
[2] *Ibid.*
[3] *Inbid.*, pp. 71ff.
[4] *Ibid.*, p. 72.
[5] *Ibid.*, p. 77.
[6] *Ibid.*, p. 76.
[7] *Ibid.*, p. 79.
[8] *Ibid.*

of reason is expressed in symbolic form.[1] This depth of reason is manifest in all functions of ontological reason, but it is also hidden in reason under the conditions or existence. In order to have an adequate conception of the rational structure of the mind, one needs to accept the ontological concept of reason and understand the depth of reason. Ontological reason, when it is united with its depth, is a response to that which (metaphorically speaking) "preceeds" reason but is manifest in it, namely Being.[2]

"Technical" reason is contrasted with both ontological reason and its specialized form of ecstatic reason. In the technical concept of reason, "reason is reduced to the capacity for 'reasoning' ".[3] It is refined in logical and methodological respects and its aim is to establish consistent, logical, and correctly derived structures of thought. Technical reason strives toward precision and clarity of expression, standardization of forms, and finality of judgment. It is in technical reason that one is concerned with formal logic[4] because of the need for correctness and

---

[1] Tillich, *Systematic Theology*, Vol. I, p. 81.

[2] *Ibid.*, Tillich declares, "Revelation does not destroy reason, but reason raises the question of revelation". I would agree and state that reason is in fact a response to revelation. But "revelation" is employed here in a broader sense than Tillich's use to mean the disclosure of Being in language. This is a disclosure through foundational thought in the symbolic dimension of language. There is also the narrower sense of revelation which refers to the disclosure of Being as holy which results in commitment and a faith relationship. This narrower view of revelation is akin to Tillich's use of ecstatic reason, "the organ with which we receive the contents of faith" (p. 53). Tillich also asserts that "revelation is the manifestation of the ground of being for human knowledge" (p. 94). In my wider sense of revelation this would again be the case because Being's self-disclosure in language does provide the foundation for human knowledge.

[3] *Ibid.*, pp. 72-73.

[4] It should be noted here that it is "formal logic", "traditional logic", or "logistics" which is associated with technical reason and limited to this sphere. Stephen Toulmin in his book, *The Uses of Argument* (Cambridge : Cambridge University Press, 1964), establishes that this notion of technical correctness with an analytic argument as a norm is in fact the stance of most contemporary logicians in regard to the definition of logic (see especially Chapter IV). Toulmin attacks this understanding of logic as resulting in a divergence between the categories of formal logic and the categories of practical argument-criticism (applied logic) (p. 146). He proposes a broader definition of logic : "Logic is concerned with the soundness of the claims we make—with the solidity of the grounds we produce to support them, the firmness of the backing we provide for them—...with the sort of case we present in defense of our claim" (p. 7). Jurisprudence rather than mathematics becomes the model for logic. Toulmin's broader notion of logic with the emphasis on "warrants" and "backing" would be

clarity of interpretation and explanation. Logic becomes a reference point upon which every discipline is dependent. Description and explanation must be in a logically correct form to establish intelligibility. In this sense theology needs formal logic as a *reference point* as much as any other discipline.[1] There is, however, a danger when formalized logic becomes the norm for all types of knowing and reasoning.[2] Technical reason in its attempt to isolate, analyze, and evaluate with a detached critical attitude makes an attempt to possess and control the object for the sake of clarity of expression and finality of judgment.

However, Tillich continually stresses that ontological and technical reason must accompany one another, that they are essentially interdependent. He asserts that in most periods of human history they have been understood in just this interrelated way, but since the middle of the nineteenth century there has been a threat that technical reason would separate itself and attempt to replace ontological reason claiming to be the only legitimate form of reason and thought; this was exemplified in some forms of logical positivism. Tillich maintains that we need both concepts of reason and that they complement one another.

> Technical reason ... dehumanizes man if it is separated from ontological reason. And, beyond this, technical reason is impoverished and corrupted if it is not continually nourished by ontological reason. ... Technical reason is adequate and meaningful only as an expression of ontological reason and as its companion.[3]

It was noted in the introduction to this chapter that not only can one distinguish between two distinctive dimensions of thought or reason, foundational and technical, but these dimensions are characterized by, or result in, two different types of knowledge : receiving and controlling. Tillich serves as the tutor in this analysis.

applicable in both technical and foundational reason. However, Toulmin makes it clear that his is not the presently accepted definition of logic. So when Urgban refers to "metalogical", what is really meant is something which transcends formal logic. So I have contended that formal logic is a "reference point" in every discipline insofar as it deals with technical reason and the conceptual dimension of language. But it is not normative for all forms of reasoning and knowing because some of these are really "meta-formal-logical".

[1] Tillich, *Systematic Theology*, Vol. I, p. 56.

[2] *Ibid.*, pp. 89-90.

[3] *Ibid.*, p. 73.

Corresponding Types of Knowledge

"Knowing is a form of union".[1] The gap between the subject and object is bridged or overcome. As a result of the act of knowing, the subject is related to the object in a specifiable kind of way. The nature of the relationship depends on the type of knowledge involved. Tillich claims that this union involved in knowing is a special kind, "it is union through separation".[2] In other words, the complete act of knowing, consummated cognition, involves a polarity between union and distance, between participation and detachment. However, there are different types of knowledge associated with different dimensions of reason where one polar element, either that of detachment or union, is dominant.

"The type of knowledge which is predominantly determined by the element of detachment can be called 'controlling knowledge' ".[3] It is the outstanding example of technical reason with its concern for possession and experimentation. "It unites the subject and object for the sake of the control of the object by the subject".[4] Controlling knowledge "objectifies" the entity with which it is concerned by transforming it into a "conditioned and calculable 'thing' ". This is not merely "thematizing" but rather what I referred to previously as a "strictly objectifying" relationship. Controlling knowledge treats every object in terms of detachment, analysis, and calculation. This results in an experimental approach to the object of knowledge. The goals of this controlling technique are preciseness and verifiability. Verifiability is based on the "public approachability"[5] of this type of objectifying knowledge. This analysis by Tillich underlines again the very characteristics I have been attributing to one dimension of thought and reason, technical reason, which produces a type of knowledge, controlling knowledge. I have also maintained that this technical dimension of thought and reason, characterized by controlling knowledge, corresponds to and is compatible with the conceptual dimension of language. This proposed schema accounts for the way in which the conceptual dimension of language functions in light of its relationship to reason and knowledge.

There is another type of knowledge in which the element of union is predominant. This cognitive stance is called "receiving knowledge".

---

[1] Tillich, *Systematic Theology*, Vol. I, p. 94.
[2] *Ibid.*
[3] *Ibid.*, p. 97.
[4] *Ibid.*
[5] *Ibid.*, p. 99.

"Receiving knowledge takes the object into itself, into union with the subject".[1] This involves a cognitive participation with the object of thought which is non-objectifying. The reality is not reduced to a "thing" by analysis and experimentation. Rather, an experiential quality persists that makes the cognitive encounter receptive and dynamic. Admittedly this type of knowledge defies preciseness, absolute clarity of expression, finality of judgment (proof), or verifiability in the same sense as controlling knowledge. Yet receiving knowledge provides significant insight, insight in the sense of healing and transforming knowledge,[2] especially in regard to those entities and realities which are non-objectifiable or which lose their significance and are demeaned by excessive objectification. The most obvious example is man himself. "Man resists objectification".[3] Some aspects of man's bodily, psychic, and mental constitution are subject to analysis by controlling reason. But this is inadequate for gaining knowledge of human nature or of any individual personality. Sufficient knowledge of man involves union and participation and only secondarily detachment and analysis. Man is dehumanized when he is dissolved by psychological, sociological, medical, or philosophical analysis into elements out of which he is supposedly composed and determined. Thus certain movements such as romanticism, philosophy of life, and, above all, existentialism, have tried to resist the dominance and claim of control over every level of reality made by controlling knowledge. "This cognitive dehumanization has produced actual dehumanization".[4] Despite the fact that claims of knowledge which involve reception and union are met today with suspicion, one must recognize their importance and necessity in giving an account of the full range of human experience about which we claim to have significant knowledge.

It should be noted here that Tillich connects the emotive or emotional element with receiving knowledge. "Emotion is the vehicle for receiving cognition".[5] Emotion is always involved in any type of union between subject and object. "This is due to the fact that an emotional element is present in every rational act".[6] However, even though the emotive element is more decisive in ontological reason and receiving knowledge

[1] Tillich, *Systematic Theology*, Vol. I, p. 98.

[2] *Ibid.*, p. 96. This is demonstrated in the healing powers attributed to "insight" by depth psychology.

[3] *Ibid.*, p. 98.

[4] *Ibid.*, p. 99.

[5] *Ibid.*, p. 98.

[6] *Ibid.*, p. 77.

than in other types of reason, these are not consequently reduced to the emotional. This position by Tillich supports my own view that there is an emotive function, although it is not itself a separate dimension, which is connected with both the symbolic and conceptual dimensions of language and the foundational and technical dimensions of reason or thought.

It is imperative to recognize that receiving and controlling knowledge cannot function properly in isolation from one another. The complete notion of knowledge is constituted by a polarity between the two. "The unity of union and detachment is precisely described by the term 'understanding' ".[1] This is identical with the notion of understanding which I described as being the necessary correlative of expression and constitutes the maturity of meaning and the realization of communication. As Tillich forcefully proclaims, in order to understand another person, a historical figure, even a religious text, it is necessary to have "an amalgamation of controlling and receiving knowledge, of union and detachment, of participation and analysis".[2]

SUMMARY

The task of this chapter has been to set forth a dimensional structure of thought and reason that is parallel and congruous with the dimensional structure of language developed in the previous chapter. This has been accomplished by utilizing the contributions of Urban, Heidegger, and Tillich as guides and supporting authorities for my schematic proposal concerning thought and knowledge. These conclusions can now be summarized in the form of an outline which indicates the lines of relationship between the various dimensions of language, the dimensions of thought or reason, and the corresponding types of knowledge. The distinguishing characteristics of the dimensions of thought and the types of knowledge proposed here will also be reviewed as well as the relationship between language and cognition that binds these two sets of dimensions together.

[1] Tillich, *Systematic Theology*, Vol. I, p. 77.
[2] *Ibid.*

Dimensions of Language		Dimensions of Thought or Reason		Types of Knowledge	
SYMBOLIC		FOUNDATIONAL		RECEIVING	
intuitive	insight	receptive	experiential	union	participation
↕	↕	↕	↕	↕	↕
indicative	illustration	possessive	experimental	distance	detachment
CONCEPTUAL		TECHNICAL		CONTROLLING	

Language constitutes man's primary access to reality. It is in language that Being discloses itself. This occurs specifically in the symbolic dimension of language. It is here that the intuitive meaning function is predominant. The capacity of the transformational symbol is such that it supplies authentic awareness and cognitive insight concerning that which it symbolizes. This disclosure of Being supplies an essential "given" for linguistic meaning that establishes the necessary foundation for intelligible discourse. However, the symbolic dimension demands interpretation in order to allow for the maturation of meaning and consummation of communication. This process of interpretation takes place in the conceptual dimension of language where the indicative meaning function is predominant and the aim is toward illustration of the insight apprehended in the symbolic dimension. This involves a concern for precision of expression, analysis, and verification. The two dimensions are dialectically and complementarily related. Each requires the other for the fulfillment of its nature and function.

The realization of the capacities claimed for these distinctive dimensions of language entails congruous dimensions of thought or reason. Being comes to word through thought. It is then a particular dimension of thought that empowers or makes possible a particular dimension of language. The symbolic dimension of language is empowered by the foundational dimension of thought. Foundational thought is determined by a receptive nature and an experiential quality, as has been illustrated. It is characterized by a non-objectifying participation in the cognitive act with the object of thought. This receptive nature allows for authentic awareness and cognitive insight to occur, and the experiential quality of this cognitive encounter guards against a distorting objectification of the object. It is this foundational dimension of thought or reason which points to its depth where Being is disclosed in the symbolic dimension of language. However, the foundational dimension of language is always accompanied by the technical dimension of language. That which is received must also be given a form. If that which is received via foundational thought and reason is to result in knowledge in a significant sense, then it must be interpreted and communicated. So technical thought is characterized by an experimental quality which seeks to isolate, analyze, and evaluate that which is received with a detached critical attitude. What becomes evident is that one cannot have an adequate understanding of thought and reason in the absence of either the foundational or technical dimension. It is consistent that foundational and technical thought or reason should be dialectically related in the same complementary way as those dimensions of language, symbolic and conceptual, with which they are respectively united.

There are also different types of knowledge which are engendered by distinctive dimensions of thought and reason and therefore become characteristic products of a certain type of thinking or reasoning. Receiving knowledge is the result of foundational thought or reason and is therefore determined by a receptive openness to the object of thought which is actualized in a kind of cognitive union or participation. Receiving knowledge constitutes insight and content upon which one may and does express opinions, make judgments, and found actions. The very nature of receiving knowledge defies preciseness of expression, finality of judgment (proof), or empirical verifiability. However, it is this receiving knowledge upon which we base some of the most critical and consequential decisions of our human experience. On the other hand, technical thought or reason is connected with controlling knowledge. Controlling knowledge strives for the preciseness, finality, and public approachability that receiving knowledge lacks. Yet in order to achieve this goal it must maintain a distance from its object, an element of detachment which secures this controlled result. Thus, controlling knowledge objectifies its object for the sake of its conclusion. The notion of understanding is composed of the unity of receiving *and* technical knowledge. They must invariably accompany each other if one is to give adequate scope to the idea of human knowledge.

Commentary on this outline has been a means of review of the content of the proposed dimensional structure of language and thought. An explication of the dimensional structure of thought or reason has been the major task of this chapter. However, a prior concern of this chapter was to consider the relation between language, thought, reason, and knowledge which would justify the need for the schema proposed here. The essential affirmation is the inseparability of language and cognition. This is based on an assumption about the ultimate inseparability of language and thought. The principle of the identity of intuition and expression asserts that language is a constitutive part of knowing. Language is ultimately involved in showing forth the nature of reality no matter how it is apprehended. However, expression also entails understanding and understanding involves communication. So communicability is seen as part of knowledge as well. If language, knowledge, and communication are so bound together, then there is no knowledge without an element of representation. This representation consists in the bi-polar relationship between the expression and that which is expressed. If, as I have maintained, there is no knowledge in a full sense without some interpretation, and if the categories of knowledge are thus the categories of language, then the central question becomes the relationship between language and reality, for language is the prime access to reality. I have maintained that language and reality are inseparable and that language is the mold in which reality, as significant, is given. Following a high evaluation of language, it was affirmed that language is not a veil on reality but rather an adequate access to it. The source of this close relationship between language and reality and the foundation for the adequacy of this access is based on Being's disclosing itself in language. Since there is no knowledge that does not ultimately involve expression and therefore language, then the problem of truth becomes a problem of the relationship of expression to that which is expressed. Truth involves adequacy of expression. The question of adequacy in turn involves some means of distinguishing between adequate and inadequate. It depends on some means of confirmation; namely, on a theory of verification and authentication.

A schematic proposal concerning a dimensional understanding of language and thought has been described. It is now necessary to inquire how the assertions made within the conceptual dimension of language might be verified and how assertions made within the symbolic dimension of language might be authenticated so that each dimension of language and reason may lay an appropriate claim to truth.

CHAPTER SIX

VERIFICATION AND AUTHENTICATION

Rudolf Carnap maintains that the meaning of an assertion is "the way in which it may be verified".[1] The crucial question is, of course, what one means by "verification". I would be willing to agree with Carnap's general thesis that there is a link between meaning and verifiability only if the scope of verification is widely enough conceived. It was previously claimed[2] that communicability is part of the notion of linguistic meaning. Meaning involves both expression and understanding. The expression of someone's intentionality and the grasping of that intentionality by another person, which constitutes understanding and therefore results in communication, brings linguistic meaning to maturation. However, this consummation of meaning requires the confirmation or acceptance of that meaning within a particular universe of discourse. There is no meaning apart from discourse. This process of confirmation is bound up with verification, with determining the verifiability of a particular assertion.

What, then, is meant by verification or verifiability? Verification in its broadest sense means a method of deciding the truth or falsity of a judgment.[3] This wider notion of verification employed by Urban and Tillich stresses the link between meaning and verifiability. I will suggest in due course a more restricted notion of verification which provides a useful terminological distinction for the dimensional theory of language. However, at this stage of the discussion, verification should be taken in the broader sense indicated above.

A judgment embodied in an assertion to which the question of truth or falsity is completely irrelevant could be said to lack meaning. In order to have linguistic meaning, as it has been defined here, there must be understanding or a confirmation of the meaning expressed. This, however, is impossible in the case of an assertion to which the question

---

[1] Rudolf Carnap, "Die Überwindung der Metaphysik durch die logische Analyse der Sprache", *Erkenntniss*, Vol. II, No. 4, p. 237.

[2] See Chapter III.

[3] This is the definition employed by Tillich in *Systematic Theology*, Vol. I, p. 102.

of truth or falsity, and thus the method of deciding about the truth or falsity of that assertion, is irrelevant. Meaning is necessarily bound up with verifiability, and it is legitimate to inquire about the verifiability of an assertion in any discipline which claims to have meaning and certainly when that claim is extended to truth. However, it ought to be noted first that I am not claiming, at least on an elementary level, that an assertion must be true in order to have meaning, but only that the question about the method of determining its truth or falsity must be relevant. The means by which the statement might be verified must be spelled out if the assertion is to be considered meaningful. Second, the stress ought to fall not on actual verification but rather on verifiability. There are many meaningful assertions, some of these in natural science, which are not capable of actual verification at this time, but the way in which these assertions might theoretically be verified can be illustrated. A contemporary illustration would be statements concerning the nature of any plant life on Mars. Every year the means of actual verification of these assertions appears to draw nearer, but even now the theoretical verifiability of these statements makes them meaningful.

Verifiability is, then, a criterion for meaning and truth if it is understood as Urban describes it, as "a certain character of one's assertion or hypothesis which marks it off from the unverifiable. ..."[1] I have been concerned up to now only with the general definition of verification. However, the more pertinent issues for this study arise as one considers the scope of legitimate verification or the notion of different means of verification. Also, the terminology involved with determining the truth of an assertion needs to be clarified. What does one mean when he speaks of a statement being confirmed, verified, or authenticated? Are there different ways in which different types of assertions, representing various dimensions of language, may be confirmed as true or false? Are there distinguishable terms to describe these different methods of confirmation which might clarify a theory of verification or authentication? It is my conviction that there are different methods of confirmation appropriate to the different dimensions of language as they have been developed in this study. It is the task of this chapter to spell out what I wish to call a theory of confirmation where assertions made in the conceptual dimension of language are verified and statements made in the symbolic dimension of language are authenticated. However, before turning to a detailed discussion of this theory, I must examine the notion of "truth"

---

[1] Urban, *Language and Reality*, p. 210.

and the relation of verifiability and truth just as I previously considered the relation between verifiability and meaning.

Truth as Adequacy of Expression

In order to indicate the relation between verifiability in the wider sense and truth, it is necessary to give some idea what notion of truth one is utilizing. Truth is adequacy of expression. I have elected to follow Urban in this understanding of the notion of truth[1] not only because it is consistent with the distinctive character of man, namely, his linguisticality, but also because it gives an interpretation to the notion of truth that allows it to be applicable to the full scope of human experience. The interpretation of meaning and communication as developed in the present study has also attempted to be applicable in a similar way. However, it is necessary to go a step beyond Urban and ask what accounts for the notion of truth as adequacy of expression and how one can claim that truth is immanent in discourse. The Heideggerian concept of Being's self-disclosure in language will be employed to supplement Urban's insight concerning truth as adequacy of expression. What is involved in this definition of truth?

It was maintained in the previous chapter that language is inseparable from thought and knowledge. If it is true that there is no knowledge that does not ultimately involve an element of expression and therefore of language, then the truth problem in the last analysis becomes a problem of the relationship between the expression and that which is expressed. It cannot be asserted that what cannot be expressed is not real; but it can be maintained that what cannot be expressed is neither true nor false. Truth in the first place concerns a quality of judgment. Objects in themselves are neither true nor false; they simply are. It is the assertions about objects that contain a certain judgment that can be designated as either true or false. It was also maintained that any form of expression, whether verbal or non-verbal, involves a form of representation. The form of representation contained in the expression always involves a degree of interpretation. There is no knowledge without an element of interpretation. The form of representation, either conceptual description or symbolic formulation, must be interpreted in order for one to grasp the intention contained in the assertion. Only then can it

[1] The notion of truth as adequacy of expression is developed by Urban in *Language and Reality*, especially pp. 375ff. My argument here is endebted to Urban's analysis.

be verified or authenticated. "Truth thus becomes in a sense ultimately a question of interpretation".[1] This is particularly the case with symbols and the symbolic dimension of language. It was asserted that all symbols demand interpretation. Ultimately the judgment about the truth or falsity of a symbol, whether it really illuminates or provides insight into some aspect of reality, depends on the adequacy of the interpretation.

The truth question arises then only when some form of representation is present. This means that the notion of "correspondence" is fundamental to the idea of truth. The question must be raised here as to which elements are in correspondence, as well as what the nature of that correspondence is. Reference to the notion of truth as developed by Alfred North Whitehead illustrates this problem.[2] Whitehead sees the essence of truth as involving a correspondence theory which emphasizes "mutual participation in a pattern". A truth relation is claimed to be present when two objects possess an identical pattern that can be abstracted on the basis of an examination of either object. Urban rejects this interpretation of the notion of truth as being too extensive. He states that this mutual participation in a pattern may exist between two objects as a result of mere similarity and no necessary truth relation. Truth becomes an issue only when the pattern of one object is intended to express the other. A truth relation is said to exist when the assertion about one object expresses the intention to stand for the other in order to make a particular judgment or draw a specific conclusion. As Urban summarizes his position, "the truth relation does not subsist between two objects, however they mutually participate in a pattern, but always between an object and an expression".[3]

This means that the essence of the notion of truth is not to be found in correspondence, coherence, or coincidence of pattern but rather in adequate expression. Truth, then is to be understood not as a quality of things but of statements or assertions. However, assertions have no significance apart from discourse. So even though we sometimes speak of truth as if it were a relation that existed between one object and another or between an object and an image in the mind, truth is in fact an assessment of the relation that exists between an expression and that which is expressed. J.L. Austin makes a similar point, "... truth and falsity are (except by an artificial abstraction which is always possible and legitimate

---

[1] Urban, *Language and Reality*, p. 377.

[2] A. N. Whitehead, *Adventures of Ideas* (New York : Macmillan, 1955), Chap XVI, pp. 240-251.

[3] Urban, *op. cit.*, p. 378.

for certain purposes) not names for relations, qualifiers, or what not, but a dimension of assessment—how the words stand in respect of satisfactoriness to the facts, events, situations, &c., to which they refer".[1]

Adequacy to "that which is expressed" refers here to adequacy to the reality that confronts the speaker and which gives rise to his thought and his language. A relationship between one object and another or between an "idea" in the mind and an object could not be determined, that is, confirmed or verified by a community, until it is expressed. Only expressions are verifiable. We recall the former thesis that language and cognition are inseparable and that ultimately "the only way to determine being or reality is in those forms in which statements aboutare possible".[2] This leads us to the conclusion that, in the last analysis, truth is adequacy of expression.

This understanding of the notion of truth is significant not only because of the avenues of communication that it could conceivably open between various disciplines, but also because of its consequences for means of confirmation or verification. It implies, first, that the truth of any expression, whether conceptual or symbolic, in any discipline, whether theology or natural science, is determined not only by the correspondence between the form of the expression and the form of that which is expressed but also by its adequacy of expression. Second, this understanding implies that adequacy can be determined or confirmed only by processes of interpretation and communication. This establishes the primacy of language not only in regard to meaning but also in regard to verification and truth. It is in the realm of language and communication that one discovers a legitimate method of confirmation for assertions about nonobservables that were previously considered to be in the area of the unverifiable.

The classical definition of truth as employed by Thomas Aquinas, *adaequatio intellectus et rei*,[3] made the notion of "adequacy" central. However, the classical notion of adequacy had to do with a relation between "mind" and "thing". The adequacy referred to in this study is one which must characterize the relationship between the expression and that which is expressed. It is specifically adequacy of expression. So an assertion can be conceived of as true when it adequately performs its function of letting us see, of illuminating a particular aspect of reality.

[1] Austin, *How to Do Things With Words*, p. 148.

[2] Urban, *Language and Reality*, p. 379.

[3] Thomas Aquinas, *De veritate*, I, 1.

There are, however, different forms of representation, and thus the criteria of truth are different in various areas or universes of discourse, but adequacy of expression is the basis for all forms of truth. Claims for truth in a particlar area or discipline are usually made in the form of an assertion or proposition. A proposition, according to Urban, belongs to a "class of sentences which have the same intentional significance for everyone who understands them".[1] Confirmation or agreement as to a common understanding makes the proposition what it is. Since a proposition can be confirmed only when it is expressed, then truth becomes a function of expression. The truth relation is dependent on the relationship between the proposition and that which it intends to represent. The more adequate the expression is, the more adequate the form of re-presentation becomes. A proposition that adequately represents that to which it refers is said to be true. Thus, truth is adequacy of expression. But just as there are different forms of representation —literal, conceptual, symbolic—so there are different forms of adequacy. Adequacy means different things in different contexts. There is no such thing as adequacy in general, any more than there is efficiency in general. Adequacy exists only in relationship to the intent of the expression, just as efficiency exists only in relationship to a particular function.

There are, then, different forms or types of truth which are appropriate to different contexts. The truth relation refers to adequacy for a particular type of consciousness and this is conditioned by a particular community of understanding. This means that every form of truth is conditioned by the context, field, or community in which it operates. There is no such thing as truth in general, or truth that is absolutely unconditioned. Since truth is adequacy of expression, a quality of an expressed judgment or proposition, and since a proposition has no reality except in some universe of discourse, then truth is truth for a particular universe of discourse. We have scientific, poetic, or theological truth. The criteria in each universe of discourse are different and depend on the accepted standards of that field or discipline constituted by this universe of discourse. It also indicates that the means of confirmation, verification or authentication, may vary from one discipline to another or even with various types of statements within a given field or discipline, such as conceptual or symbolic. This view of truth as adequacy of expression and the distinction between various forms or types of truth that are contextually oriented is a broader notion of truth and is correlate with

---

[1] Urban, *Language and Reality*, p. 380.

the wider view of knowledge taken previously. The purpose is to offer an understanding of knowledge and truth that will encompass the whole scope of human intercourse and experience.

The interpretation of contextual truth, of different types or forms of truth as associated with various universes of discourse could confront one with a serious problem. This would be the charge that the notion of truth has been diluted of all significant meaning because one can no longer talk about the comparative value of a truth claim in different fields such as one in natural science and one in theology. As a result the force of a claim for truth in every discipline has been diminished. Stephen Toulmin, to whom I have referred before, presents an answer to this accusation. He does so in his book, *The Uses of Argument*, by making an important distinction between the "force" of truth and the "criteria" of truth.[1] In fact, this distinction applies to all words in the development of an argument which Toulmin describes as "modal" terms, such as "true", "real", or "cannot". He asserts that the meaning of each modal term has two aspects : the force of a term and the criteria for its use. The force of a term refers to the "pratical implications of its use" which allow it to have the same force of meaning over several different fields. The criteria for the use of a term are the "standards, grounds, and reasons, by reference to which we decide in any context that the use of a particular modal term is appropriate".[2] The meaning of a term may be too general unless one distinguishes between these aspects.

Consider how this distinction could apply to the modal term "true" and how its use provides a response to the problem previously noted. The meaning of "true" in regard to the force of the term is to commend a statement as worthy of being believed or accepted. The criteria of true, that which establishes the commendation noted above, varies from field to field. The result is that the meaning of true is "field-invariant"[3] in force, which means that the term true is applicable over several fields because the modal term has a common force of meaning. However, the criteria of true are "field-variant" because the criteria are dependent on the presuppositions of the field or, in my definition of truth, on the presuppositions of the particular universe of discourse in which a truth claim is being made. The consequences of employing this distinction

---

[1] Toulmin, *The Uses of Argument*, pp. 30ff.
[2] *Ibid.*, p. 30.
[3] *Ibid.*, pp. 15, 37.

are, first, that it provides a legitimate answer to the charge that distinguishing between types or forms of truth dilutes the significance of a truth claim and that it prohibits comparative interdisciplinary references to truth. The distinction between these aspects of force and criteria allows a modal term like "true", or "good",[1] or "real" to have the same *force* over several fields and thus the question of how strong the case is for the truth of a theological assertion or the truth of a conclusion in mathematical physics can be generally compared. The claim for the truth of an assertion has not lost its force or its comparability despite differences in criteria.

Second, this distinction also guards against the mistake of raising one criterion to a unique philosophical position and then applying this in all fields. It is suggested by Toulmin that this happened in the case of the Utilitarians who in their single-minded concern for legislation and social action made the issue of "consequence" the universal criterion for analyzing all arguments.[2] It appears that the Logical Positivists of this century attempted to establish empirical verification as the criterion to which all standards were reducible. However, the position I wish to assume in this study is that the differences between the criteria employed in different fields or different universes of discourse are irreducible. There is no universal set of criteria for establishing the truth or goodness or reality of a given assertion or argument. The criteria of what is true are field-variant and in order to establish the claim of truth in any given area we must examine in detail the presuppositions and the means of confirmation which are operative in that field as demonstrated by the way in which statements function in a given universe of discourse.

---

[1] Tulmin, *The Uses of Argument*, pp. 32-33. An example of this distinction in regard to the modal term "good" is supplied by Toulmin in a hypothetical philosophical argument and is worth noting as a clear example of this distinction. "A word like 'good' can be used equally of an apple or an agent or an action, of a volley in tennis, a vacuum cleaner or a Van Gogh; in each case, to call the fruit or the person or the stroke or the painting 'good' is to commend it and to hold it out as being in some respect a praiseworthy, admirable or efficient member of its class—the word 'good' is accordingly defined most accurately as 'the most general adjective of commendation'. But because the word is so general, the things we appeal to in order to justify commending different kinds of things as 'good' will themselves be very different. A morally-good action, a domestically-good vacuum-cleaner and a pomiculturally-good apple all come up to standard, but the standards they all come up to will be different—indeed, incomparable. So one can distinguish between the commendatory force of labelling a thing as 'good', and the criteria by reference to which we justify a commendation".

[2] *Ibid.*, p. 34.

These different forms or types of truth must ultimately be made coherent within the realm of the totality of intelligible discourse. The notion of truth as adequacy of expression asserts that the problem of truth cannot be solved apart from the problem of language and expression. This link between truth and language is also affirmed in the examination of the relationship between truth and verification in the wider sense. As was maintained at the beginning of this chapter, truth and verification as well as meaning and verification are bound together if verification is understood broadly enough. In Tillich's words, "Statements which have neither intrinsic evidence nor a way of being verified have no cognitive value. ... The verifying test belongs to the nature of truth".[1] The scope or range of acceptable verification will be considered in detail presently; but some initial assertions noted by Urban must be made in order to fill out the notion of truth as developed here.[2] First, it has been affirmed that meaning and verifiability are inseparable. In order for meaning to come to maturity it must be accepted or confirmed by a particular community. Second, it will be maintained that empirical verification (reference to an observable entity) is not the only means of verification possible. Third, there are other legitimate means of verification or, as I wish to call it, confirmation; one can distinguish in principle between verification and authentication, which are two different forms of deciding about the truth or falsity of a judgment. Fourth, confirmation is ultimately a matter of communication.

The method of deciding the truth or falsity of a judgment always involves language and communication. It has been affirmed that language and cognition are inseparable. Therefore, that which is verified or authenticated is always an expression. In fact, only expressions are ultimately capable of confirmation because that which is claimed to be true must be expressed and that, in the last analysis, involves expression in language. If truth is a quality of a judgment expressed in language and that expression can subsist only within human discourse, then the verification or authentication of that judgment must also lie within the realm of intelligible discourse. However, the issue of verification cannot be reduced simply to an issue of the common pattern between the expression and the nexus of events represented. There is always some gap and, as I

---

[1] Tillich, *Systematic Theology*, Vol. I, p. 102. Tillich states that this was one of the valuable insights of Positivism. The problem arose in terms of the limitation the Logical Positivists placed on the range of verification, restricting it to empirical verification.

[2] Urban, *Language and Reality*, p. 384.

affirmed formerly, truth involves not only representation and expression, but adequate representation and adequate expression. Any expression involves a degree of interpretation. So the verification or authentication of an assertion involves a determination of its adequacy—also through interpretation.

The concept of truth as functional and contextual is also affirmed by J.L. Austin. The adequacy of linguistic interpretation for Austin is indicated by the way in which statements fit the facts or situation about which one is making a judgment. "There are various *degrees and dimensions* of success in making statements : the statements fit the facts always more or less loosely, in different ways on different occasions for different intents and purposes".[1] Statements in a particular situation and a particular universe of discourse may be judged true, false, or simply inept. This judgment focuses on adequacy of expression.

An objection might be raised which would claim to refute this entire notion of truth. As Urban has correctly seen, it could be argued that the crucial exception to this understanding comes in regard to perceptual truth or the truth of sense perception.[2] Here surely there is a truth that is independent of interpretation and communication. One sometimes speaks of the direct verification via sense perception. However, when one analyzes sense perception more closely, he discovers that it provides neither direct verification, if one means by this simple acquaintance or mere awareness of the sense datum, nor does it provide an exception to the notion of truth developed here. If one says, for instance, "the table is brown",the simplest form of ostensive proposition, it is not a result of mere awareness of the sense datum. Sense data themselves verify nothing. However, the expression, the proposition, interprets and expresses intention in language. As I noted previously, there is no perception without some element of description and interpretation. There is really no such thing as direct verification. "It follows ... that the verification which we call direct is always an interpretation in terms of pre-existing sentences and expressions".[3] Even then, in regard to the truth of sense perception, the key relation is between an expression and that which is expressed. All verification is therefore indirect but the degree to which this is the case obviously varies. In some assertions of natural science verification of a theory often claims to be based on observation. An

---

[1] Austin, *Philosophical Papers*, p. 98.

[2] Urban, *Language and Reality*, p. 385.

[3] *Ibid.*, p. 386.

example suggested by Urban is the confirmation of Einstein's theory that non-Euclidean geometry prevails in the space of the universe.[1] This is claimed to be verified by certain observations concerning the deflection of light passing the sun or the displacement of the perihelion of Mercury. This is confirmation of verification by observation, but is based on an incredibly complex theoretical argument. The verification occurs not in the observation of a certain sense datum but in the entire process of the interpretation of the sense datum. The question of truth is whether the interpretation expresses adequately what is inferred by the sense datum. The truth relation is one of adequacy of judgment as contained in the expression. The judgment must therefore fit into our accepted standards of intelligibility as established in this field. The verification of a theory such as this in physics takes place in a given universe of discourse. This universe of discourse is constituted by mutually acknowledged presuppositions as to rationality and intelligibility. It is here that the key to verification not only in natural science but in other fields as well is focused. In the next chapter I will turn to a more detailed consideration of science in order to support the thesis that confirmation, as verification or authentication, is finally dependent on communication and mutual interpretation of meaning.

This discussion of verifiability leads me to affirm another thesis set forth by Urban as a consequence of this notion of truth. It is that"truth, in the last analysis, is immanent in discourse".[2] This idea can be expressed in a thesis that correlates with the notion of truth as adequacy of expression; namely, that the totality of intelligible discourse is the truth, *veritas in dicto*.[3] Although this thesis at first glance appears to be unacceptable, I think that its significance can be demonstrated if it is properly understood. It first involves the relationship between meaning and truth. I have asserted that meaning and truth are linked to verifiability in the wider sense. However, meaning is really prior to and more ultimate than verification or truth. In order to be able to verify an assertion by any means and thus to be able to establish its truth or falsity, one must be clear about its meaning, about what intention is embodied in the expression. The search for the truth is finally a matter of distinguishing the meaningful from the unmeaningful. But it is necessary to recognize the presence of qualifying phrases such as "ultimately" or "in the last ana-

[1] Urban, *Language and Reality*, p. 387.

[2] *Ibid.*, p. 392.

[3] *Ibid.*, p. 394. John Macquarrie agrees with Urban in *God-Talk*, p. 75

lysis". In some universes of discourse the meaningfulness of a statement certainly does not initially establish its truth. An assertion about the nature of plant life on Mars is not true simply because it is meaningful. However, if this hypothesis about the nature of plant life on Mars were the only hypothesis that would make meaningful and intelligible other facts such as the atmospheric conditions on Mars or the chemical content of the soil, then one could call it true even if the exact nature of the plant life was forever beyond our observation and laboratory analysis. This is the case with many assertions in science where meaning and intelligibility are the ultimate terms.

I am more concerned here with basic assumptions that condition the meaningfulness of assertions in any discipline. For instance, the assumption that there are other selves[1] is the condition for all communication and thus for the meaningfulness of assertions of any type, whether they are about plant life on Mars or the nature of God. The assumption that there are other selves can be expressed in a meaningful assertion, and because of its implications, to say that this assertion is meaningful is equivalent to saying it is true. In the last analysis, meaning in the sense of intelligibility and truth tend to coincide. It is obvious that initially this is not the case. In some universes of discourse the meaningfulness of an assertion is conditioned by its reference to some observable entity. The thesis is that only ultimately in the realm of the totality of intelligible discourse do truth and intelligibility coincide.

The idea that truth is immanent in discourse holds for basic presuppositions or principles that underlie several fields. Take for example the notion of truth itself. Consider the notion of truth as developed here in comparison with other significant notions of truth. "The various notions such as the correspondence, the coherence, and the pragmatic, are themselves criteria of truth, and presuppose the more ultimate notions of adequate expression and intelligibility ...".[2] Urban defends this view quite persuasively by noting that it is not possible to show that the correspondence theory of truth is in fact true because it corresponds to something called truth, nor does the coherence theory cohere with a definite situation known as truth. Finally, it is certainly not possible to demonstrate that the pragmatic theory is true because it works. Rather, "all these theories of truth, if true, are so in some other sense than that expressed by the criterion itself. If verifiable at all—and to be meaning-

---

[1] Urban develops this example in some detail in *Language and Reality*, pp. 211ff.
[2] *Ibid.*, pp. 390-391.

ful they must be verifiable in some sense—it can only be by mutual acknowledgment in discourse. They are truths of interpretation".[1] This example of a basic principle illustrates the authenticity of the notion of truth affirmed in this study, for here truth and meaning coincide. *Veritas in Dicto* : truth is immanent in discourse. This means that "all meaningful propositions *qua* meaningful are, then, *ipso facto* true or contain elements of truth, references to reality".[2] There are in each limited universe of discourse certain specific criteria of truth. This results in types or forms of truth determined by a particular context which involves area and time. However, there is a point or dimension in each universe of discourse when fundamental principles or foundations are involved which undergird the entire discipline or field. It is here that truth and meaning must ultimately coincide. It is here in the mutual recognition and acknowledgment of basic suppositions or assumptions that it can be claimed that truth is immanent in discourse and that truth is indeed the totality of intelligible discourse.

This study has been in agreement with much that Urban has asserted about the nature of truth as adequate expression and with the assertion that ultimately truth is immanent in discourse. I think it is correct to say that truth is essentially a quality of judgment and that judgment is expressed in language. However, I think one must go beyond this and ask, "Why is truth immanent in discourse? What is there about the nature of the relationship between language and reality that makes it possible for a judgment to adequately represent reality so that it can be described as true?" Paul Tillich states the problem this way : "There must be an explanation of the fact that reality can give itself to the cognitive act in such a way that a false judgment can occur and in such a way that many processes of observation and thought are necessary in order to reach true judgments".[3] What is the way in which reality gives itself to the cognitive act? It seems to me that it is here that the Heideggerian insights about the nature of language can serve to supplement and complete the very systematic and constructive analysis of Urban. Truth is immanent in discourse because Being discloses itself in language. Language is the medium in which Being reveals itself in and to man. However, Being not only discloses itself in language but it also hides itself in language. Therefore false judgments are not only possible but frequent.

---

[1] Urban, *Language and Reality*, p. 391.
[2] *Ibid.*, p. 392.
[3] Tillich, *Systematic Theology*, Vol. I, p. 101.

Errors of judgment are made not only at the initial level of the failure to establish and then apply the proper criteria of truth for a given universe of discourse, but false judgments are also made at the levels of the universe of discourse where presuppositions and basic principles are operative. Man must be attentive to the self-disclosure of Being. Man must seek for this disclosure in the special dimension of language that we have described as the symbolic. He must utilize the foundational dimension of thought and the receiving type of knowledge which is its product. As Tillich has stated, many different forms of observation and thought are required. This attentiveness to Being demands a continual process of dialectical examination, a probing which seeks to let this disclosure of Being in language open us up to new insights into the nature of certain aspects of reality. There is a proper ontological question about the "depth" or the "essence" of things, "that which gives them the power of being".[1] Truth has a reference to the essence of things, to its power of being. A true judgment is one which grasps and expresses true being.[2] This grasping and expressing is possible because Being discloses itself in language; language is an adequate access to Being. It is this high evaluation of language combined with a dimensional understanding of the nature of language which provides an ontological foundation for the notion of truth as adequacy of expression and which ties the notions of truth and verification to the realms of interpretation and communication.

Confirmation : Verification and Authentication

It has been maintained that there is a necessary relation between meaning and verifiability and between truth and verifiability. Ultimately meaning and truth tend to coincide so that the task of one seeking the truth is to distinguish, in the last analysis, the meaningful from the unmeaningful, the intelligible from the unintelligible. However, in each case this is bound up with the question of the verifiability of an assertion with the claims to be meaningful or true. The problem which confronts us now is that of the range or scope of legitimate or acceptable means of verification.

Verifiability was defined in the broadest terms as the method of deciding the truth or falsity of a judgment. In recent years we have been confronted with normative interpretation of the means of verification which

---

[1] Tillich, *Systematic Theology*, Vol. I, p. 101.
[2] *Ibid.*, p. 102.

has become so widely accepted that it has camouflaged the fact that there are several means of verification and that this interpretation itself is normative and not absolute. This normative interpretation is based on the principle of empirical verification. This means that in order for a judgment to be meaningful and ultimately capable of making a claim to truth, it must make reference to empirically observable entities or have a logically correct form. So statements which are meaningful and true must, in fact or in principle, be verified by analytic tautologies or by evidence that is empirical. The wide acceptance of this "normative view of verification"[1] has been due in part to the growing influence of the natural sciences during this century and the somewhat simplified notion of the scientific method which had been popularized as a result. But beyond this general influence there has been the effect of a loosely-knit philosophical movement usually described by the term logical positivism or simply positivism. The initial thrust of this movement was to analyze and classify statements that could be considered meaningful and true. This form of linguistic analysis made the empirical criterion normative not only for claims of truth but also for claims of meaningfulness. The major difficulties with the position of the logical positivists have been marked out often and these critiques have caused the movement of analytic philosophy itself to be transformed. The central critiques are that the very principle of empirical verification could not be established on the basis of its own criterion and that simply too much of human experience that was considered both meaningful and true was relegated to the category of the meaningless. The presuppositions of this normative mode of verification were placed in question.

The specific results of this position, as a consequence of the dominance of the natural sciences combined with the views of the positivists, were, first, to establish a monolithic criterion of verification. Rather than operating with field-variant criteria of truth, the implication was that there existed a field-invariant criterion of truth which was constituted by reference to empirically observable entities. This meant that assertions made in certain fields, for example, aesthetics, ethics, and theology, either had to reject the thesis of positivism or say that these assertions were in fact not verifiable but were still meaningful and true on a variety of other grounds. One criterion assumed a position of philosophical primacy across multiple fields. Second, by failing to acknowledge the assumptions that underlie this empirical criterion, one did not generally

---

[1] Urban, *Language and Reality*, pp. 208ff.

recognize that this interpretation of the method of verification was only normative; it was not absolute. This position assumes the prior rights of the physical because verification on the basis of the criterion is possible only in the physical context. Any assertion that did not directly relate to the physical realm or could not be reduced to that was therefore unverifiable. This interpretation of the means of verification is normative on the basis of the often unexpressed assumption about the priority of the physical, but this interpretation is certainly not absolute or necessary. It is ironic to note, as Urban does, in light of this claim that the principle of empirical verifiability is normative, that the logical positivists claimed that normative propositions were meaningless or mere expression of feeling.[1] As I noted previously, the conclusion one draws from these reflections is that there must be other ways of verification. There are certainly meaningful assertions where reference is made to empirical, observable entities, but there are also meaningful assertions where no such reference is possible.

The task of this chapter is to distinguish at least two different means of verification, or, as I will prefer to describe it here, two different dimensions of confirmation. The question was raised earlier whether it would be helpful to have a revised terminology in regard to the method of establishing the truth or falsity of judgment. We need a terminology that allows one more readily to distinguish between the different means of verification. Truth and verification are bound together. Only expressions are finally verifiable and expressions have no reality apart from discourse. So the process of verification always involves interpretation and communication. Verification requires the confirmation of a particular meaning or truth by a particular community. Thus, in the wider definition of determining the method of deciding the truth or falsity of a judgment, confirmation in a particular universe of discourse is equivalent to verification. Terminologically, I think, it is more instructive to employ the term "confirmation" rather than "verification", because confirmation can designate a wider scope or range for the means of deciding the truth or falsity of a judgment than does verification in much contemporary discussion of language. In order to make verification refer to this wider range it must be redefined, as it is by Urban and Tillich. For purposes of clarification in regard to my own dimensional theory of language, I am suggesting a change in terminology which avoids this expanded definition of verification by substituting the term "confirma-

---

[1] Urban, *Language and Reality*, fn., p. 208.

tion". As a consequence of this change, verification can then be reserved for reference to that means of confirmation which does depend on repeatable experimental evidence and ordinarily establishes truth or falsity by reference to an empirical criterion and the correctness of formal logical structure. This association between the term verification and evidence, which is empirically observable, is already prevalent in our cultural situation. Another term should be utilized to make reference to those means of confirmation not included in the empirical criterion. The term which I propose to employ for this other means of confirmation is "authentication".[1] The following explication deals with this specialized meaning of authentication and illustrates its function in order to distinguish between the two different means of confirmation, verification and authentication.

The term "authentication" is frequently used by those making claims to truth which extend beyond the empirical criterion. It is often employed in the fields of aesthetics and ethics. One speaks of a poem as having an "authentic ring". He means more by this expression than a reference to the sincerity of the author. Ordinarily one is also expressing the judgment that the author was able to convey by his medium a "truth" about some element of experience. However, this authentic note, this reference to truth, in a work of art is not determined by the verification of its assertions in regard to an empirical criterion. Rather, "that which makes a work of art authentic is the fact that it 'shows forth', in its medium, certain qualities and values which are ... recognized as authentic and acknowledged by the 'observer' ".[2] Authentication occurs, then, in the recognition and mutual acknowledgment of this "truth element". Authentication takes place in communication and, in the case of this illustration, in the aesthetic universe of discourse.

Justification for the use of the notion of authentication in regard to the aesthetic is obvious. However, it is the contention of this study that the term is not confined to the aesthetic but is applicable to some degree in every field of human discourse. Urban continues his development of authentication by making a helpful distinction between direct and

---

[1] The term "authentication" is employed by Urban, *Language and Reality*, pp. 213ff., and forms the foundation for my own development of this notion. But whereas for Urban authentication is simply a form of verification, I wish to draw a distinction between verification and authentication by interpreting them both as forms of confirmation. These means of confirmation can be distinguished but not separated, because as elements in the dimensional understanding of language they are dialectically related.

[2] Urban, *Language and Reality*, p. 214.

indirect authentication. Direct authentication involves the " 'showing forth' (*aufweisen*) of some *quale* or relation".[1] Urban uses the field of ethical discourse to illustrate this form of confirmation. In this case confirmation focuses on the assertion of value which represents not merely an emotional response but shows forth some *quale* or relationship which is intuited and in this intuition acknowledged. Recall now the initial thesis about the essential inseparability of intuition and expression. One speaks at this point not of sensuous but of non-sensuous intuition. It is this possibility of mutual intuition and communication which constitutes authenticity. Urban demonstrates this in relation to the quality of "pride" Two people may agree that an action manifests pride They may have quite different emotional responses to the action and one may approve of the action while the other disapproves. However, both their emotional reaction and evaluation of the action are quite independent of their mutual recognition and agreement as to the quality of the action. The two people can both apprehend the quality of pride on the basis of non-sensuous intuition which is quite different from sensuous observation. In order for two people to agree that the action is proud, "it is necessary that there shall be mutual recognition and acknowledgment of the value *quale*. It is here that the authentication takes place".[2] One can therefore confirm the existence of values such as "pride" or "goodness". However, one does so not by verification, by reference to an observable entity, but rather, by authentication, by mutual recognition and acknowledgment in discourse. I concur with Urban in this definition that direct authentication is a form of confirmation which takes place in communication, in the mutual acknowledgment of values and their relations on the part of communicating subjects.

There is also indirect authentication which occurs in discourse. However, rather than being constituted by the mutual recognition and acknowledgment of something which is "shown forth", indirect authentication consists in the mutual recognition and acknowledgment of the "implications of that discourse".[3] If, in other words, it can be demonstrated that assertions with which one agrees and which one employs have certain necessary implications, then one has a forced acknowledgment of the truth of these assertions which embody the implications. This is confirmation of assertions by means of indirect authentication. Urban supplies

---

[1] Urban, *Language and Reality*, p. 215.

[2] *Ibid.*, p. 216.

[3] *Ibid.*, p. 217.

a rather simplistic illustration of this process which demonstrates the nature of indirect authentication quite clearly.[1] He suggests that a cynical sensualist maintains that the only goods are mastication and sex. He evidently intends this statement to be more than an expression of his feelings. It is an objective matter that is more than an emotional response, and he would assert it only if he thought it to be true—implying that truth is better than falsehood. However, it can be shown by the implications of his original assertion that it is not true. For if his assertion is to have any meaning, it must itself assume that truth is a value. This means it is a value other than the two he asserts to be the only values. Therefore, we have the indirect authentication of the value of truth which was not dependent on verification by empirical observation, but consists in a forced recognition and acknowledgment in the ethical universe of discourse. It seems to me evident that indirect authentication by means of the implications of specific discourse is as legitimate a means of confirmation as is the forced recognition that if certain sense data are experienced, other objects, not directly experienced, are real. In other words, indirect authentication is as legitimate as indirect verification. It is in fact this indirect authentication, not always recognized as such, which gives meaning and establishes the truth claim for many of our most important assertions.

Urban in his efforts to establish the legitimacy of authentication sets forth what he thinks is the conclusive argument which is that authentication is presupposed in the empirical criterion itself.[2] It has already been indicated that the empirical criterion cannot be confirmed on the basis of its own standards. This means that either the criterion itself is meaningless or that it can be confirmed by some other means; namely, by what has been described as authentication. As Urban notes, A. J. Ayer, who developed the classic position of logical positivism in his book *Language, Truth and Logic*,[3] has admitted that the empirical criterion cannot be established on its own means, but maintains that one need not resort to a metempirical or a metaphysical basis. Rather, Ayer concludes that the criterion may be established on practical grounds by appealing to "what people mean by meaning".[4] Urban asserts correctly, I think, that this is an appeal not to psychological fact but rather, "precisely to that mutual acknowledgment which is not psychological but epistemo-

---

[1] Urban, *Language and Reality*, pp. 217-218.

[2] *Ibid.*, p. 215.

[3] Ayer, *Language, Truth, and Logic* (London : Victor Gollancz, 1936).

[4] A. J. Ayer, *Mind*, Vol. XLIII, pp. 335-345.

logical".[1] The criterion of the meaningful and ultimately of the true is found not outside but within discourse or communication. If the principle of empirical verification is confirmed, even within a limited area of application—which is, I think, the case—it is confirmed only within intelligible discourse, or by authentication. The empirical criterion is not a statement of fact but is a normative criterion applicable to a limited area of discourse.

However, confirmation by authentication is still within the realm of experience. The need is to widen our understanding of experience. When a value or insight is shown forth and acknowledged, this is as much a part of experience as reference to sense data. The physical is not the only language open to public confirmation. The limited view of experience which tends to identify it with the sensuously observable is connected with the more limited view of knowledge and of truth and is part of an initial assumption about the prior rights of the physical. It is necessary to reevaluate the notion of experience and give it a scope that is broader than that which can be reduced to the empirically observable.[2]

The major issue in this development of the notion of authentication is that it occurs in the area of communication. Discourse and language are essential not only to the maturation of meaning but to the constitution of truth. Both meaning and truth are bound to the idea of "confirmation", or, as it was described earlier in this study, to "verification" in its broadest terms. Tracing the exposition of Urban, one sees all forms of confirmation have their locus in communication.[3] Confirmation is not an additional factor in determining the method for deciding the truth or falsity of a judgment but rather it is the essential element. In relation to knowledge, confirmability and communicability are inseparable. All knowledge must have to some degree a public character. It must be open to some degree to confirmation by other menbers of the community if it is to qualify as knowledge and make a claim to truth. The problem which arises deals with the nature or scope of that confirmation. It has been the thesis of this study that the emphasis ought to be shifted from verification to authentication. It is here that many of our most important

---

[1] Urban, *Language and Reality*, p. 221.

[2] The task of reevaluating and broadening the notion of experience, particularly in regard to theological questions, has been initiated by Smith in *God and Reason*, and has been further explicated in John E. Smith, *Experience and God* (New York : Oxford University Press, 1968).

[3] Urban, *op. cit.*, p. 223.

assertions are established, including those principles which often underlie the assertions for which we provide verification.

It is important in this discussion to note that authentication is not reducible simply to consensus or public confirmation. The emphasis on confirmation within the area of communication should not mislead one into thinking public agreement itself is decisive. Rather, the focus on language and communication is crucial because of the nature of language itself, because of the ontological element which enters into the process of authentication. Authentication results in the "showing forth" of a truth element about a particular aspect of experience. The recognition and acknowledgment of that truth element is due to Being's disclosure in language. It is in the process of sharing and communication that one is grasped by this disclosure, this encounter with Being. Truth for Heidegger is just this "unhiddenness" or "non-concealment" of Being. It is in language that this non-concealment takes place. In discourse a discovery or insight about some aspect of experience is revealed or disclosed by this lighting-up process. Professor Heinrich Ott illustrates this process of authentication when he describes having been graped in his reading of Buber's *I and Thou* with not only the awe-inspiring power of God but also God's graciousness in being personally related to us.[1] However, he declares that it was only in speaking of this with another person that these insights were really confirmed or authenticated for him. In the process of sharing in human discourse, the words seemed to light up his personal experience and "showed forth" the element of truth. The conversation shared between Ott and his friend led him on a path to an encounter with reality. This was an instance of agreement, but that agreement was not the essence of authentication. Authentication was a witness to a disclosure of reality that lies behind and within the nature of language itself as "language speaks".

Mutual recognition and acknowledgment in discourse of this process of disclosure reinforces our acceptance of the insight or discovery so that our assertions tend to be given a greater degree of confirmation by wider agreement. However, it is the quality or authentication in discourse and not simply its numerical frequency that is significant   I have maintained that this means of confirmation, described here as authentication, occurs in every principal universe of discourse in reference to the symbolic dimension of language. There is a means of confirmation that has its locus

---

[1] This experience was related in a private conversation in the spring of 1968 in Basel.

in language and communication. However, authentication can be accounted for only by the recognition of a dimensional structure of language and the capacity of language to be an access to reality. It is sometimes suggested that this shift to authentication, communication, and language is a weakening of claims to meaning and truth. It is ordinarily claimed that propositions should be confirmed by facts. But this is simply a careless way of speaking. "Facts do not confirm, but minds interpreting the facts confirm".[1] A fact is constituted by the language in which it is articulated. Sentences are really confirmed by other sentences, both of which involve interpretation, which is in turn a community affair. This is the case because, as I have asserted on numerous occasions, language has no reality except in a given speech community. It should be made clear, then, in any attempt to develop a theory of verification and authentication, that communication, either overt or potential, is essential in all forms of confirmation.

Means of Confirmation

The intent of this discussion is to expand the range or scope of legitimate verification or, as I have preferred to describe it in a revised terminology, confirmation. This interest in widening the range of confirmation is shared by Paul Tillich, and his suggestions also provide a bridge for correlating these means of confirmation with the dimensions of language and thought already outlined. Tillich notes the trend in contemporary thought which assumes that "truth can be verified only within the realm of empirical science. Statements which cannot be verified by experiment are consideredt autologies, emotional self-expressions, or meaningless propositions".[2] Tillich agrees with what he considers to be one of the contributions of positivism, which is the demand to show how an assertion is verified or, in my terminology, confirmed. In order to have cognitive value a statement must be capable of confirmation. The crucial issue for Tillich, as it was for Urban, is the range of legitimate confirmation. He denies that one can make the experimental method of verification (parallel to what I described formerly as empirical verification) the exclusive pattern of confirmation. Thus Tillich distinguishes between two basic means of confirmation : experimental and experiential.

[1] Urban, *Language and Reality*, p. 225.
[2] Tillich, *Systematic Theology*, Vol. I, p. 102.

The experimental method is characterized by its repeatability, precision, and finality of judgment at any particular moment.[1] However, this experimental process of confirmation presupposes isolation, regularity, and generality. In order to perform the experiment and subject the assertion to empirical verification, the element that is to be examined must be separable from the on-going life process. A static element must be imposed on that which is dynamic in order to control it for the purposes of experimentation and specifically in order to confirm the results. Thus the experimental method is more exact and definite, but the range of its applicability is limited by its method of operation.

In contradistinction to this we have what Tillich describes as the experiential method. Experiential confirmation occurs within the life process itself. The life processes have the character of totality, spontaneity and individuality.[2] According to Tillich, the advantage of this experiential method of confirmation is that it need not abstract from and disrupt the life process (as much as the experimental method) in order to distill elements which may be subject to confirmation. This means of experiential confirmation is less exact and definite than the experimental, but it is also more extensive and truer to the life situation.

There is, I think, a parallel in regard to the major distinctions between what I have called verification and what Tillich describes as experimental verification and between what I have designated as authentication and Tillich develops as experiential verification. Tillich then goes on to state : "It is obvious that these two methods of verification correspond to the two cognitive attitudes, the controlling and the receiving".[3] Controlling knowledge is confirmed by the process of experimental verification. Technical reason, as it functions in scientific knowledge, is the most impressive demonstration of this means of verification. Receiving knowledge, on the other hand, is confirmed by a creative union of the two natures of the knower and the known. The test is made not by controlled experimentation but in the life process itself. Receiving knowledge is not so precise or definite; it involves a risk. Receiving knowledge cannot be empirically verified; it must be authenticated. It is not less significant or persuasive; it is simply less precise and confined. Most of our cognitive confirmation is in fact by experiential authentication. I wish to go beyond Tillich and emphasize the role of language and the significance of the

[1] Tillich, *Systematic Theology*, Vol. I, p. 103.
[2] *Ibid.*
[3] *Ibid.*, p. 102.

discourse situation in the process of confirmation. Confirmation within the discourse situation may suggest that truth or falsity is being determined by community concensus. However, this suggestion disregards what I have maintained as the fundamental link between language and the process of human life. Confirmation is not merely in language, but in language which is inseparable from cognition and reality. Wittgenstein does not share my ontological commitments, yet he does affirm a type of authentication within the "form of life". "So you are saying that human agreement decides what is true or false?—It is what human beings *say* that is true or false: and they agree in the *language* they use. That is not agreement in opinions but in form of life".[1] Tillich's distinction between the experimental and the experiential method and his linking of these forms of confirmation with the types of knowledge is, I think, correct and is also supportive of the dimensional structure of confirmation outlined here. Tillich proceeds to add an observation that is important for the consistency of my entire schematic proposal. He notes that these two means of confirmation, like the two dimensions of reason and the two types of knowledge, must be dialectically related. In the same way the controlling and receiving elements of knowledge must be united, so the truth of this knowledge is confirmed partly by experimental test, by verification, and partly by participation in the life process, by authentication. Tillich calls this knowledge by participation, which results in authentication, "intuition". "Intuition in this sense is not irrational, and neither does it by-pass a full consciousness of experimentally verified knowledge".[2] Rather, confirmation in a complex situation may involve both verification and authentication. However, it is experiential authentication which is most under fire in the contemporary scene. So Tillich, like Urban, wishes to stress the scope or range of legitimate confirmation and particularly the prevalence and validity of authentication. Tillich, in an illustration of how the historian uses this experiential method, this authentication, states that confirmation in this respect "means to illuminate, to make understandable, to give a meaningful and consistent picture".[3] Authentication depends on illuminating or showing forth insight and on the ultimate intelligibility of that insight.

---

[1] Wittgenstein, *Philosophical Investigations*, p. 88.
[2] Tillich, *Systematic Theology*, Vol. I, p. 103.
[3] *Ibid.*, p. 104.

SUMMARY

On the basis of the notion of truth explicated in this chapter and the theory of confirmation consistent with this notion, I have added another and final part to my schematic proposal concerning the dimensional structure of language. This involves the means of confirmation by which one can determine the method of deciding the truth or falsity of a judgment made within a particular dimension of language and within the context of a specific universe of discourse. This can be illustrated most concisely by an expanded form of the diagram of this schematic proposal presented in Chapter V. It would now appear like this :

Dimensions of Language	Dimensions of Thought or Reason	Types of Knowledge	Means of Confirmation
SYMBOLIC	FOUNDATIONAL	RECEIVING	AUTHENTICATION
↕	↕	↕	↕
CONCEPTUAL	TECHNICAL	CONTROLLING	VERIFICATION

The analytic philosophers made an important contribution when they demanded that each discipline or field show how the assertions made within that discipline might be verified and on what basis the assertions could lay a claim to truth. I have argued that the scope or range of legitimate means of verification permitted by some analytic philosophers was too narrow, but the demand was appropriate. The crucial conclusion or this chapter is that assertions made within the symbolic dimension of language empowered by foundational thought which results in receiving knowledge can be confirmed (a term employed for the notion or verification in its broadest sense) by a process of authentication within the discourse situation. Assertions made within the conceptual dimension of language which is empowered by technical thought and results in controlling knowledge can be confirmed by a process of verification. This conclusion assumes, of course, a certain notion of meaning and truth as well as a concrete theory of confirmation which defines and illustrates what verification and authentication in this sense involve.

The notions of authentication and of truth as adequacy of expression are especially important in regard to the understanding of symbol developed here. Only truth as adequacy of expression can do justice to the notion of symbolic truth asserted previously. A symbol is an expression and thus its criterion of truth lies in its adequacy. This is its adequacy of representation and therefore its adequacy to grasp the disclosure of Being as it occurs in language. However, the adequacy involved here, regardless of what it may be in other areas, is certainly adequacy for a specific type of consciousness, symbolic consciousness, which is conditioned by a given universe of discourse, by a community of communicating subjects. The truth of the symbol in science, art, or theology is in some degree conditioned by those who employ the symbol. Therefore, its confirmation can legitimately be justified on the basis of mutual recognition and acknowledgment of a value or truth which is disclosed in language itself; namely, by the process of authentication. It is possible, I think, to meet the demands of the analytic philosophers to show the means by which even a symbolic statement can be confirmed and the basis within that universe of discourse upon which it makes a claim to truth. The first part of my response has been given in this chapter; the second part depends, of course, on an examination of the specific universe of discourse in question.

It is the thesis of this study that the dimensional structure of language is operative in every principal universe of discourse, in every major discipline. It is in fact this common dimensional structure which provides the possibility for communication between different universes of discourse. This thesis will be briefly developed in regard to several illustrative universes of discourse, employing natural science as a special, if unlikely, paradigm case, before considering the theological universe of discourse.

CHAPTER SEVEN

DIMENSIONAL STRUCTURE OF LANGUAGE
IN REPRESENTATIVE UNIVERSES OF DISCOURSE

There is, it has been claimed, a dimensional structure of language operative in every principal universe of discourse. A symbolic and a conceptual dimension are present in every major field or discipline, and although they are of necessity interdependent, these dimensions can be distinguished. The failure to identify and analyze these dimensions has resulted not only in linguistic confusion but also in a crisis in the meaning value of certain universes of discourse, such as the ethical and religious. This failure has also contributed to the isolation of certain universes of discourse from one another, such as the case with science and religion. As Ian G. Barbour notes in his introduction to *Science and Religion : New Perspectives on the Dialogue*, science and religion are often understood today as "unrelated languages". "The distinctive features of religion ... are held to be absent from science. There can be no significant dialogue if there are no common interests and no points of contact between the fields".[1] This isolation avoids conflict, but it also prevents fruitful communication.

It is the thesis of this study that a theory of unrelated language games and the resulting isolation of certain disciplines is not only unproductive for the specific disciplines, but also wrong. Such a theory springs from an inadequate understanding of the nature of language which underlies any particular universe of discourse. There is a common interest, a point of contact, for instance, between science and religion precisely in the dimensional structure of language that cuts through both universes of discourse. Not only is there a symbolic and conceptual dimension of language which operates in both disciplines, but also parallel dimensions of reason, forms of knowledge, and means of confirmation. A schematic proposal has been presented here which purports to be a comprehensive theory of language, applicable in all principal universes

---

[1] Ian G. Barbour, "Science and Religion Today", *Science and Religion : New Perspectives on the Dialogue*, Ian G. Barbour (ed.) (New York : Harper & Row, 1968), p. 17.

of discourse. In addition, if the proposal is correct, it would provide the foundation for inter-disciplinary communication and understanding.

In order to prove that this is a comprehensive and adequate theory of language, it would be necessary to show that it is an intelligible means of interpreting several representative universes of discourse; for example, theology, natural science, and history. It would be necessary to demonstrate that each universe of discourse has both a symbolic and conceptual dimension as previously defined; that assertions made in the respective dimensions are empowered by a particular type of reason ; that this results in a particular form of knowledge; and that these assertions can be confirmed respectively by authentication and verification. It is clear that this kind of proof is beyond the scope of this project. However, perhaps one can make a case for the feasibility of this schematic proposal and its warrant for further investigation by first suggesting how this dimensional structure would apply to the aforementioned representative universes of discourse in regard to its most controversial and questionable element; namely, the claim for a symbolic dimension which provides crucial insights and patterns for the discipline via transformational and pointing symbols. This could be accomplished through the tutelage of a contemporary thinker, Karl Jaspers, who employs a different terminology but whose concern for the symbolic dimension as an instrument of insight is comparable to my own.

The case for this comprehensive theory of language could also be supported by taking one universe of discourse, other than theology, as a paradigm case and thus illustrating the dimensional structure of this discipline in more detail than is possible in the brief suggestions relating to the other universes of discourse. The case would be further substantiated if this paradigm case were to represent a universe of discourse in which the proposed dimensional structure and particularly the symbolic dimension appeared least likely to be applicable; namely, in the universe of discourse employed in natural science. The task of this chapter will be to attempt to make a case for the dimensional understanding of language by considering this preliminary symbolic outline in relation to the thought of Karl Jaspers. The following chapter will concentrate on natural science as a paradigm case for the dimensional structure of language.

Philosophy of Symbolic Forms : Cipher and Symbol

The full explication of this proposed dimensional understanding of language would ultimately require the construction of a "philosophy of symbolic forms". This is, I believe, the labor which confronts those who investigate the nature of language from the perspective of a "high evaluation". Ernst Cassirer has developed one of the most thorough studies in this century. Wilbur Urban also recognized the necessity of this task and developed his own more abbreviated construction. Urban defined the project by stating that the philosophy of symbolic forms

> implies that there are different forms or types of symbols which, while all belonging to one general field of symbolism, yet have different functions and different ways of expressing reality. In other words there are different universes of discourse —let us say the poetic, the scientific, the religious—and these universes have different symbolic forms.[1]

The present study obviously cannot entail the development of a full-blown philosophy of symbolic forms, but it does demand the determination, application, and interpretation of the symbols which operate in certain universes of discourse. Presented here is a partially developed philosophy of symbolic forms which depends on the existence of certain insight symbols, their constructive interpretation, and their existential significance in the events of ordinary experience to justify its further exploration. Different universes of discourse are simply diverse contexts in which communication takes place. The consummation or adequate fulfillment of this communication depends on the capacity of symbols to apprehend the world in this context, to be an intelligible way of rendering reality and therefore of accounting for our experience. I have argued previously that the capacity of the symbol adequately to render reality is the consequence of Being's self-disclosure in this symbolic dimension of language. The assignment of this partial philosophy of symbolic forms in reference to a specific universe of discourse is to discover or recognize the insight symbols, to expand and interpret the symbol in the conceptual dimension, and to confirm or authenticate the symbol as a means of rendering reality in that context or universe of discourse. The symbol becomes a model, metaphor, or cipher for comprehending reality.

In the application of a preliminary symbolic outline I would like to take as my guide a contemporary thinker who certainly does not describe his work as the philosophy of symbolic forms and in fact uses quite different terminology but who has nevertheless the same basic concerns. His primary emphasis is on the illuminating power of certain linguistic forms in manifesting transcendent reality to human *Existenz*. The central

---

[1] Urban, *Language and Reality*, pp. 454-455.

issue is the intrinsic relltionship of certain linguistic forms to transcendent reality and thus the resulting capacity to illuminate and direct human existence. He speaks of Transcendence manifested in ciphers. I have spoken of the disclosure of Being in symbols. There are, of course, essential differences in method and content, but there is a significant parallel between Karl Jaspers' use of ciphers and my use of symbols. My choice of Jaspers illustrates here that differences in terminology may obscure a basic similarity in intent and in existential ramifications.

The crucial factor in the explication of what I have called the philosophy of symbolic forms is not merely the use of the term symbol which, as we have noted, often ambiguously refers to more than one meaning. The significant factor is the definition and interpretation of certain language forms as being so related to reality itself as to have the illuminating and transforming function indicated whether these forms are designated as symbols, ciphers, models, images, or myths. I would assert a preference for the term symbol on the basis of its historical and cultural prominence and its acceptance in present speech patterns. I would argue that it needs refining, as I have attempted to do, and not rejection because of its misappropriation. However, the danger of the term symbol being misconstrued is obvious and accounts for its replacement by other terms. But one must look beyond the selection of labels to the role given the linguistic form in the theory of language being set forth. Reference to the views of Jaspers as an illustration lends support to what is, I think, a rather widespread concern with the symbolic element in language even when it is articulated in a different nomenclature.

Karl Jaspers elucidates his theory of ciphers in a systematic manner accessible to the English reader in *Philosophical Faith and Revelation*.[1] It is a complicated and detailed argument and I do not propose here to do more than justify the claim that there is a parallel between Jasper's employment of cipher and my own use of symbol. In our consideration of Jaspers' theory we must ask first what he means by the term "cipher". Jaspers maintains that what is meant by cipher "cannot be comprehended in a definition, but it can be experienced in the use of communication".[2] We can, however, give some picture of how a cipher works in the process of communication and its potential effect of the individual who thinks in ciphers. Jaspers asserts that ...

---

[1] Karl Jaspers, *Philosophical Faith and Revelation*, E. B. Ashton (trans.) (New York : Harper & Row, 1967). Translated from the German, *Der philosophische Glaube angesichts der Offenbarung* (Munich : R. Piper & Co., 1962).

[2] *Ibid.*, p. 116.

ciphers light the roots of things. They are not cognition; what is conceived in them is vision and interpretation. They cannot be experienced and verified as generally valid. Their truth is linked with Existenz. The magnetism of Transcendence for Existenz is voiced in ciphers. They open areas of Being. They illuminate my decisions.[1]

The emphasis in this description of ciphers is on their capacity to illuminate the human situation and to enable one to receive his own self as a gift. Ciphers are crucial in the decisions that determine the form of one's life and action. "Man lives in ciphers from the day he starts to think",[2] although he may not have a self-conscious methodology in regard to ciphers. But why do ciphers have this extraordinary power? It is because, according to Jaspers, "transcendent reality, to be experienced by Existenz alone, is manifested in ciphers".[3] Man, insofar as he comes to Existenz, is related to Transcendence by means of ciphers. The answer to what Transcendence is cannot be simply or sufficiently given here, but it is "the power from which I receive the gift of self, in my freedom. I am not self-made. I did not create myself",[4] declares Jaspers. So man is dependent on Transcendence for his possible Existenz.[5] Transcendence is comparable to what I have referred to in this study as Being. Jaspers speaks of the gift via ciphers, while in a parallel way I have spoken of the self-disclosure of Being in symbols. Both the gift and the self-disclosure constitute the power of letting-be. Cipher and symbol have an intrinsic relationship to reality itself. Jaspers goes on to note the linguistic nature of cipher and his preference for this term when he states :

"Cipher", a word I prefer to the word "symbol", denotes language, the language of a reality that can be heard and addressed only thus and in no other way – while

---

[1] Jaspers, *Philosophical Faith and Revelation*, p. 92. Despite my general agreement with Jaspers, I shall wish to take exception to his denial of cognition to ciphers. I also contend that although ciphers cannot be verified as generally valid, this does not deny that their adequacy cannot be confirmed by authentication.

[2] *Ibid.*, p. 95.

[3] *Ibid.*

[4] *Ibid.*, p. 69.

[5] Some explanation of the term "Existenz" is perhaps required. For Jaspers it is to be clearly distinguished from mere "existence", which is "the observation of objectively occurring facts ... finding myself as life in the world" (p. 67). "Existenz" is, however, always only *possible* Existenz. "It is potential being ... I do not have myself; I come to myself" (p. 66). "The cause of self-being ... this cause, this freedom, this faculty of being myself, of coming to myself in communication with other selves— this is what we call possible Existenz" (p. 65).

a symbol stands for something else, even though this may not exist outside the symbol. What we mean by the symbol is the other thing, which thus becomes objective and comes to be present in the symbol.[1]

Jaspers has an understanding of symbol which is equivalent to what I have described as the "wider" or "representative" meaning of symbol. He is also worried about the process of objectification which he associates with the term symbol. However, it appears that what Jaspers means by cipher coincides with what I have called the narrower meaning of symbol as an illuminating, transformational, and pointing symbol. In addition, the foundational thinking which I understand as engendering the symbolic dimension avoids the objectification which Jaspers properly rejects in reference to Transcendence or Being. Jaspers himself admits that symbols, even in this wider meaning, "may turn into elements of the cipher language".[2] Thus symbol in the narrower sense and cipher are parallel not only in their capacity for illumination but also in their intrinsic relation to transcendent reality as the source of human Existenz.

This explication of ciphers recalls several themes which have been developed in this study concerning symbols. All symbols point beyond themselves to another reality. They bear insight and convey an "awareness" of the presence of that reality which is referred to by the symbol. I have insisted on the necessity of a dialectic of affirmation and negation in regard to the symbol which guards against the absolutizing of a particular smybol. There is a "struggle of symbols" in the sense of the continual need to balance and correct the illumination given in one symbol by that conveyed in another. Symbols are born and they die. They become authentic transformational and pointing symbols when they are received or adopted by a particular community in a particular historical and existential situation. It is perhaps the failure to recognize the symbolic character of all reference to transcendent reality, to Being, that leads to a distortion and eclipse of the awareness of the reality itself. Man and Being are in a sense co-creators of the authentic insight symbols. They have arisen out of man-made cultural structures and yet are transformed and infused with the illuminating capacity by the act of Being's self-disclosure in symbols. This is the speaking of Being in and through language. But this insight defies total comprehension and adequate conceptualization; thus this insight can maintain its power and authenticity only in its symbolic character.

[1] Jaspers, *Philosophical Faith and Revelation*, p. 95.
[2] *Ibid.*

In spite of the parallels between Jaspers' use of cipher and my own understanding of a symbolic dimension of language, there are several points of basic disagreement between Jaspers and myself. Two of these require attention. The first concerns the denial by Jaspers that ciphers that ciphers involve cognition. Jaspers was quoted earlier as stating that ciphers are not cognitive and that they cannot be experienced and verified as generally valid.[1] Jaspers maintains a distinction between the vision or illumination present in the cipher and cognition which is related to the "phenomena of reality". These phenomena can be objectified and are verifiable as generally valid by reference to sense perception. Second, Jaspers has maintained that all thinking is objectifying, so he claims that thinking reduces to an object that upon which thought focuses. Jaspers asserts that this objectification is illegitimate in regard to realities that are in their own nature non-objectifiable, such as Transcendence and Existenz.

In response to these points, I have argued that although symbols (or ciphers, if you will) do not result in the same type of knowledge associated with objectifying conceptuality and sensory verification, they do involve a significant form of knowledge and thus symbols can be considered as involving cognition. I have maintained that we need to recognize two forms of knowledge, each of which can make the claim to be cognitive, but which are distinguishable and have characteristic methods of confirmation. So the schematic proposal presented here has distinguished "receiving knowledge" from "controlling knowledge" and maintained that the former is a consequence of the symbolic dimension of language. Jaspers would not, I assume, recognize the receiving form of knowledge as being cognition. Yet does it not seem unusual to relegate the source of some of the most crucial human decisions to the non-cognitive level? Does it not border on the unintelligible to speak of the ciphers upon whose "experience depends the illumination of the meaning and the goal of our life",[2] and then interpret this insight and illumination as non-cognitive? I maintain that it is much more intelligible to recognize the distinctive cognition which is a result of the adoption of symbols or ciphers. It is necessary to indicate how this form of cognition is to be distinguished from the realm of conceptual cognition and to elucidate the form of knowledge which is consistent with each. I have attempted to do this in a tentative way in the schematic proposal contained in this

[1] Jaspers, *Philosophical Faith and Revelation*, p. 92.
[2] *Ibid.*, p. 228.

study. I would agree that ciphers cannot be verified as generally valid in the same way as the phenomena of conceptual cognition. I would, however, maintain that they can be authenticated and that there is a process of confirmation within the realm of communication and the structure of community life which saves ciphers or symbols from the charge of total ambiguity and thus from meaninglessness. The solution is not to deny cognitive status to that which is revealed in the cipher or symbol but rather to envision a dimensional structure of language with corresponding forms of knowledge.

Despite the fact that Jaspers declares quite clearly that ciphers are non-cognitive, he appears to employ them in his own work as if they were cognitive. In making the distinction between cognitive and non-cognitive, one could surely agree that what is claimed to be true or false is cognitive. Jaspers speaks throughout the book of the "struggle in the world of ciphers".[1] In speaking of this struggle he declares that "the stakes for any present Existenz are truth or untruth of individual ciphers ...".[2] Jaspers himself, for example, accepts the cipher of the personal God and repudiates the cipher of the Trinity.[3] I am convinced that despite what Jaspers says about the non-cognitive nature of ciphers, he refers to ciphers as if they supply significant knowledge. However, I think that knowledge from ciphers of symbols may be distinguished from that of conceptual cognition.

My response to Jaspers' rejection of non-objectifying thinking is to say that, while the type of thinking or reason which is understood to engender a conceptual language is objectifying, in the sense that troubles Jaspers, all thinking is not necessarily of this type. One should recognize by reflection and analysis of the rational processes that while all thinking must be objectifying in the sense of "thematizing", all thinking is not necessarily objectifying in the sense of demeaning that about which one thinks by reducing it to an object in his control and possession. Rather, there is in addition to this technical thinking or reason another non-objectifying form of foundational thinking which is open and receptive to that upon which one focuses his thinking. It is in the sphere of this foundational thinking that the symbols or ciphers are operative. It might even be proposed that when Jaspers speaks of "thinking in the direction of Transcendence in ciphers",[4] something like the foundational thinking

---

[1] Jaspers, *Philosophical Faith and Revelation, passim.* See especially pp. 126ff.

[2] *Ibid., pp.* 126-127.

[3] *Ibid.,* p. 166.

[4] *Ibid.,* p. 288.

I have been describing would make the whole discussion more intelligible. Jaspers fears either (1) reducing the illumination of ciphers to the sphere of sense observation and proof and thus perverting the ciphers, or (2) allowing ciphers to become so abstract that one can no longer hear Transcendence speaking and thus loses touch with transcendent reality. Such a conception of foundational thinking as proposed here might guard against these dangers. This form of thinking preserves the freedom of the object of thought to disclose or reveal itself and yet maintains a means of confirmation which preserves the integrity of the disclosure from charges of subjectivism, arbitrariness, emotionalism, and illusion. The proposal here suggests a dimensional understanding of thinking and reason rather than a denial of the rational character of insight and illumination in the realm of ciphers or symbols.

Jaspers warns us against identifying the cipher with transcendent reality. "Ciphers are never the reality of Transcendence itself, only its possible language".[1] Ciphers are said to "bear the message of Transcendence". One could say, I think, that Transcendence speaks in and through language. As Jaspers reminds us, "Ciphers point beyond themselves, at the root of things. They point to what we call "Being' ...".[2] I too have warned against identifying the symbol with that which it symbolizes. The symbol is intrinsically related to that which it symbolizes so as to provide insight and result in illumination, but it is not only a "transformational symbol"; it is also a "pointing symbol" which directs us beyond itself. Jaspers concurs with my interpretation of symbol when he reminds us of the inadequacy of any single cipher to grasp without ambiguity that to which it points. Ciphers are instruments of insight, heeded only as images or guidelines in a particular historic and existential moment.[3] There is no final or absolute cipher. Jaspers sees the "embodiment of ciphers" (the identifying of the content of a particular cipher with reality), which results in the claim for one absolute and final cipher, to be the basic perversion which has led to the loss of the power of cipher language, a situation described by him as a calamity of our time. I am calling for a new examination of ciphers or symbols which will give them the opportunity to regain their "old existential vigour and wealth of language".[4]

In light of the inadequacy or limitation of any single cipher, Jaspers suggests a "struggle of ciphers" in which they compete with one

---

[1] Jaspers, *Philosophical Faith and Revelation*, p. 93.
[2] *Ibid.*, p. 134.
[3] *Ibid.*, p. 93.
[4] *Ibid.*, p. 104.

another and therefore balance, supplement, and challenge the insight provided by other ciphers. Ciphers are historic; they arise, are adopted, and then lose their voice.[1] They are known from collections of mythologies and revelations and one experiences their power in great art, poetry, and speculative philosophy. Anything is capable of becoming a cipher. Ciphers ought to be held in suspension because they are in a sense man-made; they are products of the operation of the human mind and of the cultural situation, "yet, speaking through this human product will be something that is more than human".[2] Man achieves a relation to Transcendence by means of the cipher's illumination.

The emphasis thus far has been on the illuminating and pointing character of cipher and on the mystery and incomprehensibleness of that power which speaks in them. But there is an equally strong emphasis in Jaspers' thought on the necessity for the interpretation of these ciphers. Ciphers cannot be separated from critical questioning via conceptual cognition. Jaspers declares, "The ciphers lose their existential impact in the generality of concepts; but a breath of their original life remains even there. We can no more dispense with this kind of information [conceptual interpretation] than with osteology in studying the body".[3] Jaspers speaks of the interpretation of ciphers in terms of "observation", the critical form of rational, psychological, and sociological exegesis of given ciphers, and "adoption", which is one's recognition of its truth and his commitment to share in its results. "The step from observation to adoption goes from knowing this cipher world to living in it".[4] There needs to be a continual and critical examination of ciphers in order that one can speak clearly and not mumble. The truth of the cipher is not determined in the process of interpretation alone, in the reflection upon the cipher; what occurs in interpretation is the clarification of the cipher and the testing of the cipher with the experience of existential thinking. The struggle of ciphers necessitates their interpretation and this interpretation of ciphers recommends certain ciphers as being those which should be adopted because they embody illumination in this historic and existential situation. I listen to certain ciphers and I deny others. The struggle of ciphers goes on, in which men choose certain core ciphers which shape and guide their Existenz.[5] The truth of the

[1] Jaspers, *Philosophical Faith and Revelation*, p. 107.
[2] *Ibid.*, p. 204.
[3] *Ibid.*, p. 117.
[4] *Ibid.*
[5] *Ibid.*, p. 128.

cipher is finally determined by the confirmation of a cipher in Existenz which involves decision and communication.

Jaspers' demand for interpretation of and reflection upon ciphers presents a striking parallel to my insistence on the necessity of non-symbolic interpretation of symbols in the conceptual dimension of language. Jaspers does not suggest a dimensional understanding of language as the basis for this process of interpretation, but I think one is implied. I have spoken of the expansion and interpretation of symbol as a means of recommending certain symbols for further investigation and consideration. The interpretation within the conceptual dimension clarifies certain symbols and makes them more intelligible; for instance, by analogical explication. There is a sense in which the conceptual interpretation of symbols is a factor in the struggle of symbols with one another for their adoption or acceptance within a particular community. The crucial point of agreement between Jaspers and myself is the need for the interpretation of symbols in the conceptual realm in order for communication to take place. Part of the impact of the symbol is lost in the process of its interpretation. So the interpretation cannot replace the symbol; it is not a matter of reduction to the conceptual dimension. But the interpretation of the symbol is necessary in order to clarify, commend, and support the symbol so that it may be freed to provide the insight and illumination of which it is capable, and point beyond itself to its source. As Jaspers puts it, "It seems clear and simple : the source should speak, and what covers it ought to be shed".[1]

The question of the truth of the cipher has been raised and it should be clear that Jaspers specifically rejects the idea of "one sole truth"[2] or the idea of truth in general. Rather, there are different modes of truth that are appropriate to the different "modes of encompassing". The modes of truth do have a common base which lies in Transcendence.[3] There is what one could call a philosophical faith in the possibility of unlimited mutual understanding. "Truth is what unites us .... In the thinking person there is a power at work that is not he and yet is in himself, urging self-understanding and communicability".[4] This view coincides with my own insistence that there is no truth in general but only various forms of truth appearing in different contexts or various universes of discourse. However, there is a common force of truth as

---

[1] Jaspers, *Philosophical Faith and Revelation*, p. 120.
[2] *Ibid.*, p. 83.
[3] *Ibid.*, p. 70.
[4] *Ibid.*, pp. 90-91.

contrasted with the different criteria of truth in different contexts. This foundation for the common force of truth depends, I have suggested, on the belief in universel intelligibility and on the disclosure of truth by Being in various symbolic forms in particular instances.

The discovery of the force of truth then involves the discovery, interpretation, and adoption of certain ciphers or symbols in specific contexts. I have called these contexts universes of discourse and have spoken of various symbolic forms. Jaspers speaks in a similar way of modes of ciphers[1] and proceeds to classify various types of historic ciphers and to reflect on them as a means of interpretation, as a means of being open to the possible truth of ciphers. Jaspers develops, I would maintain, his own kind of philosophy of symbolic forms, since it is philosophy which becomes the interpreter of the various ciphers.

I indicated previously that perhaps the most questionable aspect of this understanding of language is the idea that there is a symbolic element (in Jaspers' terms, a cipher) which is present in every major area of human investigation and it is this symbolic element which provides insight and illumination for this discipline. Making reference to some representative areas in which Jaspers identifies and reflects on particular ciphers can illustrate this. Here is additional support for a preliminary symbolic outline by means of which one can apprehend reality. Jaspers does not classify ciphers in terms of universes of discourse as this study has done. I have felt free, however, to apply that means of classification to Jaspers' work simply for purposes of illustration. This appears to be legitimate since Jaspers denies that his list of ciphers is comprehensive and therefore a survey.[2] He also does not assert that his classification of ciphers of transcendence, immanence, and existential situation is more than a guideline for his own presentation. I am concerned here primarily with the cipher itself and with its interpretation in each of several representative areas. The ciphers to be considered here are those that become significant in the following universes of discourse : theology, natural science, and history.

Jaspers considers first the "basic ciphers of the Deity"[3] or ciphers that refer "directly to Transcendence (God)."[4] It is ciphers or symbols of God with which theology of every variety is primarily concerned. Jaspers selects certain God-oriented ciphers which have their basis in the Biblical

---

[1] Jaspers, *Philosophical Faith and Revelation*, p. 123.

[2] *Ibid.*, p. 136.

[3] *Ibid.*, p. 137.

[4] *Ibid.*, p. 136.

tradition and thus are particularly appropriate for the concerns of this study. According to Jaspers, it is the cipher that allows us to be in contact with Transcendence and which provides the illumination and guidance for our human Existenz. It is in ciphers that a man "transcends" toward the Deity. "Our only access to the incomprehensible, the inconceivable, the all-encompassing, is the ever-inadequate, endlessly variable ciphers".[1] The crucial aspect of this view is the recognition of the cipher or symbol element. Those terms which are the foundation of theological discourse and therefore the discipline of theology must be recognized as symbols and not literal references to embodied reality. It is its function as cipher which endows it with illuminating potential.

Jaspers distinguishes three basic ciphers of the Deity: the One God, the Incarnate God, and the Personal God. The One God is an illuminating cipher of man's will to unity both with Transcendence and within himself.[2] The cipher of the Incarnate God is really transformed by Jaspers into an emphasis on the human Jesus as the unique, incomparable cipher of man's capacity before his God.[3] These ciphers can only be mentioned here in passing, but I will focus more closely on the cipher of the Personal God.

The Bible is full of images of the Personal God. "God protects and commands, is mild and severe, merciful and angry. He loves man and is just. Man approaches Him trustingly and fearfully".[4] Man addresses God and is addressed by God in prayer. These images, including the idea of God itself are ciphers of Transcendence, of the power of transcendent reality. The need is present to relate to God in a personal way, in an I-Thou relationship. It is the illuminating cipher of the personal God that provides that opportunity. Our Existenz is the self-being of personality and thus man must conceive of God as a person.[5] Yet Transcendence, the source of personality, is surely more than a person and certainly not less than a person. The cipher is inadequate, but as a cipher it brings illumination and insight. It is saved from distortion by remaining a cipher. Transcendence speaks and reveals itself in ciphers. It is in the ciphers of the personal God that Transcendence relates to

---

[1] Jaspers, *Philosophical Faith and Revelation*, p. 137.

[2] *Ibid.*, pp. 137ff.

[3] *Ibid.*, pp. 145ff. With Jaspers' particular interpretation of the Christological cipher I have disagreements, but the notion of Jesus Christ as a cipher or symbol is not inappropriate if properly understood.

[4] *Ibid.*, p. 141.

[5] *Ibid.*

man in "self illumination" as God; namely, as the source of our personality, freedom, and Existenz. The suprapersonal, incomprehensible Godhead turns to man in the ciphers of the personal God, while the source, the Transcendent ground of the ciphers, stays hidden.[1] The ciphers are authenticated only in the life of a historic community by attesting to their existential impact, their capacity to provide insight and guidance.

However, there is another dimension to this explication of ciphers and that is the interpretation and reflection upon the basic historic ciphers. These "fundamental ciphers of the Godhead are inaudible without thinking".[2] Thinking, it will be recalled, is limited according to Jaspers to the objectifying conceptual sphere. The aim of this " 'cognition of faith'—whether it is philosophical or theological—seeks to unfold what is inaccessible to objective cogntion".[3] This involves the critical questioning of the ramifications of the ciphers. Cognition is part of the struggle of ciphers where a particular cipher must be interpreted, evaluated, and correlated with the other elements of one's experience in order to accept or reject the cipher as a possibility for providing illumination of man's existential situation. For instance, as a result of this critical interpretation, Jaspers accepts the cipher of the Personal God and rejects the historic cipher of the Trinity.[4]

It would be my contention that the cipher or symbol itself cannot be proved or disproved in the realm of interpretation and reflection. The cipher itself can only be authenticated as illuminating by the existential response of the individual in the midst of communication in a given community. As Jaspers asserts, "The test of the image, the extent to which it will be illuminating, inspiring, fatal, or enhancing for man, is neither logical or epistemological but existential".[5] However, the reasonableness of a particular historic cipher to struggle for and claim acceptance on the basis of its illuminating power can be clarified and evaluated by interpretation. This interpretation takes place in what I have described as the conceptual dimension of language. In this conceptual realm the qualities of God, such as God's omnipotence, which are supplementary to the cipher of the Personal God can be interpreted and clarified. Jaspers does just this and proposes a balancing of various interpretations

[1] Jaspers, *Philosophical Faith and Revelation*, p. 142.

[2] *Ibid.*, p. 148.

[3] *Ibid.*

[4] *Ibid.*, p. 166.

[5] *Ibid.*, p. 153.

of omnipotence as suspended ciphers.[1] I think Jaspers would agree that the interpretation of the cipher is necessary in order to provide the cipher an opportunity to function in a community as that which relates man to Transcendent reality, to Being.

Jaspers considers next "ciphers of immanence", "those in which an immanent concept as such comes to refer to Transcendence".[2] "Immanence is the universe in space and history in time ... all that manifests itself to our senses, our thoughts, our consciousness of physical existence".[3] Jaspers maintains that here too one must distinguish between ciphers and cognition. This is parallel to my distinction between the symbolic and conceptual dimensions. Jaspers stresses the illumination provided by these ciphers in relation to scientific cognition.

Jaspers contends that "a principle of exact natural science is to envision a unified nature".[4] Thus, the evolution of modern science, particularly in modern physics, has led to greater unifications of previously separate fields. Yet it has also been recognized that a view of nature as a whole, as a unity, or even the unity of a particular scientific field cannot be achieved on the basis of scientific cognition or scientific technical knowledge. One finds in science "systematic unities *ad infinitum*". However, an understanding of these more limited forms of unity and the unity of the whole of nature is based on ciphers of nature and ciphers of the universe or cosmic images. "The rigour of science serves to clarify the different original meanings of the ciphers and to preserve their unrestricted scope of truth".[5] The cipher of nature in terms of the structure of the atom or the cosmic cipher of the One and All, which sees a tightly ordered universe where everything has its place, is the means of existentially illuminating thinking. "Ciphers have furnished the impulses for the scientific research that is now independently valid apart from the impulses".[6] The ciphers of nature with which natural science works must always be tied to concrete tangible phenomena. These ciphers are the means of envisioning the unity which is not apprehensible on the level of conceptual or technical knowledge. There is a constant struggle between the ciphers of nature; no one is ever absolute. The value of the cipher depends on its ability to provide insight and illumination of a unity beyond our

---

[1] Jaspers, *Philosophical Faith and Revelation*, pp. 153ff.
[2] *Ibid.*, p. 136.
[3] *Ibid.*, p. 168.
[4] *Ibid.*, p. 171.
[5] *Ibid.*, p. 179.
[6] *Ibid.*, p. 184.

conceptual verification. However, the ciphers require interpretation as a means of checking on the reasonableness of their insight and motivation for the uniting urge of natural science. The ciphers of immanence come to refer to Transcendence, the source of all unity. It is important to recognize that ciphers of nature exist and to distinguish them from the facts of conceptual cognition. The two elements, ciphers and cognition (or, as I have expressed it, the symbolic and the conceptual dimension) cannot be separated, but they ought not to be confused.

Another area which illustrates the parallel between Jaspers' thought and my own within representative universes of discourse deals with the ciphers of history. " 'Understanding' is the basic category in our conception of history".[1] The historian wants to see and show how things really were and to indicate the causality of events. This can never be done conclusively, but certain methods of historical science are employed in order to present certain historic realities—events, conditions, periods, and personalities. This research is subject to conceptual analysis and verification on the basis of certain historical data. However, the theme, the selection, and arrangement of the facts proceed from motives which transcend the conceptual sphere.[2] Appraisal is an essential aspect of understanding. According to Jaspers, one "motivation of historical science is the will to know so as to learn from the past, to live and to act better".[3] This, however, requires an overall view which is available only as a cipher of history. Ciphers dealing with the overall view of history such as progress, evolution, eternal recurrence, or Divine guidance cannot be proved but "they do express a historic sense fo Being".[4] The acceptance of a historic cipher, the way of understanding the overall course of history or some aspect of it such as its "eschaton", determine the way I decide, act, and evaluate my present existence. Man seeks to know so as to learn from the past. There is a struggle among the ciphers of history. "The ciphers lay out the horizons in these struggles. They orient us to possible perspectives".[5] The ciphers illuminate the past and provide insight and guidance for man's future decisions. These ciphers of history must be interpreted and clarified in order to show their ramifications and so that they may be checked in regard to their correlation with the historical

[1] Jaspers, *Philosophical Faith and Revelation*, p. 186.
[2] *Ibid.*, p. 187.
[3] *Ibid.*, p. 188.
[4] *Ibid.*
[5] *Ibid.*, p. 196.

data itself. The cipher and the interpretation are interrelated, but it is the existence of historical ciphers and their capacity for illumination that direct the historical discipline.

I have attempted to illustrate via Jaspers that ciphers or symbols illuminate each representative universe of discourse. The issue of the source of this capacity of ciphers still remains. I have maintained that symbols have this illuminating capacity because they are ultimately the result of Being's self-disclosure in language. Therefore ciphers or symbols provide an access into the nature of reality itself. In a parallel manner, Jaspers asserts that Transcendence is the source of the language of ciphers. Transcendence, when conceived in a special way, becomes the power we call God. As Jaspers states it, "when I talk of ciphers of God, I identify God with Transcendence".[1] Only in ciphers does man experience his own ground (Transcendence[2]). Ciphers occur in language and are open to many forms of interpretation. Man shapes what he is by responding to the ciphers which are manifest in a linguistic form. Thus language and communication, the means of authenticating the cipher, are crucial to man's realization of his own self. It is by language, and specifically this cipher language, that man is related to Transcendence. "As a result, these ciphers are revelations ...".[3] The decisive role of ciphers (symbols in our definition) in each principal area of human concern, the necessity of their cognitive or conceptual interpretation, and the source of their illuminating capacity are confirmed by Jaspers' work.

SUMMARY

The task of this chapter has been to make a case for the general applicability of the dimensional structure of language. This has been done by indicating how the symbolic and conceptual dimensions of language are operative in several representative universes of discourse : theology, natural science, and history. It was maintained that there was an essential parallel between the way Karl Jaspers employs the notion of "cipher" and the way I have interpreted "symbol" as operative in a symbolic dimension of language. With Jaspers as a guide, the basic ciphers of theology, natural science, and history were analyzed, indicating in each

---

[1] Jaspers, *Philosophical Faith and Revelation*, p. 327.
[2] *Ibid.*, p. 302.
[3] *Ibid.*

case the need to interpret the cipher. The basic emphasis here has been on the presence in each discipline of an illuminating cipher or symbol which has an intrinsic relation to transcendent reality. The source of the cipher language is Trancendence; Being discloses itself in the symbolic dimension of language. Thus the schematic proposal about the dimensional structure of language is not only applicable but clarifying in regard to each representative universe of discourse.

Now I turn to natural science, as a paradigm case, to show how the dimensional understanding of language is applicable and particularly how the symbolic elment is operative in this particular universe of discourse.

CHAPTER EIGHT

SYMBOLISM AND NATURAL SCIENCE

The contemporary climate of thought would probably make one most skeptical about applying the dimensional understanding of language to the universe of discourse called natural science. This is particularly true in regard to the claim that there is a symbolic element in the assertions of natural science which provides significant insight and illumination for the scientist, but is not subject to verification in terms of observable sense confirmation. It is just this skeptical attitude which led me to select natural science as a paradigm case of the possible applicability of my schematic proposal. In addition, natural science is an area in which support for methodological similarities between science and theology might form the basis for increased interdisciplinary communication and dialogue.

The prevailing attitude in recent years has been to see science and religion in regard to method as "strongly contrasting enterprises which have nothing to do with each other".[1] The conflict between science and religion which characterized an earlier decade has been replaced by a view which sees the two disciplines as independent and autonomous and yielding "complementary perspectives". This position is reflected in the separation of science and religion as unrelated but "complementary languages".[2] In this chapter I want to maintain that the "complementary language" relation correctly recognizes the characteristic differences between the fields but prohibits authentic dialogue. I want to go beyond this tentative and neutral stance concerning the relation between science and religion by asserting that there are significant parallels in their method which, when one focuses on the nature of language, provide the basis for significant interdisciplinary dialogue and understanding. This will be done by emphasizing the functional and logical similarities between

[1] Ian G. Barbour, *Issues in Science and Religion* (Englewood Cliffs, New Jersey : Prentice-Hall, 1966), p. 1.

[2] This view is contained, for example, in Professor Herbert Feigl's vice presidential address to the Association for the Advancement of Science in 1959, "Philosophical Tangents of Science", *Current Issues in the Philosophy of Science*, H. Feigl and G. Maxwell (eds.) (New York : Holt, Rinehart and Winston, 1961), pp. 1-17.

theological and scientific symbols or models; i.e., indicating the symbolic dimension of natural science. Distinct differences between science and religion do remain. One must be aware that methodological parallels can be pushed too fast and too far. However, the existence of these parallels needs to be accentuated and their recognition by some prominent scientists and philosophers of science noted. The task of this chapter is to indicate briefly the similarities between science and religion in : the use of symbols or models, the factor of personal involvement, the role of the respective communities in confirmation, the interaction between experience and interpretation, and even in the revelatory element in interpretation which illuminates our present experience.[1] In this explication a case will be made for the applicability of the dimensional understanding of language to the scientific universe of discourse.

In a collection of articles entitled *Science and Religion : New Perspectives on the Dialogue*, Donald D. Evans expresses the skeptical attitude noted above when he insists that "although there are a few genuine similarities between religious theory (theology) and scientific theory, there are fundamental differences between religion and science ...".[2] This difference in methodology is stressed when Evans asserts that "a scientific assertion should be logically neutral, comprehensible impersonally, and testable by observation",[3] while none of these characterizes religious assertions. It should be noted that Evans' position implies, first, that all scientific assertions are fundamentally of the same type. He then contrasts these scientific assertions with religious assertions which also appear to have a monolithic nature. I wish to argue that this position is simplistic, because it fails to recognize the dimensional structure of both the scientific and the religious universe of discourse. Although there are some scientific assertions which coincide with Evans' qualifications, those which I have described as conceptual, there are other statements which do not; namely, those in the symbolic dimension of science. The symbolic dimension includes the symbols, ciphers, or models which provide insight and illumination for the discipline of natural science. My response to Evans, and to others who take this position, will be to examine the assertions of natural science and see if there are not some

---

[1] Barbour, in *Issues in Science and Religion*, proposes the same program without having my particular concern for the dimensional structure of language, which I think is the key factor in establishing these methodological parallels.

[2] Donald Evans, "Differences Between Scientific and Religious Assertions", *Science and Religion : New Perspectives on the Dialogue*, p. 101.

[3] *Ibid.*, p. 111.

important aspects of natural science which do not take the form suggested above. This study makes a claim for the existence of a symbolic element in natural science which parallels the symbolic elements in theology, history, and philosophy.

The way in which one understands the language of natural science depends to a degree on what he conceives as the purpose and scope of natural science. I would concur with those who see the aim of natural science to be not only prediction and control but also understanding and intelligibility. Werner Heisenberg, the Nobel prize winner and director of the Max Planck Institute for physics, emphasizes this aim of scientific intelligibility when he states that "every detailed question in science is subordinate to the major task of understanding nature as a whole".[1] Ian Barbour, who is both physicist and theologian, asserts that what is required is "a coherent interpretation of all experience" to which science and religion both contribute in their attempt at general understanding.[2] This recognition of the dual aims of natural science in terms of both control and understanding is supported by Charles A. Coulson,[3] Oxford mathematician and theoretical physicist, Harold K. Schilling,[4] physicist, and Frederick Ferré,[5] philosopher of language and religion. Ernest Nagel summarizes this view in an article on "The Nature and Aim of Science" by stating that practical control was one, but not the main aim of science. Rather, Nagel asserts, "science seeks to make the world intelligible ... [it] satisfies the craving to know and understand ...".[6]

This conception of natural science as having a twofold purpose is important, for if science is only concerned with control and prediction, then the conceptual dimension of language may be sufficient and one can represent the objects of science in terms of graphs and equations. How-

---

[1] Werner Heisenberg, "The Representation of Nature in Contemporary Physics", *Symbolism in Religion and Literature*, Rollo May (ed.) (New York : George Brasiller, 1960), p. 224.

[2] Ian Barbour, "Science and Religion Today", in *Science and Religion*, p. 27. This is developed in more detail in Barbour's *Issues in Science and Religion*.

[3] Charles E. Coulson, "The Similarity of Science and Religion", *Science and Religion*, pp. 57-77. See especially pp. 62-63.

[4] Harold K. Schilling, "The Threefold Nature of Science and Religion", *Science and Religion : New Perspectives ...*, pp. 78-100. For a more extensive discussion see Schilling's *Science and Religion* (New York : Charles Scribner's Sons, 1962).

[5] Frederick Ferré, "Science and the Death of 'God' ", *Science and Religion : New Perspectives ...*, pp. 134-156. See especially p. 141.

[6] Ernest Nagel, "The Nature and Aim of Science", in *Philosophy of Science Today*, Sidney Morgenbesser (ed.) (New York : Basic Books, 1967), p. 5.

ever, if an essential part of natural science involves this element of understanding and intelligibility in regard to the whole of nature or of systematic unities therein, as I would contend, then natural science involves more than a conceptual dimension of language.

In order to meet the demands of scientific intelligibility and the need for a coherent interpretation of all experience, one needs a symbolic element in the language of natural science. As Urban affirms, "The recognition of the symbolic element in science ... is perhaps the chief mark of the modern self-critical attitude of science ...".[1] The symbolic element in science appears in the attempts to reach intelligibility and comes in the form of "symbolic constructions or models which enable us to express compendiously very complicated assemblages of facts".[2] These scientific symbols are sometimes the most significant aspect of natural science as they provide a relevant and coherent interpretation of a given section of experience as well as direct and motivate further scientific investigation. As Stephen Toulmin states in *The Philosophy of Science*, "one must have also some clearly intelligible way of conceiving the physical systems we study. This is the primary task of models : for know-how and understanding ...".[3] Toulmin gives as an illustration the wave-model and particle-model of quantum mechanics.

Yet it is just these scientific symbols or models which are not verifiable on the basis of the "empirical criterion", or in Donald Evans' terminology they are precisely not "testable by observation". Rather, they are confirmed and accepted as adequate for providing the force of truth in the direction of scientific research because they are part of "self-authenticating symbolic systems".[4] The scientific symbol becomes accepted within the scientific universe of discourse at a specific historical period as providing insight and illumination in regard to apprehending a certain aspect of reality. It is the acceptance, the authentication, of a scientific symbol, model, or paradigm within the midst of the communication of the scientific community which is crucial. The scientific symbol, like the theological symbol, is not so much verified as it is authenticated. However, the question of verification will be considered again later. The emphasis here is on the existence of a symbolic element in natural science as a result of conceiving this discipline as having one of its purposes that of under-

---

[1] Urban, *Language and Reality*, p. 503.

[2] *Ibid.*, p. 504.

[3] Stephen Toulmin, *The Philosophy of Science* (New York : Harper Torchbooks, 1960), p. 35.

[4] Urban, *op. cit.*, p. 505.

standing nature as a whole or providing scientific intelligibility in relation to all of experience.

The symbolic element in science is a result of the necessary process of interpretation that always goes on in scientific research. As was asserted previously, there is no such thing as an uninterpreted fact. Sense data are interpreted initially simply by being put in a linguistic form that can be communicated. Language is inseparable from cognition, so an interpretive element enters immediately and this process continues as knowledge becomes more complex and sophisticated. As Coulson reminds us, science is not a collection of facts, but rather, what one makes of the facts. The correlation of the facts depends on an interpretive leap, a theory, a bold guess. This interpretive leap is sometimes formulated as a scientific method. Coulson, for example, asserts that natural science depends on unverifiable and often unexamined presuppositions such as the belief that facts are correlatable and that there is an "order and consistency in Nature".[1] Coulson also insists, contrary to the position taken by Donald Evans, that "The personal element plays a large role in science".[2] The symbols or models which are a result of this interpretive leap are imagined and conceived by man. Einstein remarked, concerning the models that form the basis of theoretical physics, that they "cannot be abstracted from experience but must be freely invented. ... Experience may suggest the appropriate [models] ... but they most certainly cannot be deduced from it".[3] Therefore the scientist's personal experience conditions the form of the symbol. As Coulson claims, "His data are always uncertain; his models, which he constructs within his mind to represent the reality behind his measurements"[4] are affected by his personal judgment. Even the ability of a scientist to comprehend and accept a certain scientific symbol depends on and is shaped by his personal experience within the scientific community. This point is convincingly made by Thomas Kuhn in *The Structure of Scientific Revolutions* when he maintains that the "received tradition" and standard examples of "paradigms" of a given scientific community influence how one describes the world and even control the direction of scientific inquiry.[5]

[1] Coulson, "Similarity of Science and Religion", *Science and Religion : New Perspectives ...*, p. 63.

[2] *Ibid.*, p. 66.

[3] Quoted from Toulmin, *Philosophy of Science*, p. 43.

[4] Coulson, *op. cit.*, p. 67.

[5] Thomas S. Kuhn, *The Structure of Scientific Revolutions* (Chicago : University of Chicago Press, 1962).

I have been emphasizing the existence and importance of a symbolic dimension in the language of natural science that includes the use of scientific symbols, models, or paradigms. The contemporary discussion in the philosophy of science includes opponents and defenders of the use of symbols or models. Dr. Dudley Shapere, in the introduction to *Philosophical Problems of Natural Science*, notes that some scientists think models serve only a psychological function as "mental crutches" for minds trying to visualize the point of mathematical formulas.[1] Professor Pierre Duhem, in his opposition to models, warns that they should be used with caution and discarded as soon as possible in favor of a mathematical formulation or calculus.[2] Many philosophers of science see models or theories as simply means of summarizing data and therefore the model is translatable into sense data, observable vocabulary, or mathematical calculus. Theories and models are accounted for by "hypothetico-deductive" systems. This view is developed in a fairly similar way by Rudolf Carnap, Carl G. Hempel, and Richard B. Braithwaite.[3]

There are also very strong defenders of the use of models and symbols in natural science. Ian Barbour notes that in earlier periods the symbolic character of scientific language was overlooked, but the importance of symbols, the contribution of man's mind in inventing theoretical models, and the role of imagination and creativity in the formulation of new theories is widely acknowledged today.[4] Stephen Toulmin is an advocate of scientific symbols which he describes as "explanatory paradigms" or "ideals of natural order". Models, according to Toulmin, determine what scientists take to be problems, what they see as facts, and what they consider to be satisfactory explanations.[5] Mary B. Hesse has contributed a careful study of this problem in *Analogies and Models in Science*.[6] The importance of models is emphasized by Hesse who notes that physicists "continue to use both particle and wave models, each in ap-

---

[1] Dudley Shapere, "Introduction", *Philosophical Problems of Natural Science* (New York : The Macmillan Company, 1965), p. 25.

[2] Pierre Duhem, *The Aim and Structure of Physical Theory*, P. Wigner (trans.) (Princeton : Princeton University Press, 1954). See especially Pt. I, Chap. 4.

[3] H. Feigl, "Philosophical Tangents of Science", *Current Issues in the Philosophy of Science*, p. 5.

[4] Barbour, *Issues in Science and Religion*, p. 157.

[5] Stephen Toulmin, *Foresight and Understanding* (Bloomington : Indiana University Press, 1961), p. 81.

[6] Mary B. Hesse, *Analogies and Models in Science* (New York : Sheed and Ward, 1963). See especially Chap 2.

propriate situations, even though they are at first sight mutually contradictory, and this is not only in condescension to readers of popular science
not merely to assist in the teaching of students. It [the model] is an essential part of research in these fields ...".[1] Hesse indicates that the model notion stresses intelligibility of explanation and is clearly related to the
intuitive idea of providing explanation and understanding. The model is,
however, a means of insight only in relation to a historical period as illustrated in the move from Democritan atoms to Newtonian attractive and
repulsive particles to quantum electrodynamics. [2] The defense of scientific
symbols by Thomas Kuhn has already been referred to, and the position
of Max Black will be developed presently. Ernest Nagel defends not
only the pragmatic value of models but the contribution they make
to science.[3] I have provided only a brief glance at the contemporary
debate in the field, which evidences the growing recognition and support
by leading philosophers of science of the use of symbols and models
in the method of natural science.

The scientific symbol is a consequence not only of this personal interpretive process, but also of the incomprehensible element present in any
explanation of nature as a whole or any explanation of a systematic
unity within nature. This is particularly true in dealing with complex
problems such as micro-physics or cosmic theories, There is a mysterious
or incomprehensible element which cannot be adequately represented
as a copy or picture of reality. In *Science and Secularity* Ian Barbour out-
lines the similarities between theoretical models in science and religious
models. He asserts, "Neither is a literal picture of reality, yet neither can
be treated as a useful fiction. Models are partial and inadequate ways of
imagining what is not observable. They are symbolic representations,
for particular purposes, of aspects of reality which are not directly
accessible to us".[4] So natural science in the more complicated areas no
longer attempts to picture reality but rather can be said to symbolize
reality. Ian T. Ramsey, in *Models and Mystery*,[5] has elaborated in some
detail the point I have made here. Ramsey also speaks of "models" in
the natural sciences and theology. I believe that Ramsey's "disclosure

---

[1] Mary B. Hesse, "The Role of Models in Scientific Theory", *Philosophical Problems
of Natural Science*, p. 104.

[2] *Ibid.*, pp. 108-109.

[3] Ernest Nagel, *Structure of Science* (New York : Harcourt, Brace and World, 1961),
pp. 112-114.

[4] Ian Barbour, *Science and Secularity* (New York : Harper & Row, 1970), p. 30.

[5] Ian T. Ramsey, *Models and Mystery* (London : Oxford University Press, 1964.)

models" operate in much the same way as what I have described as transformational and pointing symbols. Ramsey maintains that all disciplines have in common the use of models by which each discipline provides its understanding of a mystery which confronts them all. Ramsey's work is especially important in this regard because it brings out the mysterious or incomprehensible element in natural science and also the utilization in this discipline of insight producing models.

In attesting to the use of insight models in natural science, Ramsey draws upon an important work by Max Black entitled *Models and Metaphors*.[1] Black traces in natural science the abandoning of a copy or picture theory which produced "scale models" of reality in favor of a theory which utilizes instead "analogue models".[2] These analogue models are distinct from scale models because they provide suggestive approaches rather than identical patterns. The stress is on a similarity in structure sufficient to produce insight about the nature of that which is referred to. The reality is beyond being comprehended and represented in any other form than the analogue model. Ramsey proceeds to employ Black's analysis in order to make a comparison between the models employed in natural science and those employed in theology.[3] "The contemporary use of models in science or theology—models which are not picturing models— points us back, then, to that moment of insight where along with a model there is disclosed to the scientist or the theologian that about which each is to be, in his characteristically different way, articulate".[4] In both cases, natural science and theology, one has the element of mystery and the necessity of a form of illuminating insight, a model or a symbol, in which the mysterious element is at least partially disclosed. Ramsey also notes that these models employed by different disciplines are never final or absolute. The models are like maps used in the exploration of mystery, scientific or social.[5] The maps are adequate for a particular historic period : adequate to produce the insight necessary for understanding and intelligibility. Man is required to produce the best maps or models he can. However, models must be criticized and corrected.

---

[1] Max Black, *Models and Metaphors* (Ithaca, New York : Cornell University Press, 1962).

[2] *Ibid.*, p. 222.

[3] Frederick Ferré makes a similar attempt to compare models of natural science with those of religion emphasizing the illuminating character of both in "Metaphors, Models, and Religion", *Soundings*, Vol. LI, No. 3, Fall 1968, pp. 327-345.

[4] Ramsey, *Models and Mystery*, pp. 20-21.

[5] *Ibid.*, p. 46.

One model may at first balance and finally replace another as man's apprehension of some aspect of reality changes. The insight symbol or model is not only present in but crucial to the discipline of natural science.

The question now arises as to the nature and source of these scientific symbols. Are scientific symbols only labels finally extrinsic to that which is represented in the symbol and therefore substitutionary and nominalistic in character? Or does science contain what I have described as authentic symbols (in the narrower sense) which are intrinsic to that which is symbolized and, by virtue of this relationship, capable of producing authentic awareness and insight into the nature of the thing symbolized? I have tried to argue that natural science does involve insight symbols. Take as an example the model or symbol of the structure of the atom. The scientist began in physics by representing the structure of the atom in terms of protons and neutrons set forth in particular patterns. The model is now considerably more complex. As Coulson describes it :

> The nuclear physicist, who visits the Pic du Midi in the Pyrenees to expose his photographic plate to cosmic rediation, and then returns to develop it, will serve as an illustration. What he finds in his plate are a series of little tracks, sometimes nearly straight, sometimes changing their direction as if something had collided with something else. And how does he interpret all this? By saying that a π meson moves fast until it collides with some other nucleus, or spontaneously decays into a μ meson, and that perhaps other mesons play their part as well. Today there is an elaborate hierarchy of fundamental particles from which all things in nature may be said to be ultimately derived. Yet if an inquirer be so bold as to ask whether anyone has ever really seen a single meson, the answer has to be "No". And the same is true of electrons, and atoms, and almost all the dominant entities in modern physics.[1]

The model of the structure of the atom becomes a symbol. It is an intrinsic symbol because it is a model which provides insight into the nature of reality[2]. It is a symbol one must have in order to "understand" in a certain

[1] Coulson, "Similarity of Science and Religion", *Science and Religion : New Perspectives* ..., p. 65.

[2] Over against the "instrumentalists", such as F. P. Ramsey and Gilbert Ryle who see the model primarily as a hypothetical construct, we have the realist view which sees the symbol or model as representing and providing insight into the structure of events in the world. The realist position is represented by thinkers such as Planck, Einstein, Whitehead, and Nagel. This latter view, when it allows a place for the creative role of the subject and the ontological element, lends support to my interpretation of the role of the symbol or model. Cf. Barbour, *Issues in Science and Religion*, pp. 164-171.

way. Yet the symbol has limitations; it is partly fictional. It "breaks in our hands"[1] and points beyond itself to the reality which it represents. However, as a symbol it provides insight and understanding to a developing symbolic consciousness in science. There is an element of symbolic truth which is indispensable even though this symbol must also be expanded and interpreted in non-symbolic language.

The issue of the source of this insight symbol, this creative leap of the scientific mind, still confronts us. Coulson suggests that a clue is to be found in the way in which many of the most significant discoveries come to be made. This raises the question of the logic of scientific discovery. Richard B. Braithwaite, in his *Scientific Explanation*, rejects the idea that modern physics is significantly subjective or dependent upon the human observer and stresses that the function of science "is to establish general laws" on the basis of a deductive system.[2] However, in opposition to Braithwaite there is an emphasis on the subjective, intuitive, and communal aspects of scientific discovery in Toulmin, N.R. Hanson, Michael Polanyi,[3] and even Karl Popper. Reference to Popper may seem surprising in light of his use of the "falsification principle", but he is quite open in his work, *The Logic of Scientific Discovery*, to the imaginative and even metaphysical element in scientific discovery. He states : "... my view of the matter ... is that there is no such thing as a logical reconstruction of this process. My view may be expressed by saying that every discovery contains ... 'a creative intuition' ".[4] Popper undergirds this view in practical application with references to Einstein.

Charles Coulson, quoting the physicist Helmholz and the chemist Kekule, who both stress the inspirational character of scientific discoveries, agrees that "science is a gift,—a sort of revelation which is given to that man who has prepared himself to receive it".[5] He supports this claim by the words of a fellow scientist, Sir Lawrence Bragg, who holds the Chair of Physics at the Cavendish Laboratory in Cambridge.

> When one has sought long for the clue to a secret of Nature, and is rewarded by grasping some part of the answer, it comes as a blinding flash of revelation :

[1] Urban, *Language and Reality*, p. 516.

[2] R. B. Braithwaite, *Scientific Explanation* (Cambridge : Cambridge University Press, 1968), p. 1. See also pp. 2-21.

[3] Cf. Barbour, *Issues in Science and Religion*, p. 156.

[4] Karl R. Popper, *The Logic of Scientific Explanation*, translated by the author from *Logik der Forschung*, 1935 (London : Hutchinson, 1959), p. 32.

[5] Coulson, "The Similarity of Science and Religion", *Religion and Science : New Perspectives ...*, p. 74.

it comes as something new, more simple and at the same time more aesthetically satisfying than anything one could have created in one's own mind. This conviction is of something revealed, and not something imagined.[1]

This stress on the "revelatory" and "given" nature of certain scientific insights can be simplistic if it comes without some explanation of the methodology of this revelatory experience. It is just this methodological void that my schematic proposal concerning the dimensional structure of language has attempted to fill. I have suggested and developed in previous chapters the idea that it is the insight symbol which bares this revelation, whether it is in the area of natural science, history, or theology. The claim has also been made that the symbol has this illuminating capacity due to the self-disclosure of Being in and through language. Being comes to language through thought and thus it is a particular dimension of scientific thought, having the character of inspiration, which is receptive to this revelation. Urban summarizes the idea that the source of intrinsic symbols (what I have called transformational and pointing symbols) in every discipline rests in a transcendent power beyond the human sphere.

> Modern critical science has come to recognize that its symbols, like the symbols of any region of experience, are constructions for a special purpose. ... Art and religion are equally symbolic forms, equally ways of representing the world. ... All share in a common fundamental character, namely, that there dwells in them a common spiritual power which makes of them media of genuine communication and interpretation of experience.[2]

In addition, Coulson asserts that it is this common character of "revealed-ness" at certain critical points which establishes a fundamental methodological similarity between science and religion and thus provides the basis for constructive exchange and interdisciplinary communication.

This interpretation of the task and nature of natural science has emphasized that there are methodological parallels between natural science and theology. The exposition has also made it clear, I think, that there is one dimension of the language of natural science, the symbolic, where assertions are not "logically neutral", but rather are self-involving. In this sense they depend on the scientist's presuppositions, his personal evaluation and experience in the interpretation of the data, and even a commitment to the implications of his results as an understanding of the whole of nature in terms of a coherent interpretation of all exper-

---

[1] Coulson, "The Similarity of Science and Religion", *Religion and Science : New Perspectives* ..., pp. 74-75.

[2] Urban, *Language and Reality*, p. 539.

ience. It has also been maintained that there are some assertions of natural science that are not "testable by observation", but are confirmed only indirectly in the communication of the scientific universe of discourse. The question of the means of this confirmation will be considered in more detail. Finally, I have suggested that scientific assertions are not comprehensible impersonally, but that the personal element becomes a major factor in the endeavors of natural science.

This latter point needs to be accentuated since there is a popular myth that scientific statements involve objective observational language and that they are essentially devoid of a personal factor. However, this emphasis on pure objectivity is more a product of idealized positivist interpretation of natural science than it is an accurate representation of how the scientist does his work. N.R. Hanson, in *Patterns of Discovery*,[1] corroborates a point I made earlier when he asserts that there are no uninterpreted facts, but that even the simplest data are "theory-laden". Hanson would see the theory development as being partially an act of personal creativity. Thus the personal interpretive judgment makes objectivity a relative term. Michael Polyani has probably produced the most penetrating study of the personal role in the knower in science in his work *Personal Knowledge*.[2] Polanyi rejects the idea of an absolute dichotomy between "objectivity" in science and "subjectivity" in religion. He maintains that the scientist exercises personal judgment in the evaluation of evidence. Also, other factors besides "empirical agreement" operate in the choice of a given model or theory to guide further research. Factors which could be described as inspirational, such as intellectual beauty, symmetry, and simplicity, are also involved. Similarly, to Kuhn's discussion of "paradigms", Polanyi argues that there are no definitive rules which demand the selection of one scientific model over against another. Rather, it is like a judge weighing ambiguous evidence or a doctor evaluating many factors in making a diagnosis. The choice of a particular theory or scientific symbol depends on personal involvement on the part of the natural scientist and therefore on varying forms of moral commitment not radically dissimilar to those made in theology. Knowledge, in this case scientific knowledge, is personal. The truth which is claimed for a scientific paradigm is a function of the personal

[1] N. R. Hanson, *Patterns of Discovery* (Cambridge : Cambridge University Press, 1961).

[2] Michael Polanyi, *Personal Knowledge* (Chicago : University of Chicago Press, 1958).

commitment of the scientist. When one knows something about a person, object, or idea, this involves a degree of "tacit knowledge". Polaniy understands this process as an empathetic indwelling. "By such exploratory indwelling the novice gets the feel of the master's skill. Chess players enter into a master's thought by repeating the games he played. We experience a man's mind as the joint meaning of his actions by dwelling in his actions from outside".[1] The same participatory indwelling is operative in the judgments of natural science.

Polanyi, in an account of "intuitive discoveries in science", indicates that the defining of a "good problem is a passionate intimation of a hidden truth".[2] Not only the discovery but the confirmation and holding of knowledge are anticipations of hidden truth to be revealed. "The scientist's convition of having arrived at some true knowledge is akin ... [to] an expression of the belief that true knowledge is an aspect of a hidden reality which as such can yet reveal itself ...".[3] Barbour summarizes my attempt to underline the personal and intuitive element in natural science in stating, "Personal involvement in science and in religion differ in degree, but there is no absolute dichotomy of 'objectivity' versus 'subjectivity', since the knower makes an important contribution to all knowledge".[4]

The aim of my discussion thus far has been to establish the existence of a symbolic element in natural science which functions in the form of models or theories to provide understanding of nature as a whole or of systematic unities within nature. Frederick Ferré, who recognizes the distinction in the aims of natural science between understanding and prediction or control, asserts that "the considerations that support or threaten the acceptance of theories or models do not lend themselves to the crisp, clear-cut decision techniques that for long have been supposed to be the hallmark of scientific thought".[5] Ferré thinks it is inappropriate to speak of the "verification" of models and theories. Theories and models are weighed rather than verified. Obviously, however, there is in natural

---

[1] Michael Polanyi, "The Logic of Tacit Inference", *Philosophy*, XLI (Jan. 1966), p. 14.

[2] Michael Polanyi, "Notes on Prof. Grünbaum's Observations", in *Current Issues in the Philosophy of Science*, p. 54. This article contains a brief summary by Polanyi of his position in *Personal Knowledge*.

[3] *Ibid.*

[4] Barbour, *Issues in Science and Religion*, p. 4.

[5] Ferré, "Science and the Death of 'God' " *Science and Religion : New Perspectives...*, p. 143.

science another type of assertion involving empirical generalization which is subject to verification. These two basic types of assertions in natural science are in actual practice interdependent and complementarily related. There is, then, a dimensional structure to the universe of discourse described as natural science. Urban speaks of the "double symbolism"[1] of science, but since I employ "symbolic" in a more specialized way than Urban, I prefer to speak of dimensions of scientific language. These are the symbolic and the conceptual. At this point it is necessary to consider how the symbolic dimension of natural science is interpreted in and by the conceptual dimension, how the symbolic is related to the non-symbolic.

There is a sense in which all of natural science is symbolic in the wider use of symbolic as representation. Thus the mathematical formula and even descriptions of the results of observable experiments can be called symbolic. But it becomes clear that the notion of the symbolic element in science becomes meaningless without the notion of a non-symbolic form in which the symbolic is interpreted. Thus there is a relative distinction between the symbolic and the non-symbolic; the latter is sometimes referred to as the literal. There is the same relative distinction between symbolic or received knowledge and literal or controlling knowledge. The literal or non-symbolic refers to the "ordinary factual propositions of science, the judgments of perception of quantitative and causal relations, empirical generalization ... those sentences ... which are more or less directly referable to sensuously observable entities".[2] The symbolic element, on the other hand, deals with models or theories, with unique wholes which cannot be verified in the sense of reference to sensuously observable entities. The former results in literal or controlling knowledge, the latter in symbolic or received knowledge. There is a sense in which both dimensions of natural science need interpretation. The symbolic dimension is often interpreted in terms of other symbols or models which not only clarify the original model but balance and correct it in the process of interpretation. But I am more concerned here with the process of interpretation whereby the symbols or models of science are interpreted in the conceptual dimension where certain forms of verification are applicable.

In the first instance, the symbols or models of natural science must be expanded. One begins by seeing what experimental evidence or

---

[1] Urban, *Language and Reality*, pp. 528-529.
[2] *Ibid.*, pp. 543-544.

practical procedures are entailed by the acceptance of a certain model or theory. Second, the implications of the data are often developed by stating why this particular model was selected over against a competing theory. In other words, what types of empirical generalizations lie behind the symbol and do they recommend this particular model or theory for further investigation and acceptance? What criteria tend to give this model the force of truth in the particular area under consideration? For example, in regard to the model for the structure of the atom, the nuclear physicist would be required to expand on and thus interpret the markings on the photographic plate that he had exposed to cosmic radiation and give the reasons for his advocating a theory of interacting mesons. This process of interpretive clarification, which takes place in the conceptual dimension, often assumes an analogical form. An analogy is said to exist between the model of the internal structure of the atom and the actual composition of the material world. The analogy clarifies and illustrates the way in which the model functions. The analogy relates the model to the experimental data which represents the empirical reality. The analogy has, however, positive and negative aspects.[1] There are points at which the analogy holds and provides clarification and substantiation for the model by reference to the data of sense experience. There are also negative aspects to the analogy so that it does not adequately represent and relate what occurs in the natural world : here the analogy breaks in our hands. The analogy is merely clarifying; it depends on the content supplied by the scientific symbol or model.

It should be stated that a conceptual interpretation of the model is not sufficient to verify the model itself, since the model or theory is a symbol and as such is not subject to verification. Rather, what is provided by this process is evidence for the reasonableness of a particular model providing illumination and insight. The interpretive process provides part of the material for weighing and evaluating the model. But the acceptance of the symbol as illuminating, the authentication or confirmation of the symbol itself, can come only to a certain type of consciousness which is conditioned by a community of subjective form, by a universe of discourse. Many other things enter into the acceptance of the model than simply the verification of certain assertions upon which the model is formed. Yet this interpretive process both in terms of expansion and

---

[1] Hesse, "The Role of Models in Scientific Theory", *Philosophical Problems of Natural Science*, p. 105. Hesse indicates the role of analogical clarification in relation to scientific models, noting specifically the negative analogy and the positive analogy.

the development of the implications of the data are crucial to the operation of the symbol itself in communication and in providing insight for
certain conclusions about nature as a whole. The symbolic and conceptual are interdependent, but they must be distinguished in order to
give an adequate view of how the scientific universe of discourse functions.

Hans Margenau, a physicist and a philosopher of science, suggests
an illustration in "Methodology of Modern Physics"[1] which supports
my thesis concerning the dimensional structure of scientific language.
Margenau discusses three constructs in physics : (a) the "sensible", of
which physical forms are examples; (b) the "pseudo-sensible", which
include atoms, electrons, and many similar entities; and (c) the "abstract",
which is "wholly insensible", and of which quantum mechanics is an
example. One might draw a line of distinction between the assertions
concerning the sensible construct, which involves the conceptual dimension, and the assertions concerning the pseudo-sensible and abstract
constructs, which are in the symbolic dimension. The principal distinction
here would be the way in which assertions concerning these constructs
are verified or confirmed. The statements about the sensible construct are
subject to the empirical criterion of verifiability; the pseudo-sensible and
abstract constructs clearly are not. Yet, unless statements about the latter
two are to be excluded from science as illegitimate, a response few scientists are willing to accept today, or they are to be translated or reduced
to assertions that refer to sense data, an option also rejected by Maregnau
and other scientists, then some other means of verification or confirmation must be recognized. This would be a form of confirmation which
would allow statements about the construct to provide insight apart
from the verification of the mode of the construct's existence.[2]

Wilbur Urban also reduces the assertions of science to two basic
types which are similar to my symbolic and conceptual dimensions.
They are : (1) assertions of the nature of empirical generalizations and
(2) assertions about unique wholes and ultimately the cosmos as the
whole of reality.[3] The distinction for Urban between empirical generalizations (the non-symbolic or literal) and assertions about unique wholes
(the symbolic) is connected with the directness or indirectness of the
confirmation of these assertions.[4] Here a more serious consideration of

---

[1] Hans Margenau, "Methodology of Modern Physics", *Philosophy of Science*,
Vol. II, Nos. 1 and 2 (January and April 1935). Quoted from Urban, *Language and
Reality*, pp. 547-548.
[2] Urban, *Language and Reality*, p. 548.
[3] *Ibid.*, p. 555.
[4] *Ibid.*, p. 545.

the means of confirmation applicable to the two dimensions of the language of natural science is called for.

The classification suggested by reference to Urban and Margenau is helpful in making the distinction between the symbolic and conceptual dimensions and relating these to the means of confirmation. However, I think this classification draws the line of demarcation between the symbolic and conceptual dimensions in the wrong place. The result is a distinction of "spheres" rather than a distinction of "dimensions"; a distinction between the language about the sensate sphere and the non-sensate sphere. I would maintain that the proper distinction is between (1) the conceptual dimension : the assertions that have a logical or propositional syntax and can be confirmed by verification (using this as a limiting term) in relation to logical structure or reference to empirical data; and (2) the symbolic dimension : the assertions that have a "modular" syntax which can be confirmed only by authentication in the scientific universe of discourse. I assert this second approach to be dimensional because the symbolic dimension is present in every instance of scientific language in a dominant or recessive form. In reference to Margenau's illustration, my approach implies that there is a symbolic dimension to assertions about physical constructs as well, and they cannot be consigned solely to the conceptual dimension. The symbolic dimension may be a recessive element here and appears only if one asks, for example, why the logical structure of the proposition is self-evident or what theoretical explanation undergirds the observable scientific experiment. For example, take a basic scientific experiment such as that involving solubility.[1] One says that "sugar is soluble in water", and he can observe the results of the experiment. Yet, to understand what there is about the submicroscopic form and composition of a solid that allows water to dissolve it, he must enter the symbolic dimension of the language of natural science. The assertions which provide their explanation will not be confirmed on the basis of their observational verifiability or their logical correctness. Rather, they will be confirmed by their acceptance within the standards of intelligibility and rationality of the scientific community of that historic period; namely, by their authentication. Likewise, the assertions concerning electrons, mesons, or an interpretation of the quantum theory (described above as pseudo-sensible and abstract constructs) will find the symbolic dimension of language dominant and the conceptual dimen-

---

[1] This example was suggested by Willard V. Quine, "Necessary Truth", *Philosophy of Science Today*, pp. 49f.

sion recessive. The language concerning the theoretical model must not be separable from the language of the experimental data and logical analysis. There are a symbolic and a conceptual element in the language of natural science, but they are dimensions characterized by universality of application and inseparability.

It was noted previously that verification should be taken as a limiting term. All verification is ultimately indirect since no sentence or proposition, even an empirical generalization, which enters into the discourse of the natural sciences describes or refers directly to an immediate datum of sense experience. There is always the process of interpretation and linguistic formulation. The simplest sentence in such discourse refers to other sentences and it is ultimately these, not the sense data, that do the actual verifying. It is linguistic formulations that verify things, and truth is adequacy of expression.But it is possible and important to make a relative distinction between direct and indirect verification, or confirmation, as I have preferred to refer to it here. For the empirical generalizations of science, the conceptual dimension, the criterion of empirical verifiability accompanied by logical correctness works reasonably well. The reference to sensuously observable entities is the key factor in what one can describe in my terminology as "verification". But as I have already indicated, the empirical criterion is not applicable to the symbolic dimension and specifically not to many of the central models of modern theoretical physics. What then is the means of confirmation of the scientific symbol? How does it avoid being rejected as subjectivistic and finally meaningless since it has no means of empirical verification? How does it come to have the force of truth which allows for the recognition of its cognitive value? I will maintain that the scientific symbol, like the theological or any other insight symbol, is confirmed by authentication in the process of communication within the scientific universe of discourse.

Verification of scientific symbols, for instance what Margenau has called the pseudo-sensible symbols (atoms and electrons) and abstract symbols (quantum mechanics), is certainly more indirect than in the case of the conceptual dimension. As Urban notes, between the "facts" and the symbol lie the most complicated theoretical arguments.[1] It seems clear that in regard to scientific symbols the locus of verification is shifted more and more to the sphere of intelligibility. This is sometimes a matter or mathematical intelligibility. Therefore, verification tends to become "authentication" within a symbolic system. This "authenti-

---

[1] Urban, *Language and Reality*, p. 549.

cation" becomes a question of the degree to which this symbol or model fits into the scientific community's accepted notions of rationality and intelligibility. The communal nature of the scientific inquiry and confirmation is being increasingly recognized. Nagel remarks in his discussion of the nature of science that "scientists are members of a self-governing intellectual community, dedicated to the pursuit of truth in a manner conforming to standards that have evolved and have proved to be sound in a continuing process of mutual criticism".[1] These communal criteria, Barbour notes, allow scientists in a given field to share "patterns of expectation and conceptions of regularity and intelligibility".[2] The introduction of a new paradigm may cause a scientific revolution, as Thomas Kuhn has attempted to demonstrate in *The Structure of Scientific Revolutions*. Yet the success of the revolution depends on the acceptance of the new paradigm by the scientific community.

I think it is clearer not to speak of verification here but rather to speak of confirmation in terms of authentication. Scientific symbols are authenticated. Where does this confirmation of the symbol take place? Urban maintains that this confirmation "takes place within a universe of discourse conditioned in its very character and constitution by mutually acknowledged assumptions as to rationality and intelligibility".[3] Truth and intelligibility tend ultimately to coincide even in natural science. Confirmation of the symbol occurs in the process of communication, in language. Truth for natural science too becomes ultimately adequacy of expression. Urban provides a summary of this confirmation within communication as it relates to the nature of the scientific symbol.

> These symbols or constructs are necessary for comprehensibility and intelligibility. As constructs, they share in the character of all symbols, namely, that they are conditioned by a community of subjective form and are "true" for our type of consciousness. The pseudo-sensible symbols—the atoms and electrons ... do not belong to nature but to the "parables with which we seek to make nature comprehensible". This comprehensibility or intelligibility is in principle as much determined by a community of subjective form as is the intelligibility of any other type of symbol.[4]

Scientific symbols are confirmed, if at all, only within the scientific universe of discourse. It is the nature of language itself and its essential relationship to reality which is the basis for this confirmation, for this

---

[1] Nagel, "The Nature and Aim of Science, *Philosophy of Science Today*, p. 9.
[2] Barbour, *Issues in Science and Religion*, p. 153.
[3] Urban, *Language and Reality*, p. 551.
[4] *Ibid.*

authentication which allows us to ascribe the force of truth to an assertion of natural science.

The problem of the grounds for knowing, i.e. the basis of confirmation, is a concern of Langdon Gilkey in *Religion and the Scientific Future*. He argues that there are religions dimensions in science and that, "Religious language and its symbols have one of their secular foundations in the tacit experience of ultimacy revealed in the passions, the theoretical structures, and the rational judgments of science itself".[1] Gilkey also understands that the grounds of knowing transcend knowing itself. "One may couch this aspect of transcendence in the idealistic language of a principle of identity between thought and being, a principle which itself cannot be explicated rationally; ... [one may explicate it] in Heidegger's heavier mythology, that Being speaks to and in us when we know..."[2] Gilkey sees this terminology of Heidegger as one phrase or option to explain that, "our language transcends even the philosophic discourse ... and our language penetrates into a deeper region of mystery, where affirmation and assertions are based more on deep intuitions and on faith than on argument ...".[3]

The method of confirmation by means of authentication in a particular universe of discourse can be even more clearly illustrated if one considers the abstract constructs of natural science. These symbols embody what science says about unique wholes and particularly about the cosmos as a whole. These abstract symbols include the theory of the universe as "running down" based on the second law or thermodynamics, and Heisenberg's principle of indeterminancy which implies that "nature is simply not completely determined". I think it can be properly argued that the cosmological propositions of scientific symbols about the whole are what science says "implicitly" and not "explicitly". The second law of thermodymanics holds for finite conservative systems with which we may experiment and is applied to the whole of the physical universe by extrapolation. It says something about the "whole" only impliclity. The principle of indeterminancy says something explicitly about the inaccuracy of determining both the location and velocity of an electron and only implicitly about the indeterminate structure of nature as a whole. Yet it seems to me that it is precisely what these generalizations and cosmo-

---

[1] Langdon Gilkey, *Religion and the Scientific Future* (New York; Harper & Row, 1970), p. 62.

[2] *Ibid.*, p. 63.

[3] *Ibid.*

logical principles of science say implicitly about the world that interests us most. This includes what natural science says even implicitly about the world's nature, ultimate origin, and possible destiny.[1] It could be maintained that these assertions in the form of models or theories about unique wholes and particularly about the cosmos as a whole are not a legitimate part of natural science. However, this reduces natural science to an operational level about what science says explicitly; namely, to empirical generalizations which are empirically verifiable. If this is the case, then science is considerably less significant than is usually assumed. It is limited primarily to matters of prediction and control and must repudiate its task to provide understanding and intelligibility. How far is one willing to take this delimitation of natural science? Must scientific models or symbols, such as atoms and electrons, also be denied as inappropriate speculation? I have argued that many scientists refuse to accept the operational limitation and insist that one of the tasks of natural science is to provide symbols or models for understanding about unique wholes. In doing so, they must deal with the symbolic dimension of natural science, with a metempirical sphere that defies verification and depends instead on authentication within the scientific universe of discourse.

I have already attempted to illustrate this in regard to what Margenau describes as pseudo-sensible symbols. With the atom and electron, the tie with the sensible is indirect and "verification", as it has been defined here, does not occur. However, it is conceivable that at some future time atoms and electrons might be so verified. However, in regard to the abstract symbols, there is no possible way, by any stretch of the epistemological imagination, that cosmological propositions about the universe as a whole might be verified, since they are metempirical in nature. They can be and are confirmed by the process of "authentication" within the process of scientific communication.

Two illustrations of this are supplied by modern physics. The second law of thermodynamics is sometimes described as the most metaphysical of all scientific laws because it leads to statements about a metempirical whole. The law can be summarized from the observations on heat by stating that "in every energy transformation, some of the original energy is always changed into heat energy not available for further transformations".[2] It is claimed that this law of the wastage of energy applies quite

---

[1] Urban, *Language and Reality*, p. 561.

[2] Arthur Beiser and Konrad Krauskoph, *Introduction to Physics and Chemistry* (New York : McGraw-Hill, 1964), p. 139.

universally. "The radiant energy of stars, the mechanical energy of planetary motions, the chemical energy of food, all are being steadily changed into the energy of disordered molecular motion'".[1] This means the universe in the past had more energy available for constructive work than it will in the future, so this leads to the theory of the universe "running down" or the "heat death" of the universe. This theory or scientific model which is accepted by many physicists does say something at least implicitly about the nature and possible destiny of the physical world. It is a scientific symbol and can be confirmed by the degree to which it fits into the assumptions of the scientific community about intelligibility. It is accepted to have the force of truth because it is authenticated within a given universe of discourse. This scientific symbol is confirmed in an essentially parallel way to the means by which confirmation occurs in other disciplines and universes of discourse including the theological. We should note that a dimensional distinction can be made between the scientific symbol, e.g., the theory of the "heat death" of the universe based on the second law of thermodynamics, and the conceptual interpretation and clarification of that symbol, which involves the empirical observations and experiments in regard to heat energy. The conceptual dimension employs an analogical interpretation of the way in which energy is wasted in heat experiments and how energy is wasted in the physical universe as a whole, but the positive and negative aspects of the analogy are specified in the process of experimental interpretation and clarification. The scientific symbol is evaluated by the degree to which it fits future empirical observations and conforms to criteria of coherence and consistency. The two dimensions, the symbolic and conceptual, are interdependent. However, the assertions in the conceptual dimension are verified and those assertions in the symbolic dimension are authenticated.

Another example involves the Heisenberg principle of indeterminancy. Prior to this development in physics the principle of determinancy was assumed in naturel science, as the underlying assumption of all verification. However, this was more of a tacit assumption than a formal principle. As a result of the Heisenberg "principle of indeterminancy", it is now asserted by many scientists that the whole of nature as conceived by the physicist, and particularly in regard to its microscopic character, cannot be understood as completely determined. This is an assertion with metempirical significance involving a scientific symbol which is certainly not capable of verification. When one looks at the principle in

---

[1] Beiser and Krauskoph, *Introduction to Physics and Chemistry*, p. 139.

more detail the dimensional structure emerges. Heisenberg shows that one must make a choice either to determine the place of a flying electron or to ascertain its speed with precision, but there can be no experiment that will fix location and velocity at once with maximum accuracy. The conceptual interpretation and clarification of this theory indicates that what natural science says explicitly here results in a principle of inaccuracy. This principle of inaccuracy becomes one of the factors which leads to the metempirical principle of indeterminancy in reference to the natural world. The conceptual dimension employs a clarifying analogy between the inability to predict accurately the changes in an electron and the indeterminant element in nature. There are clearly positive aspects where this analogy holds and negative aspects where the analogy is misleading : both of these become factors in weighing the reasonableness of this scientific model. The conceptual dimension which results in an assertion about inaccuracy cannot be said to verify the principle of indeterminancy except by an epistemological misunderstanding. Rather, the principle of indeterminancy as a scientific symbol or model is confirmed and authenticated by acceptance within a universe of discourse with mutually acknowledged assumptions as to rationality and intelligibility. Confirmation takes place in language by means of adequate expression. Once again the symbolic and conceptual dimensions of language are seen as interdependent when their distinctive functions and means of confirmation are recognized.

SUMMARY

The task of this chapter has been to make a case for the general applicability of the dimensional structure of language. Natural science was taken as a paradigm case and it was shown that even in this most unlikely universe of discourse the dimensional structure of language was relevant. Special attention was given to the fact that not only is there a distinctive symbolic and conceptual dimension in natural science, but that each one has its respective means of confirmation. I would suggest that this common dimensional structure of language might provide the basis for interdisciplinary dialogue and communication as illustrated in the methodological similarities between science and theology when these dimensional distinctions are recognized. I maintain that this dimensional understanding of language forms the basis of a more adequate understanding of theological language, specifically in reference to theological symbolism. This investigation into the nature of language should help us understand the source and nature of theological symbols, what form of reason engenders them, what type of knowledge they produce, by what means they are confirmed, and, finally, how they are interpreted in the conceptual dimension of language.

CHAPTER NINE

THEOLOGICAL LANGUAGE
AND THE SYMBOLIC DIMENSION

This study has maintained that the dimensional understanding of language is applicable to the major universes of discourse and makes a case for its being a comprehensive understanding of the nature of language. Therefore, the applicability of this theory to theological language should provide another avenue for understanding the claim of theological language to be meaningful and significant. It is precisely this applicability to theological language which must now be examined, giving special attention to the role of theological symbolism.

The symbolic dimension of theological language can be distinguished from the conceptual dimension. In fact, it is the failure to make this distinction and to recognize the crucial function of the symbol in theological language which leads to a kind of credibility gap between the theologian and his academic colleagues. As Tillich says, "if we are not able to make understandable to our contemporaries that we speak symbolically when we use such [theological] language, they will rightly turn away from us, as from people who still live in absurdities and superstitions".[1] However, our contemporaries may turn from us anyway unless we can not only indicate that we are speaking symbolically but also give a viable account of the nature and function of the theological symbol. In order to demonstrate the applicability of this dimensional understanding to theological language, I want to explicate what is probably the most influential theory of the religious symbol developed in this century, that of Paul Tillich. It is my contention that there is a parallel between Tillich's notion of symbol, particularly the religious symbol, and my own development of the symbolic dimension of language so that the latter can be seen as applicable to the former. Beyond this I wish to maintain that the dimensional understanding of language as developed here provides a foundation in the nature of language itself for Tillich's doctrine of symbol. This dimensional understanding of language may also supply a means of supplementing and reinforcing Tillich's original insight about

[1] Tillich, "The Nature of Religious Language", *Theology of Culture*, p. 63.

the unique function of the symbol and thus provide a means of defending his position against certain charges of subjectivism and unintelligibility. The initial contribution of the dimensional understanding of language is indicated in just this type of grounding and support for specific theories of theological language.

I am in basic agreement with Tillich's understanding of symbolism and his adaptation of this to theological language. However, the difference between Tillich's position and the one developed in this study is that Tillich has a "theory of symbol" and I have a theory of language with a "symbolic dimension". Tillich, as a result of his lack or concern for the nature of language, allows his theory of symbol to degenerate into a "sphere" approach to language which endangers the claims he makes for the power and significance of symbols. For Tillich, symbols in relation to language are confined to specific linguistic forms that occur only in certain realms. Gill, who also shares a concern for the dimensional understanding of experience and language, agrees that Tillich's employment of dimensions "almost invariably reveals that the term is being used merely as a synonym for 'realm' or 'world' ".[1]

Tillich's use of symbol refers to a sphere of language within specific forms of discourse. The symbolic for Tillich is not only separable but also independent. The present study of the symbolic dimension of language, on the other hand, maintains that the illuminating and transforming power of symbols can be dicsovered in all universes of discourse and is an element, even if latent, in virtually every instance of speaking. This "dimension" is characterized by universality of application and inseparability from the other basic dimension of language. The symbolic form by virtue of being a dimension is interdependent with the conceptual dimension of language. If the illuminating and transforming power manifested by the symbol is not a specialized and isolated sphere but a constantly accessible dimension, then it should be readily discoverable and therefore more intelligible. This is so if the nature of language is understood as having this dimensional structure. The dimensional understanding of language presented in this schematic proposal not only supports

---

[1] Gill, *The Possibility of Religious Knowledge*, p. 119. Gill advocates a "two-dimensional" structure of theological language (Chapter VIII). However, it is clearly different from the theory presented in this study despite similar terminology, since it employs Ian Ramsey's "model" and "qualifier" distinctions as the basis of dimensions. Gill's position is more a technique for understanding theological language as "odd-talk" about God than an attempt to explicate the dimensional structure of language itself as exemplified in theological discourse.

and defends Tillich's insight about symbolism, but also suggests the need for a revision in his position as a consequence of an analysis of the nature of language. This revision involves a move from a "sphere'" approach to a "dimensional" understanding of all language, especially theological language. This move would make the symbolic language of theology more viable and thus responsible. In the following explication of Tillich's "theory of symbols" the points at which I think Tillich's view is inadequate and requires revision will be scrutinized.

Tillich developed his understanding of symbolism in a series of articles spanning a period of some thirty-three years beginning in 1928.[1] Over

---

[1] The study of Tillich's theory of symbolism is rendered more difficult by the fact that not only does each major essay show some slight modification of the previous one, but the articles were republished from time to time without always specifying the original dates and places of publication so that the sequence of the material sometimes gets confused. It is not always clear in this series of essays whether Tillich wished to stress the shift in emphasis or the continuity of his position with only points of clarification. I think both a comparison of the 1928 and the 1961 articles plus this practice of republication argues for the latter view, but this is open to debate.

There appear to me to be seven major essays where Tillich's understanding of symbolism is developed. These are :

(1) Paul Tillich, "The Religious Symbol", James Luther Adams (trans.), *Journal of Liberal Religion*, 2 (1940), pp. 13-33, from the original German article "Das religiöse Symbol", *Blätter für deutsche Philosophie* (Ed. 1, H. 4, 1928). This article was first reprinted in *Religiöse Verwicklung*, Berlin, 1930. The English translation has appeared also in *Daedalus*, Proceedings of the American Academy of Arts and Sciences, 87, Summer, 1958, pp. 3-21; in *Religious Experience and Truth*, Sidney Hook (ed.) (New York : New York University Press, 1961), as an "appendix", pp. 301-321; in *Symbolism in Religion and Literature*, Rollo May (ed.) (New York : George Braziller, 1960), pp. 75-98; and in *Myth and Symbol*, F.W. Dillistone (ed.) (London, S.P.C.K., 1966), pp. 15-34.

(2) "God as Being and the Knowledge of God", *Systematic Theology*, Vol. I (Chicago : The University of Chicago Press, 1951), pp. 238ff. Another important reference to symbol, because it notes this shift in the range of symbolic reference to God, occurs in *Systematic Theology*, Vol. II (Chicago : The University of Chicago Press, 1957), in the Introduction, pp. 9-10.

(3) "Theology and Symbolism", in *Religious Symbolism*, F.E. Johnson (ed.), The Institute for Religious and Social Studies (New York : Harper & Brothers, 1955), pp. 107-116.

(4) "Religious Symbols and Our Knowledge of God", *Christian Scholar* XXXVIII, 3 (September 1955), pp. 189-197. This was reprinted in Paul Tillich, "The Nature of Religious Language", *Theology of Culture*, R.C. Kimball (ed.) (New York : Oxford University Press, 1964), pp. 53-68.

(5) "Existential Analysis and Religious Symbols", in *Contemporary Problems in Religion*, H. A. Basilius (ed.) (Detroit : Wayne University Press, 1956), pp. 35-57.

the years there have been certain modifications in terminology, typology, and even the range of reference of symbolic language in relation to God. However, I believe Tillich's theory of symbolism has remained substantially the same and the modifications have constituted attempts at clarification rather than a major shift in his position. This view is supported by Tillich's last major lecture on symbolism given to a conference of philosophers and theologians in 1960.[1] Tillich had the 1928 article, "The Religious Symbol", distributed to all participants prior to the conference, and his address, "The Meaning and Justification of Religious Symbols", was a restatement of his position in light of the criticism raised about his notion of symbolism.[2] Thus, in explicating Tillich's theory of symbolism we have a relatively well developed and consistent body of material from which to draw. I will rely on the final article as my principal guide on the assumption that this response to his critics represents the most adequate restatement and clarification of his position. This certainly does not deny, however, that some problems about the theory remain and even that there is, as critics have maintained, a certain vagueness connected with Tillich's notion of the "participation" of the symbol in that which it symbolizes, despite his attempts at clarification.

It is clear that, for Tillich, symbolism is not just one aspect of his discussion of theological language but rather is the very core of his theological system. Theology is constituted as a discipline by the religious symbol. When one asks what the material of theological thought is, Tillich responds by stating :

> The answer is that the direct object of theology is not God : the direct object of theology is His manifestation to us, and the expression of that manifestation is the religious symbol. This is the basic relation between theology and symbolism. The object of theology is found in the symbols of religious experience. They are not God but they point to God. God may be said to be the object of theology but only indirectly. The direct object of theology is found only in religious symbols.[3]

This was reprinted in *Four Existentialist Theologians*, Will Herberg (ed.) (Garden City, New York : Doubleday Anchor Books, 1958), pp. 41-55.

(6) "Symbols of Faith", Chapter 3 in Paul Tillich, *Dynamics of Faith* (New York : Harper & Row, 1957), pp. 41-54.

(7) "The Meaning and Justification of Religious Symbols", *Religious Experience and Truth*, Sidney Hook (ed.) (New York : Harper, 1955), pp. 3-11.

[1] The fourth annual New York University Institute of Philosophy, October 21-22 1960. The major contributions to this conference were published in *Religious Experience and Truth*, Sidney Hook (ed.).

[2] See *Religious Experience and Truth*, preface xiii.

[3] Tillich, "Theology and Symbolism", *Religious Symbolism*, p. 108.

It is not surprising in light of this to hear Tillich say, in his "Reply to Interpretation and Criticism" in the book edited by C. W. Kegley and R.W. Bretall entitled *The Theology of Paul Tillich*, that "the center of my theological doctrine of knowledge is the concept of symbol ...".[1] Not only are religious symbols the object of theology but, also, theological methodology is determined by the theologian's relationship to religious symbols. "Theology, then, is the conceptual interpretation, explanation, and criticism of the symbols in which a special encounter between God and man has found expression".[2] Tillich's theological system can be said to depend on an understanding of both cognition and language which attributes a significant role to the symbolic. In an understanding of of knowledge and language which denies the legitimate function of the symbol there could be no significant knowledge of the divine and no way in which one could speak about him meaningfully.

It is the contention of this study that Tillich's theological system, focused as it is on symbolism, requires a conception of language, reason, and knowledge such as that which is developed in the dimensional structure of language set forth here. Although Tillich never explicitly works out a philosophy of language in which his system could adequately be grounded, I think he was cognizant of the problem. This is indicated in his reaction to nominalism in its ancient and modern form which not only denies a significant role to symbolism but denies that language in any form can be an adequate access to reality. As Tillich maintains, "the nominalistic presupposition—that words are only conventional signs— must be rejected. Words are the results of the encounter of the human mind with reality".[3] This encounter with reality is focused on the symbol. Tillich states that all symbols "are results of a creative encounter with reality. They are born out of such an encounter".[4] Symbols cannot be invented or abolished; they are "given" in this encounter with reality. This is particularly true of religious symbols which find their source outside of themselves in this encounter. A religious symbol has "a special character in that it points to the ultimate level of being, to ultimate reality, to being itself, to meaning itself".[5] I have argued that it is in the sym-

---

[1] *The Theology of Paul Tillich*, C. W. Kegley and R. W. Bretall (eds.) (New York : The Macmillan Company, 1964), p. 333.

[2] Tillich, "Theology and Symbolism", *Religious Symbolism*, p. 108.

[3] Tillich, *Systematic Theology*, Vol. II, p. 19. All subsequent references in this chapter and the next will abbreviate *Systematic Theology* to *S.T.*

[4] Tillich, "Theology and Symbolism", p. 109.

[5] *Ibid.*, pp. 109-110.

bolic dimension of language that this encounter comes to expression. Being discloses itself in and through symbols. Although Tillich does not talk precisely in this way about the nature and function of language, it is clear that this concept of a symbolic dimension of language would add support for the intelligibility and the persuasiveness of his theory of symbolism. Tillich notes, in speaking about the need to guard against the confusion of literalism and symbolism : "That is the great problem of Protestantism. It must develop an attitude in which it is again able to accept symbols".[1] I am convinced that a fresh look at the structure of language itself will help prepare Protestantism to do just that.

In order to recover the power of the symbol, Tillich has asserted that one needs to develop a "clearing house"[2] for language. The present investigation could be conceived as being an effort in that direction. The first step in the clearing of concepts for Tillich is to distinguish between a "sign "and a "symbol". "A fundamental difference between them is that signs do not participate in any way in the reality and power of that to which they point. Symbols, although they are not the same as that which they symbolize, participate in its meaning and power."[3] The question of what this participation involves will be considered in more detail. The point at issue here is to define a special status for the authentic "symbol" to distinguish it from other forms such as those in mathematics, which are sometimes described as symbols but do not have the special quality attributed to symbols by Tillich. This is really a functional distinction. The sign-symbol contrast appeared briefly in the first article[4] and was later developed[5] in more detail until it became the standard distinction for authors discussing the nature of religious language. However, in the final article Tillich no longer stresses this sign-symbol distinction per se, perhaps as a result of the criticism from those who maintained that the line between the two was not so clear-cut and that they often overlapped. Thus, in the final article[6] Tillich, responding to a suggestion by John Randall, distinguishes between "representative symbols" as the genuine symbols and "discursive symbols", which

---

[1] Tillich, "Theology and Symbolism", *Religious Symbolism*, p. 116.

[2] See Tillich, *S.T.*, I, p. 54, and Tillich, "The Nature of Religious Language", *Theology of Culture*, p. 53.

[3] Tillich, "The Nature of Religious Language", *Theology of Culture*, p. 54.

[4] Tillich, "The Religious Symbol", *Myth and Symbol*, pp. 16, 31.

[5] Cf. Tillich, "The Nature of Religious Language, p. 54ff.

[6] Tillich, "The Meaning and Justification of Religious Symbols", *Religious Experience and Truth*, p. 3.

lack this distinctive quality. Tillich's emphasis is that the special character of the genuine symbol should be recognized by adding an adjective[1] or some means of description.[2] The principal concern is to establish a specialized and limited use of "symbol" when it is applied in the narrower sense. A dimensional understanding of language, such as I have proposed, which acknowledges that special status of the symbol in its very structure certainly supports this concern of Tillich's. This is a functional concern so one must consider the function of genuine symbols as exhibited in their common characteristics.

Tillich was certainly open in principle to the type of grounding for the notion of theological symbols that I have suggested here. This is denoted by his assertion that "in order to understand religious symbols we must first understand the nature of symbols generally".[3] The notion of the religious symbol should be rooted in an adequate understanding of symbolism that is applicable and comprehensible in other areas. I think this implies the need for an understanding of language that makes symbolism intelligible. Although Tillich does not take this second step, an analysis of the nature of language, I think he is on the methodological road that leads to that destination. The question must be raised here whether Tillich had an adequate understanding of "the nature of symbols generally" or whether the "sphere" approach mentioned previously has not limited his own interpretation. For instance, the sphere-like under-standing of symbolism is noted by Tillich in his final article when he limits the realms in which genuine symbols appear. He states, "The realms in which representative [genuine] symbols appear are language and history, the arts and religion".[4] The implication is that symbols appear only in certain realms or universes of discourse and not others. This is

---

[1] Tillich, "The Meaning and Justification of Religious Symbols", p. 3.

[2] I indicated previously (see Chapter I) that the term "sign" is probably more in-telligibly employed as a generic term to indicate linguistic meaning in general. I prefer-red the parallel distinction between "symbol" and "signal". I also suggested that rather than seeing these terms as an exhaustive division, the notion of a continuum which recognizes various linguistic forms is more helpful. This does not counter Tillich's major intent and might even provide some clarification. Also, Tillich happens to use "representative" here to refer to a genuine symbol where I have used "represen-tative" in the sense of "merely representative" and therefore not a genuine symbol. The stress must be on the special character of symbol and not the particular adjective selected.

[3] Tillich, *op. cit.*

[4] *Ibid.* There is an initial problem of interpretation in that the four classifications are not coordinate. The problem noted refers to the restriction in the operation of genuine symbols indicated by this reference.

supported by Tillich's failure to speak of genuine symbols appearing in a realm such as natural science. The symbol for Tillich appears to designate a separable sphere which appears only in certain fields and under special conditions. In opposition to this view, I would maintain that a symbol is distinguished by the nature and function of a linguistic form within the symbolic dimension. If the dimensional aspect is taken seriously, then genuine symbols should be present in every principal universe of discourse, even that of natural science, as I have attempted to demonstrate. The dimensional structure means that the power and significance of genuine symbolism is founded in the nature of language itself. This understanding of symbolism, recognizing its dimensional quality, would contribute to the intelligibility of symbolism as found in all disciplines and universes of discourse. This revision in Tillich's position, or one might even say clarification of his understanding of the notion of symbolism in relation to the dimensional understanding of language, would support Tillich's claims for the nature and function of symbols. Such an understanding of language as proposed by this revision would also tend to undergird the common characteristics Tillich attributes to all genuine symbols.[1]

Characteristics of Symbols

"First and most fundamental is the character of all symbols to point beyond themselves".[2] The symbolic material does not refer in the first instance to the ordinary meaning of the word but rather, uses a linguistic form to orient the inner attitude of a person to that which is symbolized. It points specifically to that which cannot be grasped directly but only expressed indirectly. That to which the symbol points may be a person, an aspect of reality that is not open to an ordinary encounter, or it can be ultimate reality, Being itself. The symbol is not to be identified with

---

[1] It is interesting how essentially consistent Tillich's description of the symbolic function is from the first to the last major essay. The four basic characteristics marked in the 1928 article, "The Religious Symbol", are : (1) figurative, (2) perceptibility, (3) innate power, and (4) acceptability (pp. 15-16). All four ideas are substantially included, although often with a change in terminology, in the six characteristics of the symbol noted in 1957 in "Symbols of Faith", in *Dynamics of Faith* (pp. 41-42), and the five characteristics described in 1961 in "The Meaning and Justification of Religious Symbols". In all these cases there had been some expansion of the original idea but no essential change.

[2] Tillich, "The Meaning and Justification of Religious Symbols", *Religious Experience and Truth*, p. 4.

that which it symbolizes. To make the symbol literal denies its ability to point beyond itself and thus distorts the symbol.

The symbolic dimension of language as developed in this study not only parallels this characteristic of symbol by Tillich but lends support to this interpretation. In the dicussslon of the symbolic dimension of language, I asserted that the genuine symbol must be interpreted as a "pointing symbol".[1] It points beyond itself to an experiential encounter with the thing symbolized. The symbol has an intrinsic relationship to that which it symbolizes but it is not identical with it. It is precisely in the symbolic dimension of language, via the symbol, that Being discloses itself in and to man. It is, however, this quality of pointing beyond itself which allows the symbol to protect the mystery of Being. The incomprehensible and inexpressible element of the reality that is symbolized is not abolished but rather is preserved by the very nature of the symbol. The symbol calls one to be attentive to Being. It points to foundational thinking where the subject-object split is overcome by the receptiveness to the object of thought. This understanding of the nature of language on the basis of a "high evaluation" where Being discloses itself in a dimension of language that is an adequate access to reality provides foundation for the "pointing beyond" quality of the symbol. However, this is possible only because the symbol is also an insight or illuminating symbol. That leads us to Tillich's second characteristic of the symbol.

"The second characteristic of all ... symbols is to participate in the reality of that which they represent".[2] The symbol radiates or mediates the power of being and meaning of that which is symbolized. The basis for Tillich's notion of "participation" is the idea that there is an intrinsic relationship between the symbol and that which is symbolized. It is this intrinsic relationship which allows the symbol to function in a certain way, to do something for the person who employs the symbol. The symbol's function is to significantly relate the reality pointed to in the symbol to our human existence. The clue to the meaning of "participation" in Tillich is, I think, in the first instance functional and this in turn has a linguistic foundation with ontological implications.

It is generally agreed that Tillich's notion of "participation" is one of the most perplexing elements in his theory of religious language. It has often been analyzed ontologically on the basis of Platonic or neo-platonic

---

[1] See Chapter IV.

[2] Tillich, "The Meaning and Justification of Religious Symbols", *Religious Experience and Truth*, p. 4.

overtones. However, as John Macquarrie asserts, "[Tillich's] notion of 'participation' is not made very clear, though it seems obvious that it is something much more concrete that the participation of a particular in a universal, the way in which the notion of 'participation' (methexis) has usually been understood from Plato onward".[1] Rather than examining "participation" in the first instance from an ontological perspective, it may be more helpful to interpret it from a functional position. This functional approach is suggested by David H. Kelsey when he says, "ontology does not provide independent information about the referent of religious symbols. ... Instead, when Tillich sets out to explain religious symbols, he describes the distinctive way in which they function. ...".[2] It is this distinctive way in which symbols function that makes possible this claim of participation. Macquarrie has suggested that the word "affinity" has some advantages over "participation".[3] "Affinity" stresses a point of contact that allows something to occur without suggesting either the idea of "looking alike" or that of "ontological identity". The degree of affinity may vary, but some intrinsic relationship remains. The symbol provides an illuminating insight and authentic awareness of that reality to which the symbol points. The symbol is constituted by the fact of what it does; it has the power to awaken an existential response.

Tillich then proceeds to indicate the function of the symbol in opening up levels of reality that are otherwise closed to us. However, one must ask what could account for the symbol having this function, this illuminating power. The answer may rest in the nature of language itself as determined by the nature of Being in relation to language. The symbol may possess this illuminating power because Being discloses itself in language. Language provides not the barrier or veil to reality but the mold in which reality as significant is given. It is in the symbol that this disclosure takes place. Man must open himself up in his mediative pro-

---

[1] Macquarrie, *God-Talk*, pp. 197-198.

[2] David H. Kelsey, *The Fabric of Paul Tillich's Theology* (New Haven : Yale University Press, 1967, p. 43. This functional approach is merely suggested by Kelsey, and I do not mean to imply that he would agree with my analysis or with my linguistic concern. Kelsey asserts that "religious symbol" may be another term for "miracle". He sees the dynamics of revelation as providing the warrants for theological judgments about the general theory of religious symbols. However, even if he is correct, his focus on religious symbol and revelation does not provide the broader intelligible support for symbols I am seeking in this analysis.

[3] Macquarrie, *op. cit.*, p. 220.

cesses to Being's speaking in language. It is through thought that Being comes to word. It is foundational thought that allows the person to be receptive to the object. The symbol is the way of making that which is symbolized present and manifest for the person or group that meaningfully employs the symbol. Thus this dimensional understanding of language which recognizes the illuminating functional power of the symbol supplies support for Tillich's notion of "participation" and perhaps some clarification. It is interesting to note that Tillich was most often criticized for his use of examples in relation to participation, particularly those of the "flag" or the "king". It may have helped had he stressed the verbal aspect of the symbol where this notion of functional illumination might have been clarified. It is a question whether a "flag" or a "king" is a particularly appropriate example of a symbol in our contemporary American culture. However, the "flag" might have this illuminating function insofar as it manifests insight and elicits an existential response on the part of the individual who employs the symbol as a symbol. The nation's flag could be a compact way of representing what the nation does or should stand for : freedom, equality of opportunity, etc. However, these qualities are difficult to define and the illuminating insight and the existential demand are lost in the complexity of conceptual description and the contradictions in historical experience which are present. Yet the flag as a symbol can be incorporated in the linguistic and cognitive processes so as to imaginatively represent the whole in its complexity. The flag participates in the power and meaning of what the nation stands for because it appeals to our symbolic consciousness and thus provides insight and demands an existential response. However, it was asserted that something *may* have this illuminating function; it *may* become a symbol. This depends on the symbol being accepted as a symbol by an individual or a group. The question of the source and the acceptance of the symbol is thereby raised.

"This leads to the third characteristic of the ... symbol : it cannot be created at will".[1] It is impossible to invent a symbol as one can a sign. The symbol may in fact arise from the individual creativity of the thinker, artist, or prophet, but "it is the unconscious-conscious reaction of a group through which it becomes a symbol. No representative symbol is created and maintained without acceptance by a group".[2]

[1] Tillich, "The Meaning and Justification of Religious Symbols", *Religious Experience and Truth*, p. 4.
[2] *Ibid.*

Tillich in his initial article spoke about the "acceptability"[1] of the symbol. A symbol is not invented or created by an individual or a community; rather it can be said metaphorically by Tillich that a symbol is born and it may die. It is born when a particular group or community "acknowledges, in this thing, this word, this flag, or whatever it may be, its own being".[2] It means that something is opened up or illuminated by the symbol in the sense just described. When the symbol no longer "speaks", when it fails to provide this insight and illumination which provokes an existential response, then the symbol can be said to die.

Once again the dimensional understanding of language supports this notion of the birth and death of symbols as related to their acceptability. I asserted that a symbol's birth begins when a linguistic sign (in the generic sense of sign) is developed into a genuine symbol by its encounter with Being's self-disclosure in regard to some aspect of reality. As Tillich maintains, the symbol is born out of "a creative encounter with reality".[3] However, before the symbol can function as a pointing and illuminating symbol it must be interpreted and accepted. This process of interpretation and acceptance is cultural and historical and it takes place in the context of language, in communication. The symbol requires what I have called "authentication". I asserted that authentication occurs in the recognition and acknowledgment of the insight, of the truth element, which is shown forth in the symbol. The acceptance of the symbol entails its authentication. When the symbol is no longer an authentic means of providing illumination for a community, then the symbol is said to die. Tillich does not assert that the authentication takes place in the sphere of language and communication, but there is the realization by Tillich of the way in which language operates and there is the focus on the acceptability of the symbol. My explicit concern with the nature of language, which Tillich did not share, drives me beyond Tillich to assert that the authentication of the symbol occurs within a particular universe of discourse. In the case of a religious symbol, this is a historic community of faith. This is not, however, simply a matter of group consensus. Rather, the authentication of the symbol is possible because of an ontological factor that enters into the situation of human discourse. I have maintained that the symbol comes to be accepted and thus authenticated because of the nature of language itself—because Being

[1] Tillich, "The Religious Symbol", *Myth and Symbol*, p. 16.
[2] Tillich, "The Nature of Religious Language", *Theology of Culture*, p. 58.
[3] Tillich, "Theology and Symbolism", *Religious Symbolism*, p. 109.

discloses itself in the symbolic dimension of language. It is the source of the genuine symbol, Being's relation to language via the birth of the symbol, which justifies the claim of Tillich and myself for the illuminating and transforming power of symbols. The nature of this "acceptance" of symbol in Tillich has often been misinterpreted and I think a new look at the dimensional nature of language as suggested here might avoid or limit this misunderstanding. Let us consider the major critique of Tillich's position on this matter.

Tillich has been criticized[1] for this notion of "acceptability" in his theory of symbol because this notion is thought to indicate a "subjectivistic bent" which implies that symbols are merely products of the human mind or the "collective unconscious". His recognition of the necessity of acceptance on the part of the community is thought to deny the objective character of symbols, to make them void of cognitive content, to make them "only symbols". However, in the full scope of Tillich's writing on symbolism it is clear that he intends to combine the notion of acceptance on the part of a community with the participation of the symbol in the reality of that which it symbolizes. The insight or the illumination which characterizes the symbol is the result of a "given" which is disclosed in language. The illuminating power of the symbol is not created by the individual or community; this power is transformed from a potentiality into an actuality by the acceptance of the symbol. Acceptance is merely a confirmation or an authentication of the illuminating function of the symbol for a particular community.

This raises the question of the source of the symbol. The understanding of language set forth in this study gives a basis for Tillich's dual concern. However, the interpretation presented here goes beyond Tillich and establishes a position distinct from but not contradictory to his own. It was asserted previously[2] that Being and man are mutual creators of language as the bearer of meaning. Being can be spoken of as the source of the genuine symbol, or as having primacy in the symbolic dimension of language, because meaning is "given" in the symbol. This "given" is a result of the mind's encounter with reality which illuminates the mystery surrounding some aspect of experience. It is this objective

---

[1] E.g., G. H. Tavard, *Paul Tillich and the Christian Message* (New York : Charles Scribner's Sons, 1962), pp. 57-58; and especially Battista Mondin, *The Principle of Analogy in Protestant and Catholic Thought* (The Hague : Martinus Nijhoff, 1963), pp. 125-126.

[2] See Chapter III.

"given", a result of the non-concealment of Being, which establishes the foundation of meaning. Heidegger's interpretation of language as the "house of Being" provides support for this view of the revelatory nature of language. There is a sense in which a "word" or a meaning comes from Being to man. Heidegger phrases it by saying, "Being comes to Word". It is the fact that Being does disclose itself in language which allows us to talk intelligibly about having things revealed or disclosed to us about some aspect of reality. Illuminating symbols are the result of this encounter between man and Being via language. There is a giftlike character to significant discoveries or insights in any area of experience and the assertion of this study is that their source can be understood by the nature of language itself. However, meaning cannot come to maturity apart from man's contribution of the initial verbal sign and the later acceptance and interpretation of the symbol as an illuminating and pointing symbol for some aspect of reality. Both the disclosure of Being in the symbol and man's acceptance are required to account for understanding and communication as developed here.[1] Recognizing a symbolic dimension of language makes the nature and function of the symbol, both in regard to its source and acceptance, more intelligible.

The fourth characteristic of symbols indicates what the illuminating function of symbols is and relates this to the question of meaning just raised.

> The symbol opens up a level of meaning that is otherwise closed. It opens up a stratum of reality, of meaning and being which otherwise we could not reach; and in so doing, it participates in that which it opens. And it does not only open up a stratum of reality, it also opens up the corresponding stratum of the mind. Symbols open up, so to speak, in two directions—in the direction of reality and the direction of the mind.[2]

The symbol is the instrument of access to certain dimensions of reality from which we would otherwise be cut off. It opens up, or one could say it illuminates, some aspect of experience that would otherwise elude him. It does this by opening up or illuminating some dimension of the mind, some depth of the human spirit that is not otherwise awakened. A great play may illustrate this event of duel illumination because the artistic symbols employed give us not only "a new vision of the human scene, but ... [they] also open up hidden depths of our own being".[3]

---

[1] See Chapter III.
[2] Tillich, "Theology and Symbolism", *Religious Symbolism*, p. 109.
[3] Tillich, *Dynamics of Faith*, pp. 42-43.

Only symbols have this power of illumination and as a result have the power to transform one's life by the existential response the symbol evokes. Tillich's conception of opening up levels of reality and of the self is undergirded by the dimensional understanding of language where the symbol is seen as a "transformational symbol" because it has the power to make the reality symbolized present and manifest for the person or group that meaningfully employs this symbol. The philosophy of language affirmed here asserts that by the act of Being's self-disclosure in language and the structure thus constituted, the symbol is capable of providing an authentic awareness and cognitive insight concerning that which it symbolizes. This cognitive insight occurs via the attentiveness of foundational thinking and results in a receiving type of knowledge. That this *does* happen is witnessed by the experience of those who claim to be moved, awakened, and transformed by the hearing and accepting of certain transformational symbols. These symbols become the means of orienting and guiding one's human existence. However, the symbols can also be a source of anxiety and disorientation. This depends on what the symbol points to and the reaction of those who accept or are grasped by the symbol.

The fifth and final characteristic of the symbol identified by Tillich also concerns the function of the symbol in relationship to individuals and groups. Genuine symbols have "integrating and disintegrating power"[1] for those who employ the symbol. The integrating power of symbols has been emphasized continually by Tillich and he has lamented the loss of the power of symbols as reflected in the phrase "only a symbol".[2] The integrating power of symbols is seen in the fact that they provide a structure of understanding in very complex and ambiguous areas of life and thought. The integrating function of symbols is particularly evident in the history of religion where certain symbolsh ave the power of "elevating, quieting and stabilizing".[3] In the sphere of religious symbolism one can speak of the "healing" power of symbols since they supply meaning to our experience which allows one to reach a kind of "wholeness" of self-understanding. However, this integrating function can be illustrated as an event in history, a document in politics, a theory in natural science, an epic work in literature, etc. Rollo May insists that

---

[1] Tillich, "The Meaning and Justification of Religious Symbols", *Religious Experience and Truth*, p. 5.

[2] Tillich, S.T., II, p. 9, and *Dynamics of Faith*, p. 45.

[3] Tillich, "The Meaning and Justification of Religious Symbols", p. 5.

this integrating function of symbols is particularly prominent in psychollogy and psychiatry where symbols are used to build up the individual's self-image.[1] In fact, the breakdown of cultural symbols and myths is tragic because these symbols are the means by which members of a society can deal with problems of guilt, anxiety, and despair.[2]

Symbols may also have a disintegrating power, causing restlessness, depression, anxiety, or fanaticism.[3] However, it seems to me that the key to this disintegrating power appears to lie with the reaction of an individual or group to the symbol. If the symbol provides insight about or awareness of a reality with which the individual or group is unable or unwilling to come to terms (i.e. free man, compassionate father, or suffering servant) it may have this disintegrating power. To avoid this disintegrating power one must either transform or adjust himself to the implications of the symbol, challenge the acceptance of the symbol by the community, or help reinterpret the original insight embodied in the symbol.

How are we to account for the integrating and disintegrating power of the symbol? This is possible only if we have a theory of language that gives a significant role to the symbolic dimension of language; only if the symbol is seen as providing an adequate access to reality that would entail the kind of power that could result in the integration or disintegration of an individual or a group. The nominalistic or "low evaluation" of language makes unintelligible this claim for the power of symbols. However, a "high evaluation" of language, such as that proposed here, provides an intelligible basis for this integrating and disintegrating power of symbols that I think is manifested in every major universe of discourse and therefore in significant aspects of human experience.

If Being does disclose itself in language, as Heidegger claims, and if this disclosure occurs in the symbolic dimension of language, as I have maintained, then this power of symbols to point beyond themselves, to be illuminating, to be transforming, and finally, to be integrating or disintegrating (depending on one's response) would have its foundation in the nature of language and in its relationship to reality. Specifically, this foundation is provided in a dimensional understanding of language such as that presented in the schematic proposal of this study.

---

[1] Rollo May, "The Significance of Symbols", *Symbolism in Religion and Literaturə*, Rollo May (ed.) (New York : George Brasiller, 1960), p. 22.

[2] *Ibid.*, p. 33.

[3] Tillich, "The Meaning and Justification of Religious Symbols", *Religious Experience and Truth*, p. 5.

Symbols of Theology

What can be said now about those symbols which are the direct objects of theology, those symbols in which a special encounter between God and man has been expressed? Tillich refers to these as "religious symbols" and since they are the objects of the theological universe of discourse, I have referred to them as the symbols of theology. The first thing to be asserted is that "the general characteristics of the symbol hold for the religious symbol also ...".[1] Tillich recognized the necessity of a coherent general theory of symbolism. "Religious symbols do exactly the same thing as all symbols do—namely, they open up a level of reality, which otherwise is not opened at all, which is hidden".[2] The distinctive feature of the religious symbol is determined by the nature of the reality which is opened and by what happens to the individual or group as a consequence of this illumination. The religious symbol opens up the "depth dimension of reality itself ... the level of being itself, or the ultimate power of being".[3] At the same time, the symbol opens up the depth dimension of the human soul[4] so that man can respond to that which is illuminated. The symbol results for the individual in illumination, transformation, and commitment.

What distinguishes the religious symbol from other symbols is that it represents that which is "unconditionally beyond the conceptual sphere".[5] It points to that which concerns us ultimately, to that which can never be made an object and to that which is the ground of all other forms of being and meaning. The aim of the religious symbol is the intuition of that which is "unconditionally transcendent".[6] Tillich continually describes that to which the symbol points and that which it illuminates as the "holy"; "religious symbols are symbols of the Holy".[7] The "holy" or the "sacred" are terms used to indicate "the presence of the ultimate power of being or meaning in an individual thing or situation".[8] However, as Tillich clearly indicates, "the holy is a 'quality in encounter', not an object among objects, and not an emotional re-

---

[1] Tillich, "The Religious Symbol", *Myth and Symbol*, p. 17.
[2] Tillich, "The Nature of Religious Language", *Theology of Culture*, pp. 58-59.
[3] *Ibid.*, p. 59.
[4] *Ibid.*
[5] Tillich, "The Religious Symbol", p. 17.
[6] *Ibid.*, p. 30.
[7] Tillich, "The Nature of Religious Language", p. 59.
[8] Tillich, "Theology and Symbolism", *Religious Symbolism*, p. 110.

sponse without a basis in the whole of objects".[1] The symbol is not to be identified with the holy. Rather, what the symbol has the power to do is draw the subject into the holy and have him experience the power and meaning of his own ground of being. The crucial factor is what the symbol does in opening up or illuminating this new level of reality and of the self. The functional power of the theological symbol is described by Tillich as producing the experience of holiness, or elevating, quieting, stabilizing, integrating, and even of "healing".[2]

The dimensional understanding of language helps account in an intelligible way for this power of the religious symbol. First, it recognizes a symbolic dimension of language and attributes to it this illuminating and transforming capacity. It is a means of representing, as Tillich says, that which is "unconditionally beyond the conceptual sphere". In addition, there is a means of acknowledging the special function of the religious or theological symbols in this conception of the nature of language. Heidegger maintains that Being discloses itself in language. I have asserted that this occurs specifically in the symbolic dimension of language. Yet Being discloses itself in the symbolic dimension of each principal universe of discourse. The dimensional understanding of language involves more than just a "theory of symbols" as presented by Tillich. The dimensional understanding claims to be a comprehensive view of language which can account via the symbolic dimension for the illuminating and transforming capacity of all genuine symbols and by this procedure render more intelligible the power claimed for religious or theological symbols.

In light of the position developed in this study and moving beyond Tillich, what can be described as distinctive about theological symbols? The symbols of other universes of discourse point to and illuminate a mystery about some aspect of experience as revealed by Being. These symbols do point to Being and they do reflect an encounter of the mind with ultimate reality. However, this is done indirectly since these symbols are concerned primarily with the insight provided about some specific aspect of experience. The theological symbol points directly to and provides an awareness of Being, of ultimate reality, of the ground of being. It does this because there is a special "quality in encounter" with Being.

---

[1] Tillich, "The Meaning and Justification of Religious Symbols", *Religious Experience and Truth*, p. 6.

[2] *Ibid.*, p. 5.

The theological symbol represents Being as holy. This means that Being is understood as that power which lets-be or provides the ground for our being and existence. It is in symbols that Being becomes present and manifest to us. It is this apprehending of Being as holy that results in an existential response of acceptance and commitment on our part. This response to Being as holy is what could be called an attitude of faith, a response to that with which we are ultimately concerned. Therefore, "God" is not to be identified with Being but rather, "God" is a symbol which we use to refer to holy Being. God is a term that expresses a certain kind of encounter with the power of Being. It expresses an encounter which evokes our acceptance of Being's power as gracious and elicits commitment toward and trust in Being.[1] One can say with John Macquarrie that " 'God' is synonymous with 'holy being' ".[2]

It is clear that for Tillich the symbolic dimension is the key to responsible and intelligible talk about God. He declares, "Thus it follows that everything religion has to say about God, including his qualities, actions, and manifestations, has a symbolic character and that the meaning of 'God' is completely missed if one takes the symbolic language literally".[3] However, Tillich was challenged by critics about his use of symbolism. As he notes, "An early criticism by Professor Urban of Yale forced me to acknowledge that in order to speak of symbolic knowledge one must delimit the symbolic realm by an unsymbolic statement".[4] Tillich's first response to this critique was to assert that the one unsymbolic statement was that God is being itself.[5] However, Tillich later came to realize that being itself was also a symbolic term and his recognition of this in a rather ambiguous passage in the Introduction to Volume II of his *Systematic Theology*[6] is sometimes overlooked by critics. It seems to me that Tillich gives a more appropriate response

---

[1] It should be noted that the Christological symbols would also be a factor in seeing the "graciousness" of Holy Being in my position just as the Christological question is central for Tillich's view.

[2] Macquarrie, *Principles of Christian Theology*, p. 105. For the source of much of my own thought and a fuller explanation of what the notion of "holy being" involves see Macquarrie's *Principles*, especially pp. 105-110. I am indebted for the basic ideas in this interpretation to the work of Macquarrie, although he does not utilize symbol in the way in which it is employed here as the means by which Being discloses itself.

[3] Tillich *S.T.*, II, p. 9.

[4] Kegley and Bretall, *Theology of Tillich*, p. 334.

[5] *Ibid.*

[6] Tillich, *S.T.*, II, p. 9.

to Urban's critique when in his final article on symbolism he approaches the problem of non-symbolic statements about the referent of religious symbols in terms of a phenomenological and an ontological analysis.[1] However, both of these approaches, the phenomenological analysis of the experience of the holy and the analysis of the kind of being man is, are really means of expanding and interpreting that to which the religious symbols point. They are, in other words, means of confirming the religious symbols. These methods of interpretation tend to support the reasonableness and intelligibility of the religious symbols. Although the religious symbols always transcend and therefore cannot simply be reduced to their non-symbolic meaning, neither can they function in separation from their non-symbolic interpretation. The contention of this study is that Tillich's own theory of symbolism would have been strengthened by a dimensional understanding of language that not only recognizes the unique function of the symbolic, but which also acknowledges the necessity of interpreting these symbols in a non-symbolic dimension which I have described as the conceptual.[2]

Types of Religious Symbols

Tillich indicates that in an encounter with reality everything can become a bearer of the holy. It can become a religious or theological symbol. Whether it does or not depends on the action of God, or in my terms, the disclosure of holy Being, and on the acceptance of the individual and group in a given historical period. In an attempt to clear up some of the semantic and material confusion about religious symbols, Tillich distinguishes types or kinds of religious symbols. This is a move toward constructing a clearing house for theological language. The problem is that Tillich has not just one but several classifications of the types of religious symbols.[3] However, I would argue, despite the shifts in terminol-

---

[1] Tillich, "The Meaning and Justification of Religious Symbols", *Religious Experience and Truth*, pp. 6-7.

[2] It is interesting that Tillich's critic on this issue, Wilbur Urban, should provide in his own study of language the basis for a theory that would bolster Tillich's own position; or at least that is the contention of this study.

[3] E.g., Tillich distinguishes in "The Religious Symbol" two basic levels : (1) objective, which includes four classes, and (2) self-transcending; in "The Nature of Religious Language" two levels : (1) transcendent, with three classes, and (2) immanent, also with three classes; in "Theology and Symbolism" three levels : (1) transcendent, (2) sacramental, and (3) liturgical; and finally, in "The Meaning and Justification of Religious Symbols" two levels : (1) primary, with three classes, and (2) secondary.

ogy and the arrangement of types of symbols under different groupings, that there is a basic consistency in the content of the types of symbols listed even though their classification may vary. In order to provide some illustration of religious symbols, as I have done in relationship to other universes of discourse discussed in this study, I will enumerate some of Tillich's basic types of religious symbols, employing the basic distinction of the final article between "primary" and "secondary" religious symbols.

The first symbol that Tillich names and describes as "the fundamental symbol of our ultimate concern"[1] is God. This first class of the primary symbols points directly to the referent of all religious symbols; namely, to being itself, ultimate reality, the holy, the unconditioned transcendent. The symbol God refers to "the Supreme Being" which takes on the form of an entity to which man ascribes certain attributes. "The word 'God' involves a double meaning : it connotes the unconditional transcendent, the ultimate, and also an object somehow endowed with qualities and actions".[2] In man's relationship to the ultimate he does and must symbolize. He must symbolize for purposes of relation and communication. Man could not be in relationship with God if He were only "ultimate Being"; one must encounter Him as a person.[3] In order to speak of God meaningfully as living and acting in relation to man, one must use "anthropomorphic symbols".[4] It is the use of the symbolic which allows one to preserve not only the element of the "unconditional", but also the I-Thou relationship which makes it possible to communicate with God and to speak to and about Him. The word "God" "has the peculiarity of transcending its own conceptual content—upon this depends the numinous character that the word has in science and life in spite of every misuse through false objectification".[5] God is, then, a symbol for the God beyond traditional theism, for the ground of all meaning and being. In the terminology of this study I would assert that the "symbol of the personal God" is a symbol which expresses the encounter with holy Being. The crucial issue is that in order to speak of God as a symbol, as I think one must, and in order to speak of God intelligibly and responsibly, this requires a viable understanding of the power of

---

[1] Tillich, *Dynamics of Faith*, p. 45.

[2] Tillich, "The Religious Symbol", *Myth and Symbol*, p. 28.

[3] Tillich, "The Nature of Religious Language", *Theology of Culture*, p, 61.

[4] Tillich, *S.T.*, I, p. 242.

[5] Tillich, "The Religious Symbol", p. 28.

the symbolic as founded in the nature of language. Therefore, the most fundamental religious symbol is God.[1]

The second class of primary religious symbols concerns itself with the attributes or qualities of God. These symbols ascribe to Him qualities of personality, power, love, justice, etc.[2] The attributes of God are taken from man's finite experience and applied symbolically to the unconditioned transcendent.

> ... the attributes of God, whatever you say about him : that he is love, that he is mercy, that he is power, that he is omniscient, that he is omnipresent, that he is almighty. These attributes of God are taken from experienced qualities we have ourselves. They cannot be applied to God in the literal sense. If this is done it leads to an infinite amount of absurdities. This again is one of the reasons for the destruction of religion through wrong communicative interpretation of it. And again the symbolic character of these qualities must be maintained consistently. Otherwise every speaking about the divine becomes absurd.[3]

To say that these attributes are symbolic is not to say that they are lacking in truth. Just the opposite, since only symbols have the capacity to represent the holy. Genuine symbols can be described as true in that they provide a true awareness of the power of Being.[4] Speaking of the attributes of God, Tillich says, "Religious symbols have the reality of the religious encounter from which they come. They ... express truth about the ground of being. They are true, but true as symbols and not in a non-symbolic sense".[5] In my terms the symbol is true for a symbolic consciousness and it provides illuminating insight about holy Being. Yet this claim requires not only a recognition of a symbolic dimension of language but also a type of knowledge which is related to it; namely, receiving knowledge. Two specific attributes might be noted as illustrations of this second type of religious symbol. Divine power is expressed in terms of the symbol of omnipotence. The idea of the symbol of omnipotence as applying to a highest being who is able to do whatever he

---

[1] This view is based on Western theistic assumptions, the context of Tillich's classification. This would not necessarily hold for all religious traditions.

[2] Tillich, "The Meaning and Justification of Religious Symbols", *Religious Experience and Truth*, p. 8. The qualities or attributes are sometimes included by Tillich in the classification of the first type of religious symbols as is the case in this article and sometimes they are considered as a second class; i.e., in "The Nature of Religious Language", p. 62, as I am doing here.

[3] Tillich, "The Nature of Religious Language", *Theology of Culture*, p. 62.

[4] Tillich, "The Religious Symbol", *Myth and Symbol*, p. 29.

[5] Tillich, "The Meaning and Justification of Religious Symbols", p. 11.

wants must be rejected. "It is more adequate to define omnipotence as the power of being which resists non-being in all its expressions and which is manifest in the creative process in all its forms".[1] We also say that God is love; "one speaks symbolically of God as love".[2] "And since God is being-itself, one must say that being-itself is love".[3] Tillich notes that there are three basic types of love that contribute to the symbolization of divine love, but the only adequate symbol is *agapē*. *Agapē* strives toward union of the lover and the beloved and it seeks the fulfillment of the other.[4] These two qualities may serve as illustrations of the second type of religious symbol. Their power is as symbols but the necessity of their interpretation must be considered in relation to the conceptual dimension of language.

The third class of primary religious symbols is often classified with the attributes of God and may be mentioned here only briefly. This third level includes the way we speak of the divine actions such as creation and incarnation. If one understands these acts literally, he appears to refer categories of time, space, substance, and causality to ultimate reality which leads to absurdities.[5] This also produces insoluble conflicts with the scientific interpretation of reality.[6] Therefore, the symbolic character of the acts attributed to God must be recognized and acknowledged.

The fourth class of primary religious symbols is in "the realm of divine manifestations in finite reality, divine incarnations in holy things or objects".[7] Natural and historical objects are drawn into the sphere of the holy and thus become holy objects. The holy is present in concrete persons, things, and actions. These objects are symbols because "they represent the presence of the unconditioned transcendent in the empirical order".[8] Their function as religious symbols depends precisely on their historical reality. Yet they are symbols insofar as they possess a holy character, "insofar as the unconditioned transcendent is envisaged in them".[9]

[1] Tillich, *S.T.*, I, p. 273.
[2] *Ibid.*, p. 280.
[3] *Ibid.*, p. 279.
[4] *Ibid.*, p. 280.
[5] E.g., Tillich, "The Nature of Religious Language", *Theology of Culture*, p. 62.
[6] Tillich, "The Meaning and Justification of Religious Symbols", *Religious Experience and Truth*, p. 9.
[7] *Ibid.*
[8] Tillich, "The Religious Symbol", *Myth and Symbol*, p. 30.
[9] *Ibid.*

But they are symbols that have at the same time an empirical, historical aspect and in whose symbolic meaning the empirical is involved. Therefore both aspects, the empirical and the transcendent, are manifest in this kind of symbols and their symbolic power depends upon this fact.[1]

The most important form of this level of symbol, divine manifestation, is in historical personalities. Tillich makes this quite clear for Christian theology when he talks of Jesus as the Christ as being a symbol or of having an important symbolic character.[2] When Tillich is describing this type of religious symbol he says, "When we speak of Jesus. ... He is the bearer of what in symbolic terms is called the Christ".[3] Jesus as the Christ, the bearer of the New Being,[4] becomes for those that receive him as the Christ the transformational symbol that is an adequate envisagement of the unconditioned transcendent, of the ground of meaning and being. To say with Tillich that Jesus as the Christ has a symbolic character is not to devalue Christology if one recognizes and acknowledges the power of the symbolic, the importance of what it means to be a genuine symbol.

The discussion has dealt thus far with the level of primary religious symbols. These are also described by Tillich at various times as "objective religious symbols" or as "transcendent religious symbols". This distinction coincides with what I have described as the level of "insight" or "integrative" symbols that provide the foundation for a particular universe of discourse.[5] There are in addition to this what I have called "explanatory" or "corroborating" symbols that point to or lead to the apprehension of the insight symbols. In a similar way Tillich distinguishes a level of "secondary" religious symbols.[6] These secondary symbols provide support for the primary symbols. They do this by pointing to or containing a reference to religious symbols of the primary level. They are a means of interpreting the symbols via other corroborating symbols.

This secondary level of religious symbols includes a host of supporting symbols like water, light, or oil.[7] It refers to special objects, special ges-

---

[1] Tillich, "The Religious Symbol", *Myth and Symbol*, p. 30.

[2] See *ibid.*

[3] Tillich, "Theology and Symbolism", *Religious Symbolism*, p. 115.

[4] See Tillich, *S.T.*, II, pp. 97ff.

[5] See Chapter IV.

[6] Tillich, "The Meaning and Justification of Religious Symbols", *Religious Experience and Truth*, p. 9.

[7] *Ibid.*

tures, or special garb that a religious community has come to recognize as pointing to the holy. These items have become consecrated by tradition and still contain sacral power or else they would lose their right to be called symbols. However, they contain less illuminating power than the primary symbols and their role is to direct our attention to the primary symbols. This is a broad area for Tillich; it seems to include the materials in the Lord's supper, the water of baptism, the cross, candles, etc.[1] Note the way in which these secondary symbols are expressed in language and the means by which they manifest their symbolic power in so doing. One could take the material of the Lord's supper as a concrete example of this level of religious symbols. The bread and wine are more than just signs (in Tillich's term): rather, they maintain a genuinely symbolic character which gives them their sacramental significance. They point to the atoning act of Jesus as the Christ and thus to a primary religious symbol. Tillich sometimes includes the cross in this classification,[2] but it is difficult to know if he is referring here to the cross which appears in all Christian churches and that this in turn points to the cross of Jesus Christ which, as holy object, is a primary religious symbol. It would seem strange to make the cross of Jesus Christ, which Tillich refers to as "the center of all Christian symbolism",[3] merely a secondary symbol. This example illustrates Tillich's point that religious symbols may fit into different levels depending on how they are interpreted. Tillich himself notes in speaking of the types of religious symbols that "the distinctions made here are neither exclusive nor static. The levels are mixed with each other".[4] Tillich maintains, however, that the relative distinction is helpful in producing semantic clarity.

There has been no explicit attempt to discuss in this study the relation of symbol and myth. However, since Tillich sees these two linguistic forms as integrally related and since his view of myth supports his theory of symbolism, a passing word is in order. "The symbols of faith do not appear in isolation. ... Myths are symbols of faith combined in stories about divine-human encounters".[5] What is required is to "break the myth" by making conscious its symbolic element. Thus, if

---

[1] Tillich, "The Nature of Religious Language", *Theology of Culture*, pp. 64-65.

[2] *Ibid.*

[3] Tillich, "The Meaning and Justification of Religious Symbols", *Religious Experience and Truth*, p. 10.

[4] *Ibid.*, p. 9.

[5] Tillich, *Dynamics of Faith*, pp. 48-49.

"demythologizing" is to be interpreted as the necessity to recognize a symbol as a symbol and a myth as a myth, then Tillich both accepts and supports it. But if the implication is that we need the removal of symbols and myths, then Tillich rejects this notion.[1] For he asserts that "there is no substitute for the use of symbols and myths : they are the language of faith".[2] This view is even further substantiated by the theory of language set forth in the present study which understands symbols to be the basis not only of the language of faith but of all types of discourse. The symbols of faith "have a genuine standing in the human mind, just as science and art have. Their symbolic character is their truth and their power".[3] The criteria of religious or theological symbols, that which establishes the truth of the symbol, must now be examined.

Symbolic Truth

The truth of a symbol is a question of "adequacy"—adequacy of expression in relation to a certain type of religious experience and adequacy to a certain type of consciousness.

> The criterion of the truth of the symbol naturally cannot be the comparison of it with the reality to which it refers, just because this reality is absolutely beyond human comprehension. The truth of a symbol depends on its inner necessity for the symbol-creating consciousness.[4]

Symbols are true for a particular kind of consciousness; namely, for a symbolic consciousness. This means that symbolic truth, the truth of any genuine symbol including the religious symbol, is not dependent on the validity of the factual statements concerning the symbolic material. Tillich claims that the truth of a symbol is "independent of any empirical criticism".[5] The danger in evaluating the truth of a symbol is the temptation to reduce or translate it into literal assertions and then determine the truth of these assertions. This fails to recognize the realm of symbolic truth and the existence of a symbolic consciousness. Tillich warns against this literalistic reduction and states : "The truth of a religious symbol has nothing to do with the truth of the empirical assertions involved in it, be they physical, psychological, or historical".[6]

[1] Tillich, *Dynamics of Faith*, p. 50.
[2] *Ibid.*, p. 51.
[3] *Ibid.*, p. 53.
[4] Tillich, "The Religious Symbol", *Myth and Symbol*, p. 29.
[5] Tillich, "The Nature of Religious Language", *Theology of Culture*, p. 65.
[6] Tillich, *S.T.*, I, p. 240.

The other aspect of adequacy is that the religious symbol must be adequate to express the religious situation or experience to which it refers. This adequacy to the religious experience "is the basic criterion of all symbols. One can call it their 'authenticity' ".[1] The symbol is true or authentic insofar as it expresses a true revelation,[2] since a religious symbol is the result of the encounter between the mind and ultimate reality. Or, as I have expressed it, the theological symbol is a result of the disclosure of holy Being. However, there are negative and positive elements involved in the truth of a religious symbol. There is always the danger with a religious symbol that it will be identified with that to which it points. This is the risk of the symbol becoming idolatrous or demonic by claiming for itself ultimacy in power or meaning. To be adequate, authentic, or true the symbol must have a self-negating aspect in which its limitations are noted so that the symbol will not be confused with that to which it points.[3] The positive element in the truth of a symbol of faith is how adequately it expresses our ultimate concern. " 'Adequacy' of expression means the power of expressing an ultimate concern in such a way that it creates reply, action, communication. Symbols which are able to do this are alive".[4] When a symbol loses its experiential basis, when it no longer evokes our commitment, then it is dead as a symbol. This means that the truth of a symbol is bound to its authentication within a given religious community. The truth of a symbol, its life, depends on whether it is accepted and acknowledged by a community as having the power of a symbol. Tillich provides an example of this in the case of the death of the symbol of the virgin birth of Jesus within many Protestant church groups.[5]

The truth of the religious symbol involves the dialectic of affirmation and negation within the symbol itself. And Tillich suggests that the Cross of the Christ is the standard of all other Christian symbols precisely because it indicates in the most radical way this self-negation. "He who himself embodies the fullness of the divine's presence sacrifices himself in order not to become an idol, another god beside God ...".[6] Yet the symbol of the Cross of the Christ also contains the affirmation of the

---

[1] Tillich, "The Meaning and Justification of Religious Symbols", *Religious Experience and Truth*, p. 10.

[2] Tillich, *S.T.*, I, p. 240.

[3] See Tillich, "The Meaning and Justification of Religious Symbols", p. 10.

[4] Tillich, *Dynamics of Faith*, p. 96.

[5] Tillich, "The Nature of Religious Language", *Theology of Culture*, p. 66.

[6] *Ibid.*, p. 67.

transforming power of God in relationship to man. It has been the Cross which has evoked the greatest commitment, reply, action, and communication in the history of the Christian tradition. This symbol of the Cross "includes the valuation in an ultimate perspective of the individual persons".[1]

SUMMARY

The application of the dimensional understanding of language and the supporting value of the schematic proposal of this study could be summarized in the following manner. First, the dimensional structure of language acknowledges within the nature of language itself a symbolic dimension and relates this specifically to a type of symbolic consciousness. Tillich does not attempt to work out a specific philosophy of language, so a dimensional understanding of language such as that developed here implies a revision in Tillich's theory of symbolism. This revision does not undercut Tillich's fundamental insight about the power of symbols, but it does provide a measure of grounding and intelligibility for the assertions he makes about the function of symbols and their truth. Second, my notion of truth as adequacy of expression coincides with Tillich's assertion that the most important criterion of a religious symbol is adequacy to the religious situation it expresses. Although Tillich does not emphasize the linguisticality of truth or the fact that truth is immanent in discourse due to the disclosure of Being in language, this view would not contradict his notion of the truth of a symbol; rather, in its developed form this view might offer support for Tillich's own position. Third, to claim that the truth of a symbol is independent of any empirical criticism and that evaluation of truth is on the basis of adequacy to that which is revealed in the symbol implies a dimension of reason and a type of knowledge which is appropriate to this symbolic sphere. I attempted to demonstrate previously[2] that Tillich had at least the basis of such a notion of reason in his reference to "ontological" reason and, in regard to theology, in his use of "ecstatic" reason. A parallel view of knowledge is also presented in his idea of "receiving" knowledge. Tillich's method of structuring man's conception of reason and knowledge is rendered more intelligible by the schematic proposal concerning dimen-

---

[1] Tillich, "The Meaning and Justification of Religious Symbols", *Religious Experience and Truth*, p. 11.

[2] See Chapter V.

sions of reason and types of knowledge as suggested in the present study. Fourth, Tillich speaks of the "authenticity" of religious symbols and their need to have an experiential basis, to be accepted by an individual or a community in order to be alive and efficacious as a symbol. Tillich does not specifically describe the means by which a symbol is confirmed as authentic despite the fact that such an attempt would make his notion of the truth of a symbol more intelligible and persuasive. I have proposed an outline for a means of confirming the symbol by its authentication; that is, the recognition and acknowledgment of its truth element, which occurs in the area of communication. Language and discourse are essential not only to the maturation of meaning but to the constitution of truth. This view of the means of confirmation supplements Tillich's own notion of the "authenticity" of the religious symbol. Fifth, Tillich has warned against the danger of elevating a specific religious symbol to ultimacy and thus allowing it to become demonic. The safeguard against this is the dialectic of affirmation and negation which must constantly occur in relation to a symbol; its truth as a symbol depends on this. My proposal has also emphasized the necessity of this process of affirmation and negation in regard to the symbol. The reason for this in the case of the theological symbol is that holy Being not only reveals but also conceals itself in the symbolic dimension of language. Thus, one symbol must be employed to balance another, just as the birth and death of symbols witness to the historical character of Being's self-disclosure. In conclusion, I have criticized Tillich's view as being limited to a "sphere-like" theory of symbol and suggested that an emphasis on a comprehensive theory of language which includes an understanding of a "symbolic dimension" would constitute a revision in Tillich's position which would strengthen and make more intelligible his own claim for the illuminating and transforming power of symbols.

In this discussion of the symbolic dimension of theological language I have taken Tillich as my guide to focus on religious or theological symbols, examining their nature, characteristics, functions, types, and truth. Tillich emphasizes perhaps above all else the special place and power of genuine symbols. Tillich claims in fact that "religious symbols need no justification if their meaning is understood".[1] The problem is precisely that of how their meaning can be properly apprehended. The proper apprehension of the symbol's meaning depends not only on an

---

[1] Tillich, "The Meaning and Justification of Religious Symbols", *Religious Experience and Truth*, p. 3.

intelligible theory of symbolism as found in the nature of language, but also on the interpretation of religious symbols. Tillich asserts that the truth or authenticity of the religious symbol is not dependent for that truth on factual statements concerning the symbolic material or on any empirical criticism. At this point I want to express reservations about this view. The truth of a symbol may not be completely dependent on non-symbolic assertions. It is the contention of this thesis that every symbol, including the religious symbol, demands interpretation. Only then is the symbol capable of being properly understood. Then the symbol is freed to make its claim to truth or authenticity. The genuine symbol which operates within the symbolic dimension of language must be interpreted primarily within the conceptual dimension of language. The importance of non-symbolic interpretation of the symbol is not adequately emphasized by many advocates of religious symbols, including Paul Tillich. This indicates further evidence of the need to revise Tillich's "sphere" approach to the nature of language which tends to separate the symbolic from the non-symbolic and stress the absolute independence of symbols from conceptual interpretation and evaluation. A theory of the dimensional structure of language would tend to correct this separation and imbalance. The structure and the function of the conceptual dimension of theological language must now be considered.

CHAPTER TEN

THEOLOGICAL LANGUAGE
AND THE CONCEPTUAL DIMENSION

When I say that the symbolic, in order to allow that term any significant meaning, must be interpreted by the non-symbolic, one must remember that non-symbolic is primarily a limiting term. It is misleading to describe the non-symbolic as "literal" language because the dimensions of language cannot be absolutely separated and there is a representative or non-literal aspect to all human language. The non-symbolic, as a limiting term, can be defined as that dimension of language which provides more precise information (than the symbolic), allows linguistic meaning to come to maturity, facilitates intelligible communication, is subject to verification, and provides a means of recommending certain symbols by establishing their depth and reasonableness. I have described this non-symbolic realm as the conceptual dimension of language. I will continue to use the thought of Paul Tillich as he interprets religious symbols, particularly Christian theological symbols. The dimensional understanding of language requires some revision in Tillich's method of symbolic interpretation. However, if this revision is accepted, then the dimensional structure of language will serve to supplement and undergird Tillich's own demand for the interpretation of theological symbols.

Interpretation of Symbols

"Theology, then, is the conceptual interpretation, explanation, and criticism of the symbols in which a special encounter between God and man has found expression".[1] This statement by Tillich marks the necessity of the interpretation of symbols, but the important thing for this analysis is what he means by these modes of conceptual interpretation. The first point to be noted is that theological interpretation has neither the power to create nor the power to destroy religious symbols. The authenticity or truth of the symbol is rooted in its encounter with ultimate reality.[2] If the nature of the encounter changes, then the symbol will change. In this

---

[1] Tillich, "Theology and Symbolism", *Religious Symbolism*, p. 108.
[2] *Ibid.*, p. 111.

way symbols are said to die and to be born. In this sense the truth of the symbol is claimed by Tillich to be independent of its conceptual interpretation. I will assert that Tillich has exaggerated the degree of this independence as a result of his failure to appreciate the dimensional structure of language.

It is my contention that what this conceptual interpretation does is to open up the symbol so that it can function as a symbol. The interpretation removes conceptual barriers, clarifies the reference of the symbol, and thus frees or liberates the symbol to have its illuminating and transforming power within a community or for an individual. The interpretation can also raise questions about whether the symbol is still alive in the sense of being a relevant and adequate expression of this encounter. This takes the form of the evaluation or criticism of the symbol. But this critical process can only function in terms of raising questions; the final judgment about the authenticity of the symbol rests on the symbolic, not the non-symbolic or conceptual dimension. The interpretation of symbols becomes a means of guarding genuine symbols against distortion and liberating the symbols by providing for their possible recognition as symbols. On the basis of this interpretation it is clear that the symbolic and conceptual dimensions are interrelated; one requires the other in order to fulfill its own nature. A dimensional understanding of language makes this evident. My critique of Tillich is that this interdependent character of language is not made clear.

How, then, does Tillich employ these modes of interpretation? The first aspect in the interpretation of religious symbols is conceptualization. "Conceptualization discloses the relation of the symbols to each other and to the whole to which they belong".[1] The first means of opening up or clarifying a symbol is to indicate its context. The other symbols with which it is related and those with which it is not associated need to be defined. Tillich offers as illustrations the Christian theological symbols that are expressed in the Bible, Church, and Christian tradition. The relation between the symbols of God and Christ, creator and creature, or divine love and divine justice are considered here.[2] Tillich attempts to free symbols from misunderstanding by setting the context and range of their reference. Creation as a religious symbol illuminates the creature's relation to holy Being and not man's understanding of the origin and development of the physical world.

---

[1] Tillich, "Theology and Symbolism", *Religious Symbolism*, p. 111.
[2] *Ibid.*

The explanation of symbols, the second mode of interpretation, is quite closely related to conceptualization. Explanation does not refer to the invention of arguments on a non-symbolic level to establish the validity of symbols.[1] This would be an attempt to interpret symbols by reducing them to a non-symbolic form and would simply result in violation of the symbol by confusing it with the literal. " 'Explanation' in theology ... [is] the attempt to make understandable the relation of the symbols used to that to which they point".[2] One example would be the theological symbol noted before, Jesus as the Christ. Here, explanation involves asking about the message of Jesus as the "messiah". How does it happen that an historical figure called Jesus of Nazareth should be called the Christ? How does "Christ" as a symbol point to the New Being? These are questions that Tillich deals with in the process of explanation in his *Systematic Theology*, II.[3]

Tillich's notion of conceptualization and explanation are comparable to what I have described as the interpretation of symbols by means of "expansion".[4] My position understands the symbol to be a condensation of meaning; thus expansion involves expanding the unexpressed reference of the symbol and elucidating the reality to which the symbol refers. This view is based on an understanding of the nature of language itself which recognizes that the symbol expresses something which cannot be expressed in any other way. One must have interpretation and not substitution in regard to the symbol. The interpretation must enrich and liberate the symbol, not dissolve it. The dimensional structure of language guards against this distortion and thus supports both the power of the symbol and its necessary interpretation in the conceptual dimension.

The third mode of Tillich's interpretation of the religious symbol is criticism. He appears to set this criticism of symbols, however, completely within the symbolic dimension. He states, "... no symbol can be criticized on a non-symbolic level".[5] Tillich equates this non-symbolic criticism with taking the symbol literally. It would be my judgment that this is not necessarily the case and in fact one needs to have a non-symbolic criticism of symbols, or what I have called an evaluation, in order to establish their intelligibility and free them to function as symbols.

According to Tillich, theological criticism has three responsibilities

---

[1] Tillich, "Theology and Symbolism", *Religious Symbolism*, p. 112.
[2] *Ibid.*
[3] Tillich, *S.T.*, II, pp. 97ff.
[4] See Chapter IV.
[5] Tillich, "Theology and Symbolism", p. 113.

in relation to symbols. "First, it has to prevent the reduction of the symbols to the level of non-symbolic thinking".[1] The moment a symbol is taken as literal then its real meaning and power are lost. This means that the job of theological criticism is to guard the symbolic function. However, it is difficult to see how the necessity of the symbolic function can be substantiated within the symbolic realm alone since this makes an appeal to a symbolic consciousness which already acknowledges the capacity of the symbol. Rather, theological criticism requires the contrast between the symbolic and non-symbolic to guard the legitimate role of the symbol. The task of criticism set forth by Tillich is thus more effectively accomplished in the non-symbolic or conceptual dimension with its empirical base. Tillich, I think, implies this himself in another article when he is discussing one of the central theological symbols, Jesus as the Christ.

> It is the task of historical criticism ... to prevent these groups of symbols from degenerating into false objectifications. Religion is greatly indebted to modern research on the life of Jesus, in that it has accomplished this task by recognizing the problematic character of the empirical element and by emphasizing the importance of the symbolic element.[2]

The second task of criticism is "to show that some symbols are more nearly adequate than others to the encounter which expresses itself in symbols".[3] The third task involves the other side of this question of adequacy; namely, "some symbols must be shown to be inadequate in the light of the totality of the symbolic meaning which they represent; they contradict the fundamental symbolic structure".[4] Tillich is correct in insisting that the final judgment of the adequacy or the inadequacy of a symbol, the question of symbolic truth, must be left to the symbolic consciousness. This insures the freedom of the revelatory encounter. However, the preparatory stage to this final judgment is that of criticism or evaluation. This involves those factors which tend either to recommend or put in question the adequacy of certain symbols. The question of adequacy raises the issue of whether symbols are alive and capable of being received as such by a particular historic community. It seems to me that it is just this preparatory stage of criticism which ought to be carried out in the non-symbolic sphere if this criticism is to be intelligible

---

[1] Tillich, "Theology and Symbolism", *Religious Symbolism*, p. 113.
[2] Tillich, "The Religious Symbol", *Myth and Symbol*, p. 30.
[3] Tillich, "Theology and Symbolism", p. 113.
[4] *Ibid.*

and persuasive. Tillich seems to suggest this himself when he discusses the cognitive function in the Church which appears in theology. "In it [theology] the churches interpret their symbols and relate them to the general categories of knowledge ... theology expresses them in concepts which are determined by the criteria of rationality".[1] This is illustrated in Tillich's discussion and criticism of the Christological symbols and their development.[2] I would agree with Tillich's concern to protect the independence and authenticity of the symbolic insight from final criticism and rejection by the non-symbolic or conceptual sphere. However, in emphasizing this concern he has tended to minimize and even repudiate the contribution of non-symbolic criticism and evaluation which, although it is not sufficient, is important in establishing the intelligibility of certain symbols and thus liberating them from misinterpretations that prevent their reception as genuine symbols.

A dimensional understanding of language demands that the symbolic and conceptual be interdependent. Although one can distinguish the symbolic dimension from the conceptual for purposes of analysis, one cannot separate them. Each dimension requires the other to fulfill its function. Tillich in his unwillingness to accept the non-symbolic or conceptual evaluation and criticism of symbols, particularly religious symbols, tends to separate the symbolic from the conceptual, thus making them spheres and not dimensions of language. The result is Tillich's refusal to recognize or be held accountable for the evaluation of theological symbols in reference to their coherence or consistency with our experience in the modern world. This kind of refusal leads to legitimate charges about the subjectivism, arbitrariness, and intelligibility of theories of theological symbolism. Tillich is correct in wishing to protect the genuine theological symbols from reduction or complete translation into the non-symbolic and thus the loss of their unique illuminating capacity. Yet Tillich is, I believe, mistaken in denying the interdependent relation of the symbolic and the conceptual.[3]

I am convinced that the notion of the interpretation of symbols in the conceptual dimension as presented in this study supports Tillich's primary concern of guarding the symbol and also clarifies his notion of

---

[1] Tillich, *S.T.*, III, p. 201.

[2] Tillich, *S.T.*, II, pp. 108-113.

[3] In contrast to what I have described as Tillich's "sphere" approach to language, he does recognize and emphasize the dimensional structure and interdependent nature of types of reason (technical and ontological) and types of knowledge (controlling and receiving). See Chapter V.

symbolism by revising his view of the criticism of symbols. The dimensional interpretation does this by asserting that there is a non-symbolic criticism of the symbols which, when properly understood, contributes to the intelligibility of symbols and yet does not challenge their unique relationship to ultimate reality. This was discussed previously when I maintained that the role of the "evaluation" of symbols in the conceptual dimension was to recommend certain symbols for consideration as being more likely to be authentic than others.[1] One pursues this evaluation on the basis of whether the expansion and interpretation of the symbol in the theological universe of discourse results in declarations which are coherent and consistent with the views one holds concerning other aspects of his experience in the modern world. If this occurs, then the symbol is recommended for further consideration, exploration, and elucidation. It is not finally and positively validated or confirmed; that can happen only in the symbolic dimension by authentication. However, it is recommended and provided with intelligible and rational support. This could be applied, for example, to Tillich's view of Jesus as the Christ, the bearer of the New Being. The analysis of the kind of being man is and his relation to the world indicates man's essential estrangement and his anxiety. New Being fulfills all finite being by conquering its estrangement. Thus Jesus as the bearer of the New Being can be said to bring salvation and healing to man. This Christological symbol is coherent and consistent with the phenomenological analysis of man's existence and relation to his world and thus is recommended for further consideration, whereas the Christological assertion that "God has become man" is, according to Tillich, nonsensical without radical reinterpretation.[2] If, on the other hand, the expansion or interpretation of the symbol results in conclusions which are evaluated as standing in contradiction or violent contrast with the other views we hold about the nature of our existence, then the authenticity of the symbol or its interpretation is placed in question. This critical evaluation does not have the power to finally reject the symbol, but it does call the adequacy of the symbol into question. This could be illustrated in Tillich's notion about God as "a being" who, as the highest being, is omnipotent and can do whatever he wants in relation to his creatures or the world. This means making God subject to categories of finitude such as space and

---

[1] See Chapter IV.
[2] Tillich, S.T., II, p. 94.

substance which make him only a being alongside others.[1] Also, this notion of omnipotence contradicts the apparent freedom of individuals and events which man observes. These problems cannot themselves result in the rejection of a symbol, but they can and do call this symbol into question and for Tillich recommend instead the symbol of God as "ground of being" and of omnipotence as "the power of being to resist non-being".

I have asserted that the conceptual dimension *with* its function of interpretation is necessary in order to allow linguistic meaning to come to maturity. In terms of our previous analysis,[2] meaning is dependent, among other factors, on the recognition of a common type of meaning function. To determine whether the theological assertions in a given context have primarily an indicative, emotive, or intuitive meaning function requires the process of interpretation. This can be illustrated by different statements about the Church which may intend to convey that the Church is a sociological entity, a source of emotional response, or an "assembly of God" with intuitive connotations. In each case a different meaning function is involved and this can be clarified by conceptual interpretation, especially expansion. I have also maintained that intelligible communication, as defined here, requires this process of interpretation. Intelligible communication was defined as a linguistic transaction in which verbal signs are understood by the hearer in all relevant aspects in a similar way to that intended by the speaker.[3] Understanding is the necessary correlate to expression. In order for a sharing of mutual understanding between speaker and hearer to occur, there must be a common speech community, a common universe of discourse, and the recognition of a common meaning function. This type of precise information which defines the range of meaning for purposes of communication must be spelled out in the non-symbolic or conceptual dimension of language. Some of the confusion in recent theological language has resulted from a lack of clarity not only about the meaning function of a term but also about the universe of discourse in which it is operating. The issue is raised here, for instance, whether "God" is equally a theological, philosophical and scientific term or whether there is a distinction between holy Being in theology, Being as source of existence in philosophy, and Being as disclosing something about the mystery of the universe

---

[1] Tillich, *S.T.*, I, pp. 235f.
[2] See Chapter III.
[3] *Ibid.*

in natural science. Terms constantly require greater specification as to their range of reference. There is a need to develop a linguistic clearing house, and it is the conceptual dimension of language with its concern for clarity of expression which is essential to this endeavor.

Reason, Knowledge, and Confirmation

The symbolic dimension of language was declared as entailing a relationship to foundational reason or thinking and to receiving knowledge. In a comparable way it is possible to indicate the dimension of reason and the type of knowledge associated with the conceptual dimension of language. It is here that technical reason and controlling knowledge are operative. If my discussion of the necessity to expand and evaluate symbols is correct, then the symbolic dimension is not completely consigned to foundational thought. Rather, the interpretive and critical functions of technical reason are applicable and important to theological symbols. As I suggested,[1] this is implied in Tillich's contrast between technical reason and ontological reason. The importance of technical reason, as I have employed the idea, is that it strives toward precision and clarity of expression, standardization of forms, and finality of judgment. It is concerned with formal logic as a reference point; description, explanation, and criticism must be in a logically correct form in order to be intelligible. Technical reason strives to isolate, analyze, and evaluate with a detached critical attutide. As Tillich notes, "Technical reason always has an important function, even in systematic theology".[2] That function is related to the sytsem, to the interpretation and explanation of theological symbols in a consistent and coherent way. Technical reason is important because it guards against illusion and superstition within the theological discipline. "Technical reason is an instrument",[3] however, and it cannot be used as the sole understanding of reason. As Tillich states, "It follows that the theologian must consider reason from several different perspectives. In theology one must distinguish ... ontological from technical reason ...".[4] It is the view of this study that the schematic proposal presented here concerning the dimensional structure of language and reason provides a basis for this distinction and yet concurs with Tillich that ontological reason (in my terms, foundational reason) and

[1] See Chapter V.
[2] Tillich, *S.T.*, I, p. 73.
[3] *Ibid.*, p. 74.
[4] *Ibid.*

technical reason must accompany one another; they require one another. The theologian cannot be deaf to the voice of technical reason, but it is not his final court of appeal. This is to maintain not a rationalistic but a reasonable approach to the interpretation of theological symbols.

There is a distinctive type of knowledge that is the product of technical reason or thought. This is described as "controlling knowledge"[1] because it seeks to possess or control the object of its thought for a specific purpose. The purpose of this technique of detachment, analysis, and comparison is to make possible preciseness and clarity of expression and verifiability in regard to the consistency and coherence of an interpretation within a particular universe of discourse, theology for example. Tillich illustrates this concern when he responds to the critique of men like Kenneth Hamilton who, in *The System and the Gospel*,[2] attacks Tillich because he developed his theology within a tightly structured system. Tillich responds by saying that the systematic form, and by implication the concern for technical reason and controlling knowledge, is not in his case an attempt to "rationalize revelatory experience".[3] Tillich warns against confusing the demand for consistency and clarity in one's statements with the unjustifiable attempt to seek non-revelatory experience as the source of theological statements. The "systematic-constructive form" is valuable because it demands consistency which is difficult in theology. The method of checking this mutual compatibility, it appears to me, involves the use of technical reason and controlling knowledge. Tillich maintanis that this also allows one to discover relations between symbols and concepts which otherwise would not come to light.[4] I am convinced that theology must be sensitive to the ways in which the technical and critical functions of reason can fulfill an important role in making theological symbols more intelligible by the process of consistent and coherent interpretation.

In this study I have employed "confirmation" to refer to a wide range of deciding the truth or falsity of a judgment. I have affirmed that confirmation has its locus in communication, that language and discourse are essential to the maturation of meaning and the determination of truth. In the theological universe of discourse it is also necessary to distinguish different means of confirmation which are appropriate for different

---

[1] Tillich, *S.T.*, I, p. 97.

[2] Kenneth Hamilton, *The System and the Gospel* (New York : The Macmillan Company, 1963).

[3] Tillich, *S.T.*, III, p. 3.

[4] *Ibid.*

dimensions of language and related dimensions of reason and types of knowledge. In the discussion of the symbolic dimension of thelogical language, I have already maintained that authentication is the proper means of confirming religious symbols. Authentication takes place in a specific religious community at a given historical period when there is recognition and mutual acknowledgment of the pointing, illuminating, and transforming power of a symbol. When a symbol is accepted which adequately expresses an encounter with holy Being so as to evoke existential commitment and trust, a faith attitude is the consequence. However, when theological symbols are interpreted in the conceptual dimension of language where technical reason and controlling knowledge are operative, then another means of confirmation functions. This has been described as verification (employing this as a limiting term), which I have reserved for reference to that means of confirmation which does depend on repeatable experimental evidence and correctness in logical form. Verification, in this sense, establishes truth or falsity by reference to empirical criteria. Theological language cannot be reduced to statements which are verifiable, in this sense, but there is an aspect or dimension of theological language which maintains this tie with the empirical and results in assertions which are capable of verification.

The present study employs "empirical" in the broader sense of that which is "open to testing by experience, or ... that relates to some observable facts".[1] Thus the interpretation of theological symbols in the conceptual dimension is subject to this type of verification. Illustrations of this cover a wide range : a critical examination of the texts of the Christian tradition, historical research about persons or events crucial to the experience of the religious community, an analysis of the acts and events of individuals or communities in response to an encounter with the holy which is sometimes called "religious" experience, and the content of arguments which are based on observable facts in the world. The key factor about all these assertions is their element of public approachability. Anyone can examine the texts or the historical evidence, observe the activities of those who claim a religious experience, or examine the content and structure of arguments about the natural world. Anyone is free to experiment with the evidence, of whatever nature, that is offered.

An explicit example of this is the historical research about the life

---

[1] Macquarrie, *God-Talk*, p. 231. Macquarrie goes on to support this broader use of "empirical" by reference to the variety of ways the term has been used in philosophical and theological thought. He also provides some examples of empirical language in theology which coincide with and support my own dicussion.

of Jesus. This obviously cannot establish faith in the person of Jesus as the Christ, but it is important insofar as this historic information is part of the material for the interpretation of a central Christian symbol. To be indifferent to this research calls into question the adequacy of one's interpretation and of the symbol itself. There is an empirical basis or a "minimal core of factuality"[1] which protects against illusion and fantasy in regard to theological assertions. The verification of the conceptual interpretation of theological symbols is not sufficient in itself to confirm the adequacy or truth of a theological symbol or an assertion that contains a reference to that symbol. Nor can the failure of a conceptual interpretation to be verified result in the final rejection or destruction of that theological symbol or assertions about it. However, the verification of assertions within the conceptual dimension certainly tends to recommend this symbol for further consideration as being more likely to be adequate. Also, the expansion of the symbol in conceptual terms that are verifiable in regard to experience or observable facts not only establishes the intelligibility of the symbol, but also may remove barriers which free the symbol to function in an illuminating and trans- forming way.

I indicated previously[2] that Tillich also has a concern for broadening the range of legitimate confirmation and that he distinguishes two types of verification (or, as I have called it, confirmation) : experimental and experiential.[3] This parallels, I think, my use of verification and authentication. The experimental method of confirmation, which is what concerns me here, is characterized by its repeatability, precision, and finality. It requires the isolation and regulation of the object in order to obtain empirical verification. The range of its applicability is limited, but its results are important. The experiential method is character- ized by totality, spontaneity, and individuality and cannot be abstracted from the life process. It is involvement, the experiential basis, that results in confirmation, or, as I have described it, authentication. Tillich goes on to assert that these two methods of confirmation correspond to the two types of knowledge, controlling and receiving. Tillich does not go on to ground this distinction in the discourse situation, as I do, nor does he work out in detail the ramifications of this distinction in relation to specific theological symbols. However, I think the foundation

---

[1] Macquarrie, *God-Talk*, p. 235.
[2] See Chapter VI.
[3] In reference to these distinctions, see Tillich, *S.T.*, I, pp. 102-104.

for the distinction and the application is present in Tillich. Finally, Tillich notes that, despite the need to distinguish these two types of confirmation in practice, the two must be united. Thus I have spoken of the dialectical relationship between authentication and verification which makes both of them essential in arriving at understanding and thus in bringing meaning to maturation and in consummating intelligible communication.

In discussing the symbolic dimension of theological language I focused on one particular type of verbal sign because of its unique function and essential power. This was the theological symbol, defined in a narrower and specialized sense, as that linguistic form which is an illuminating, transforming, and pointing symbol which provides authentic awareness and cognitive insight concerning man's encounter with holy Being. We have suggested that other terminology may sometimes be employed such as cipher, metaphor, or model, and while there may be subtle differences between these terms, the nature and function of the symbolic element that distinguishes this dimension of language remains singular and constant. However, it is quite a different matter when one turns to the conceptual dimension of theological language where the symbols come to be interpreted. In the conceptual dimension there is not just one type of verbal sign which is operative, but a great many. As has been suggested, all types of verbal signs which are capable of providing conceptual information are applicable. The ways of speaking included here are those which attempt to provide objective or controlling knowledge, via their use of technical reason, precision, and clarity of expression. When the intention and result of the employment of a verbal sign is to supply conceptual information, descriptive definition and illustration, or direct denotation concerning theological symbols, then one is involved with the conceptual dimension of theological language. I have already indicated that the range of verbal signs employed in the conceptual dimension runs from denotative signals and direct declarative statements to analogical statements. The specific analysis of the various types of verbal signs that are operative in the conceptual dimension of theological language is beyond the scope of this study and is not crucial to my case for the importance of a dimensional understanding of language in making theological language more responsible and intelligible. However, I would like to consider briefly the notion of analogy because of its importance in the present debates about the nature of theological language.

The Conceptual Dimension and Analogy

It had been my expectation in the initial stages of the research on theological language to show that analogy is definitely operative in the conceptual dimension of language. However, my conclusions at the end of
my research are more cautious. Analogy is presently defined and employed
even in theological circles in such a variety of ways[1] that to confine
it to the conceptual dimension on the basis of the contemporary discussion would be arbitrary and unjustified. Tillich has been our guide in
much of the discussion of theological language, and he often uses analogy
and symbol as if they were synonymous.[2] Also, John Macquarrie,
who has been very influential in my own understanding of the nature and
function of theological language, states that the expressions "symbol"
and "analogy" often overlap,[3] and that the distinction between the
two is not entirely clear so that the problem of symbolism resolves itself
into the problem of analogy.[4] I agree that on the basis of the present
usage the line of demarcation is not clear and this leads to confusion
about the nature and function of both symbol and analogy.

Therefore, I wish to suggest that a more limited and specialized understanding of analogy, particularly in relation to theology, might make
our language about God more intelligible not only in intra-theological
discussions but with those in other disciplines as well. As in the case
with symbol, a definitive definition for analogy is impossible to provide
in the contemporary situation. However, a provisional or working definition is that an analogy is a type of verbal form operating in the conceptual dimension of language which refers to a relation of *likeness*
between two things (entities, conditions, or situations) or to a relation
of one thing to and with another. It is my suggestion that analogy in
this sense ought to be understood primarily as a descriptive tool or
a principle of interpretation which is operative in the conceptual dimension of language. Analogy in the theological universe of discourse should
not be seen as a means of obtaining radically new knowledge or insight
about God or, in my terms, about the encounter with holy Being.
Rather, analogy should be understood as a conceptual tool for expressing,

[1] Mondin, *The Principle of Analogy in Protestant and Catholic Thought*. Mondin
demonstrates the multiple ways in which analogy has been defined and employed
in philosophy and theology.

[2] E.g., Tillich, *S.T.*, I, p. 131.

[3] Macquarrie, *God-Talk*, p. 196.

[4] *Ibid.*, p. 216.

expanding, interpreting, evaluating and illustrating a new cognitive insight gained prior to this in an existential encounter with holy Being which is constituted by authentic awareness and cognitive insight. Awareness and insight come via the symbol. Analogy could be understood as a means of interpreting that insight. Symbol illuminates; analogy illustrates. Analogy on this basis could be understood as a means of providing objective knowledge about theological symbols, which have been described as the proper object of theology. This analogical interpretation becomes a means of liberating the symbol for its illuminating and transforming work. Theological symbols are the means by which Being discloses itself as holy through foundational thought and results in receiving knowledge. However, these symbols demand interpretation, and it is analogy which could be conceived as functioning in this interpretive and clarifying role. John Macquarrie, when he attempts to draw a relative distinction between symbol and analogy, maintains that analogies are almost self-interpreting while symbols frequently require explanation before we can see clearly where they are pointing.[1] I do not wish to suggest that Macquarrie draws the same conclusion I do: namely, that it is analogies which provide the explanation for symbols. I only suggest that he also recognizes the interpretive function of the analogy.

Let us see what might lead to such a proposal about the relationship of symbol and analogy. In my judgment that which especially characterizes the notion of symbol is "participation" or "affinity". It is this affinity that allows the theological symbol to be illuminating and transforming as it opens up an aspect of ultimate reality, namely, its holy character, and also opens up a dimension of the self to respond to holy Being in commitment and trust. In the symbolic dimension there is no particular need to discuss the "likeness" or "similarity" between God or man or between the symbol and that which it symbolizes. The concentration is on the function of the symbol, on what occurs as a result of this encounter. Emphasis here is placed on the power of certain linguistic forms as a result of the disclosure of holy Being in and through language. The very pointing nature of a symbol and the necessary element of negation which it incorporates defy the static isolation and analysis of the nature of the relationship. The symbol provides in this illuminating function insight and awareness. However, for this insight and awareness to come to fruition and result in the transformation of an individual or group, one must interpret it by means of expansion and evaluation.

---

[1] Macquarrie, *God-Talk*, p. 196.

Analogy, on the other hand, is characterized by this notion of "similarity" or "likeness". It must not be understood in the crude way of "looking alike", but the notion of comparison is certainly involved. Analogy involves the comparison of statements, entities, conditions, attributes, circumstances, effects, etc. The analogy takes the form of asserting a particular kind of relationship between the analogates or components. The comparison of one with another, their analogous character, results in knowledge of or clarification about the nature of the lesser known of the elements involved in the analogy. The point is that in an analogy one has two components in mind, whether they be statements, conditions, entities, etc., about which he has some definite knowledge, information, or awareness. The assertion of an analogical relationship between the two components furnishes further clarification about them as a result of the declared relationship. I quoted Niels C. Nielson previously when he stated that "analogy is not so much a method for gaining new knowledge as a means of making clear what is already implicit in a particular context".[1] It is this clarifying or descriptive function of analogy, as proposed here, that makes it a reliable methodological instrument not only for theology but for other disciplines as well.

The understanding of analogy as a descriptive tool or principle of interpretation places the emphasis on precision and clarity of expression. The aim is to indicate what the nature of the comparison or relationship is between two elements and what this relationship clarifies or fails to clarify about the components concerned. This means that one should specify the positive and negative aspects of the analogy employed. One should indicate those respects in which the analogates resemble each other and provide objective knowledge, the positive analogy. But one must also indicate the respects in which the analogates differ from one another, the negative analogy, and thus tend to mislead. The positive and negative aspects of analogy must be dialectically related or, as John McIntyre suggests, "held in suspension".[2] If analogy is to be considered in the conceptual dimension of language, then assertions made in regard to this methodological tool, whether positively or negatively, are subject to the laws of formal logic and to appropriate forms of verification. Here is an empirical foundation or reference point for this notion of analogy.

---

[1] Niels C. Nielson, Jr., "Analogy as a Principle of Theological Method Historically Considered", *The Heritage of Christian Thought*, p. 198. (See Chapter IV.)

[2] John McIntyre, "Analogy", *Scottish Journal of Theology*, 12:1, 1959, p. 18.

It seems to me that the reason analogy is not usually conceived in this way is because "analogy" is employed in such a loose and general way, comparable to the manner in which "symbol" is frequently utilized. There are several famous examples of this in the theological universe of discourse. Probably the most well-known reference to analogy in contemporary theology is that developed by Karl Barth. In his basic definition of analogy in his *Church Dogmatics* II/1 he states : "... 'analogy' means similarity [*Ähnlichkeit*], i.e., a partial correspondence and agreement ...".[1] He rejects the Thomistic notion of *analogia entis* in favor of *analogia fidei* which he considers to be the proper form of analogy. The question I want to raise is whether *analogia fidei* ought properly to be considered an analogy at all. Certainly Barth was not indicating that there was some condition known as faith held by the Deity that could be compared in degree of similarity to a faith condition in man. Nor did Barth want to imply that there was a basic similarity between man and God that was constituted by faith. There simply do not appear to be two concrete components or analogates between which an element of similarity or likeness could be claimed to exist. Rather, what Barth wants to assert is that faith has a cognitive aspect. Faith involves an act of apprehension (*Vernehmen*) of a proper and unique object, God.[2] Knowledge of God is made possible only by God in the act of revelation. This apprehension by faith appears to be beyond the subject-object split. The concern here is with what occurs as a result of this apprehension by faith. It is faith which establishes the point of contact between God and man. One could argue in light of this discussion that what is operating here is much closer to what I have defined as a symbolic relationship than an analogical one.

A similar analysis might be made in regard to the Thomistic notion of *analogia entis*. Although the nature of this analogy has been interpreted in different ways, there is some agreement now that it must involve both an analogy of attribution and an analogy of proportionality.[3] However, the analogy of attribution tells us only about our relation to God as the supreme cause and nothing about the nature of the cause. The analogy

[1] Karl Barth, *Church Dogmatics*, II-1, G. W. Bromiley and T. F. Torrence (eds.) (Edinburgh : T&T Clark, 1957), p. 225.

[2] Hans W. Frei, "Analogy and the Spirit in the Theology of Karl Barth" (unpublished essay), p. 2.

[3] I.e., George F. McLean, O.M.I., "Symbol and Analogy", *Paul Tillich in Catholic Thought*, Thomas O'Meara (ed.) (Dubuque, Iowa : Priority Press, 1965), p. 183.

of proportionality, i.e., creature : its being : God : His being, purports to say that when we know the proportion of the terms on the left then we know the proportion of the terms on the right and thus something positive about God.[1] However, the problem, as Tillich argues, is that both terms concerning God are unknown. Analogy cannot give us objective or controlling knowledge about God. *Analogia entis* does not seem to me to make a direct comparison between the being of God and the being of man. Rather, it says that there is something about the nature of being which provides an access between God and man or, as Macquarrie puts it, an "ontological bridge".[2] But saying that there is the power of being in everything that has being, as Tillich does, or that Being discloses itself in and to the beings via language, as I have maintained, does not imply an analysis of the points of similarity and dissimilarity between God and man. Such an analysis is beyond the capacity of man. It means only that there must be an ontological foundation for symbolism or analogy. It is perhaps this which Tillich implies when he asserts in a letter to Father Weigel that in speaking of symbolic knowledge he means what St.Thomas means by *analogia entis*.[3] It may be that a more limited utilization of analogy which distinguishes it from symbol would be a step toward greater clarity in our reference to symbol and analogy.

Analogy and Its Interpretive Function : Love

An illustration of this suggested understanding of analogy can be given in regard to one of the principal Christian theological symbols, love. The Scriptures as well as Christian tradition declare that "God is love".[4] Love is perhaps the most important attribute of God. The attributes of God were designated in this study as primary theological symbols. This means that one has no means of knowing directly and in itself what the nature and function of love is as referred to God. As Tillich states, "one speaks symbolically of God as love".[5] To say that one speaks symbolically about God's love does not imply that he has

---

[1] McLean, "Symbol and Analogy", *Paul Tillich in Catholic Thought*, p. 182.

[2] Macquarrie, *God-Talk*, p. 52.

[3] Paul Tillich, Letter to G. Weigel, S.J., cited in *Theological Studies* XI, 1950, p. 201. I think one can argue that St. Thomas meant more by *analogia entis* than Tillich implies in this casual reference. Lewis E. Ford does just this in an article, "Tillich and Thomas : The Analogy of Being", *Journal of Religion*, Vol. XLVI, No. 2 (April 1966), pp. 229-245.

[4] I John 4:8.

[5] Tillich, *S.T.*, I, p. 280.

no significant knowledge of this love. Quite to the contrary, love understood as a symbol may provide authentic awareness and cognitive insight about the nature of God's love. This is the power of the genuine symbol. This occurs as a result of an encounter with Being as holy and the symbol is an expression of this encounter. However, the dimension of knowledge, the result of this encounter, is receiving knowledge which is the result of being attentive or receptive to the object of knowledge via foundational thinking. The symbol appeals to the symbolic consciousness wherein it may be authenticated as having illuminating and transforming power in relation to an individual or group. Many have experienced at one time or another this power of the symbolic to open one up to new dimensions of reality and of the self. In the sphere of the Christian faith something takes on the quality of the holy and demands ones commitment and trust. This experience, say of God's love in Jesus Christ, has a content, a given, yet in cannot be reduced to or translated into non-symbolic forms. The insight provided by this symbol has both a content and an authenticity of its own. Yet when one wishes to speak of this experience and clarify it for oneself and for others in order to communicate the experience and make it viable as a symbol for someone else, then he must interpret it. The cognitive insight provided by the symbol is a concentrate of meaning that must be expanded and evaluated if it is to be meaningful for and communicable to others. It is here that analogy becomes operative. The task of analogy is to compare the experiences man has of love with the content of the symbolic insight about God's love. This is a question of similarity or of likeness between the analogates about which we already have some knowledge, even if the form of that knowledge is different. Analogy provides clarification and therefore valuable objective knowledge by means of the comparison, but this is knowledge by means of comparison between present experience and that which is already implicit in the context. It is not knowledge by a leap of insight or the disclosure of radical new understanding. The latter is supplied not by analogy, an instrument of explanation, but by symbol, an instrument of insight.

The analogy then proceeds to specify those points at which there is a positive analogy between our human understanding of love and our symbolic apprehension of God's love. In terms of the positive analogy one might speak of the liberating or freeing aspect of human love. Macquarrie interprets this, I think, in a very creative manner when he speaks of love as "letting-be" .This does not mean standing off from someone or something, but rather it is to be understood in the positive and active sense of "enabling-to-be". This is indicated in human love when one loves someone so as to help him realize his full potential for being—even if this is at some considerable cost to one's own desires and requires the "spending of one's own being".[1] Macquarrie goes on to note the analogous relation to God's love by asserting that the essence of God as Being is just this act of letting-be, which is "to confer, sustain, and perfect the being of the creatures".[2] The positive aspects of the analogy could be spelled out further, as they are, for instance, in a recent work by Daniel Day Williams where he lists the categorical conditions of human love as individuality, freedom, action and suffering, causality, and impartiality.[3] These aspects cannot be developed here, but it is Williams' contention that this "analysis of love in human experience might open up possibilities of understanding the meaning of the love of God ...".[4]

But there are also negative analogies between human love and the symbolic apprehension of the love of God. For instance, there is a possessive element in human love which seeks union with the beloved, but this is a union that seeks to care for and protect the beloved and may place a limitation on the individuality and freedom of the beloved. These elements may constitute negative analogies in comparison with the symbol of the love of God. I say that they *may* because there have been instances in the Christian tradition when the love of God has been understood in terms of omnipotent but gracious care which tended toward possession and control of His creatures. The point is that the interpretive function of analogy in expansion and evaluation allows one not only to clarify what the love of God might mean but also to either recommend or call into question a certain understanding of this theological symbol. But it should be noted again that the conceptual interpretation which occurs for example via analogy is not capable in its own right of confirming or rejecting the theological symbol as adequate; that occurs only within the symbolic dimension itself via authentication.

It is clear that if my proposal concerning the function of analogy is accepted, then symbol and analogy are neither synonymous, as Tillich sometimes suggests, nor contradictory, as some Roman Catholic scholars

---

[1] Macquarrie, *Principles*, pp. 310-311.

[2] *Ibid.*, p. 311.

[3] Daniel Day Williams, *The Spirit and the Forms of Love* (New York : Harper & Row, 1968); see especially Chapter 6.

[4] *Ibid.*, p. 122.

like McLean have implied by rejecting symbol as too subjectivistic and relativistic.[1] Rather, they are complementary and strategically interconnected insofar as they fulfill their respective and appropriate functions. It becomes obvious that in the theological universe of discourse the symbol and analogy (or some other verbal form in the conceptual dimension) require one another. The symbol requires the analogy to expand and interpret it if the symbol is to reach maturity of meaning and thus facilitate intelligible communication. The analogy requires the symbol to provide insight, illumination, and finally an access to ultimate reality. This integral and complementary relation is congruent with a dimensional understanding of the structure of language and thus makes the notion of both symbol and analogy in theological language more intelligible.

SUMMARY

The aim of these last two chapters is to show that the dimensional understanding of language as developed in this thesis is applicable to theological language. The principal concern has been to indicate the nature and function of the symbolic dimension of theological language. Paul Tillich's "theory of symbol" has illustrated the fundamental insight concerning the need to recover an understanding of the illuminating and transforming capacity of authentic theological symbols. However, I have maintained that Tillich's view is inadequate because it fails to recognize that the symbol is more than just a sphere of language restricted to certain realms or universes of discourse. Rather, the symbol is properly understood as operating in a symbolic dimension which is present, even if in a latent manner, in all significant instances of human discourse. If this revision in Tillich's position is made on the basis of a comprehensive dimensional understanding of language and a high evaluation of that language as an access to reality through Being's self-disclosure in language, then Tillich's own fundamental claim for the power of symbols in relation to theology is supported and made more intelligible.

The major thesis of this study is that the dimensional understanding of language provides a basis for the idea of theological symbolism in the nature of language itself. If this dimensional understanding of language is applicable to all principal universes of discourse, as I have main-

---

[1] McLean, "Symbol and Analogy", *Paul Tillich in Catholic Thought*, pp. 145ff.

tained, then it makes our speaking of God in the symbolic dimension of language not only necessary but also intelligible. However, the theological symbol must be interpreted in order for meaning and communication to occur. The symbol, I have maintained, must be interpreted in the conceptual dimension of language. The dimensional understanding of language recognizes not only these two distinct dimensions of language but also their necessary and complementary relation. The dimensional structure of language in order to be intelligible itself entails the explication of parallel dimensions of thought or reason, types of knowledge, and means of confirmation. This constitutes a schematic proposal which attempts to account for the nature and function of symbolic language about God by founding it in a particular understanding of the nature of language. However, the schematic proposal contained in this study is just that—an attempt at understanding the nature of language, utilizing particularly the insights of Heidegger and Urban, which might make all our speaking—but particularly our talk about God—more responsible and intelligible. It is experimental in design and is presented as one step toward the construction of a clearing house for theological language.

BIBLIOGRAPHY

A. Books

Adams, James Luther. *Paul Tillich's Philosophy of Culture, Science, and Religion.* New York : Harper & Row, 1965.

Altizer, Thomas (ed.). *Truth, Myth and Symbol.* Englewood Cliffs, New Jersey : Prentice-Hall, 1962.

Austin, J. L. *How To Do Things With Words.* Cambridge : Harvard University Press, 1962.

——. *Philosophical Papers.* London : Oxford University Press, 1961.

Ayer, A. J. *Language, Truth, and Logic.* London : Victor Gollancz, 1936.

—— (ed). *Logical Positivism.* Glencoe, Illinois : The Free Press, 1959.

Barbour, Ian G. *Issues in Science and Religion.* Englewood Cliffs, New Jersey : Prentice-Hall, 1966.

—— (ed.). *Science and Religion : New Perspectives on the Dialogue.* New York : Harper & Row, 1968.

——. *Science and Secularity.* New York : Harper & Row, 1970.

Barr, James. *Semantics in Biblical Language.* London : Oxford University Press, 1961.

Barth, Karl. *Church Dogmatics.* 12 vols., eds., G. W. Bromily and T. F. Torrence. Edinburgh : T & T Clark, 1936-1962.

Beiser, Arthur and Konrad Krauskoph. *Introduction to Physics and Chemistry.* New York : McGraw-Hill Book Company, 1964.

Bevan, Edwyn. *Symbolism and Belief.* New York : Macmillan, 1938.

Black, Max. *Models and Metaphors.* Ithaca : Cornell University Press, 1962.

Braithwaite, R. B. *An Empiricist's View of The Nature of Religious Belief.* Cambridge : Cambridge University Press, 1955.

——. *Scientific Explanation.* Cambridge : Cambridge University Press, 1968.

Bridge, A. C. *Images of God.* London : Hodden and Stoughton, 1960.

Bultmann, Rudolf. *Essays, Philosophical and Theological,* trans. J. C. G. Greig. London : SCM Press, 1955.

——. *Jesus Christ and Mythology.* London : SCM Press, 1960.

——. *Theology of the New Testament.* 2 vols., trans. K. Grobel. New York : Scribners, 1951-55.

Buri, Fritz. *How Can We Still Speak Responsibly of God?* Philadelphia : Fortress Press, 1968.

——. *Thinking Faith,* trans. H. Oliver. Philadelphia : Fortress Press, 1968.

Carnap, Rudolf. *The Logical Syntax of Language.* London : K. Paul, Trench, Trubner and Co., Ltd., 1935.

Cassirer, Ernst. *Die Philosophie der symbolischen Formen.* 3 vols. Berlin : Bruno Cassirer, 1923-29. English translation, *The Philosophy of Symbolic Forms.* 3 vols.; trans. Ralph Manheim. New Haven : Yale University Press, 1953-57.

——. *An Essay on Man.* New Haven : Yale University Press, 1944.

——. *Language and Myth,* trans. Susanne Langer. New York : Dover Publications, Inc., 1953.

Caws, Peter. *The Philosophy of Science*. Princeton : D. Van Nostrand Company. 1965.

Croce, Benedetto. *Aesthetic as Science of Expression and General Linguistic*, trans. Douglas Ainslie. New York : Noonday Press, 1960.

Cohen, L. J. *The Diversity of Meaning*. New York : Herder and Herder, 1963.

Crystal, David. *Linguistics, Language, and Religion*. Urbana : University of Illinois Press, 1963.

Danto, Arthur and Sidney Morgenbesser (eds.). *Philosophy of Science*. Cleveland : Meridan Books, 1960.

Dilley, Frank B. *Metaphysics and Religious Language*. New York : Columbia University Press, 1964.

Dillistone, F. W. *Christianity and Symbolism*. London : Collins, 1955.

—— (ed.). *Myth and Symbol*. London : S.P.C.K., 1966.

Duhem, Pierre. *The Aim and Structure of Physical Theory*, trans. P. Wigner. Princeton : Princeton University Press, 1954.

Ebeling, Gerhard. *God and Word*, trans. J. W. Leitch. Philadelphia : Fortress Press, 1967.

——. *Word and Faith*, trans. J. W. Leitch. Philadelphia : Fortress Press, 1964.

Eliade, Mircea. *Images and Symbols*, trans. Philip Mairet. London : Harvill Press, 1961.

Evans, Donald. *The Logic of Self Involvement*. London : SCM Press, 1963.

Farrer, Austin. *The Glass of Vision*. Westminster : Dacre Press, 1948.

Feigl, Herbert and G. Maxwell (eds.). *Current Issues in the Philosophy of Science*. New York : Holt, Reinhart and Winston, 1961.

Ferré, Frederick. *Language, Logic and God*. New York : Harper & Row, 1961.

Flew, A. G. N. and Alasdair Mac Intyre (eds.). *New Essays in Philosophical Theology*. London : SCM Press, 1955.

Foss, Martin. *Symbol and Metaphor in Human Experience*. Princeton : Princeton University Press, 1949.

Fuchs, Ernst. *Hermeneutik*. Bad Cannstatt : R. Müllerschon Verlag, 1954.

Funk, Robert W. *Language, Hermeneutic and Word of God*. New York : Harper & Row, 1966.

Gilkey, Langdon. *Naming the Whirlwind*. Indianapolis : Bobs-Merrill, 1969.

——. *Religion and the Scientific Future*. New York : Harper & Row, 1970

Gill, Jerry H. *The Possibility of Religious Knowledge*. Grand Rapids, Michigan : William B. Eerdmans, 1971.

Gollwitzer, Helmut. *The Existence of God as Confessed by Faith*, trans. J. W. Leitch. Philadelphia : Westminster Press, 1965

Hamilton, Kenneth. *The System and the Gospel*. New York : The Macmillan Company, 1963.

Hanson, N. R. *Patterns of Discovery*. Cambridge : Cambridge University Press, 1961.

Hartshorne, Charles. *The Logic of Perfection and Other Essays in Neo-Classical Metaphysics*. Lasalle, Illinois : Open Court Publishing Company, 1962.

Heidegger, Martin. *Einführung in die Metaphysik*. Tübingen : Niemeyer, 1953.

——. *Existence and Being*, ed. Werner Brock. Chicago: Regency, 1965.

——. *Holzwege*. Frankfurt : Klostermann, 1950.

——. *Platons Lehre von der Wahrheit. Mit einem Briefe über den "Humanismus"*. Bern : Francke, 1947.

——. *Sein und Zeit.* Tübingen : Niemeyer, 1949. English translation, *Being and Time,* trans. John Macquarrie and E. Robinson. New York : Harper & Row, 1962.

——. *Unterwegs zur Sprache.* Pfullingen : Neske, 1959.

——. *Vom Wesen des Grundes.* Frankfurth : Klostermann, 1949.

——. *Was ist Metaphysik?* Frankfurt : Klostermann, 1955.

Hepburn, Ronald W. *Christianity and Paradox.* London : C. A. Watts & Co., 1958.

Herzog, Frederick. *Understanding God.* New York : Scribners, 1966.

Hesse, Mary B. *Analogies and Models in Science.* New York : Sheed and Ward, 1963

Hick, John (ed.). *The Existence of God.* New York : The Macmillan Company, 1964.

——. *Faith and Knowledge.* Ithaca : Cornell University Press, 1957.

Hordern, William. *Speaking of God.* New York : The Macmillan Company, 1964.

Hutchison, John A. *Language and Faith.* Philadelphia : Westminster Press, 1963.

Jaspers, Karl. *Philosophical Faith and Revelation,* trans. E. B. Ashton. New York : Harper & Row, 1967.

——. *Truth and Symbol,* trans. J. T. Wilde, W. Kluback, and W. Kimmel. New Haven : College and University Press, 1959.

Johnson, F. E. (ed.). *Religious Symbolism.* New York : Harper and Bros., 1955.

Kant, Immanuel. *The Critique of Judgment,* J. H. Bernhard, trans. New York : Hafner, 1914.

Kaufman, Gordon D. *God the Problem.* Cambridge : Harvard University Press, 1972.

Kegley, Charles W., and Robert W. Bretall (eds.). *The Theology of Paul Tillich.* New York : The Macmillan Company, 1964.

Kelsey, David H. *The Fabric of Paul Tillich's Theology.* New Haven : Yale University Press, 1967.

Kirk, G. S. *Myth : Its Meaning and Functions in Ancient and Other Cultures.* London : Cambridge University Press, 1970.

Kuhn, Thomas S. *The Structure of Scientific Revolutions.* Chicago : The University of Chicago Press, 1962.

Langer, Susanne. *Feeling and Form.* New York : Scribners, 1953.

——. *Philosophy in a New Key.* New York : Mentor Books, 1951.

Leibrecht, W. (ed.). *Religion and Culture.* New York : Harper & Row, 1959.

Lyttkens, H. *The Analogy Between God and the World.* Uppsala : Almquist, 1952.

Mac Intyre, Alasdair (ed.). *Metaphysical Beliefs.* London : SCM Press, 1957.

Macquarrie, John. *An Existential Theology.* New York : Harper Torchbooks, 1965.

——. *God and Secularity.* Philadelphia : Westminster Press, 1967.

——. *God-Talk.* London : SCM Press, 1967.

——. *Principles of Christian Theology.* New York : Scribners, 1966.

——. *Studies in Christian Existentialism.* Philadelphia : Westminster Press, 1965.

——. *Twentieth-Century Religious Thought.* New York : Harper & Row, 1963.

Martin, J.A., Jr. *The New Dialogue Between Philosophy and Theology.* New York : Seabury Press, 1966.

Mascall, E. L. *Existence and Analogy.* London : Longman's, 1949.

——. *Theology and Image.* London : A. R. Monbray, 1963.

May, Rollo (ed.). *Symbolism in Religion and Literature.* New York : George Brasiller, 1960.

McKelway, Alexander. *The Systematic Theology of Paul Tillich.* New York : Delta
    Book, 1966.
Mitchell, Basel (ed.). *Faith and Logic.* Boston : Beacon Press, 1957.
Mondin, Battista. *The Principle of Analogy in Protestant and Catholic Thought.*
    The Hague : Martinus Nijhoff, 1963.
Morgenbesser, Sidney (ed.). *Philosophy of Science Today.* New York : Basic Books,
    1967.
Morris, Charles. *Signs, Language and Behavior.* New York : Prentice Hall, 1946.
Nagel, Ernest. *Structure of Science.* New York : Harcourt, Brace, and World, 1961.
Ogden, C. K., and J. A. Richards. *The Meaning of Meaning.* New York : Harcourt,
    Brace & Co., Inc., 1923.
Ogden, Schubert M. *The Reality of God.* New York : Harper & Row, 1966.
O'Meara, Thomas (ed.). *Paul Tillich in Catholic Thought.* Dubuque, Iowa : Priority
    Press, 1965.
Ott, Heinrich. *Denken und Sein.* Zürich : EZV-Verlag, 1959.
Polanyi, Michael. *Personal Knowledge.* Chicago : University of Chicago Press, 1958.
——. *The Tacit Dimension.* Garden City : Doubleday, 1966.
Popper, Karl R. *The Logic of Scientific Explanation,* trans. Karl R. Popper. London :
    Hutchinson, 1959.
Ramsey, Ian T. *Models and Mystery.* New York : Oxford University Press, 1964.
—— (ed.). *Prospects for Metaphysics.* New York : Philosophical Library, 1961.
—. *Religious Language.* London : SCM Press, 1957.
Richardson, W. J., S. J. *Heidegger : Through Phenomenology to Thought.* The Hague :
    Martinus Nijhoff, 1963.
Robinson, J. M. and J. B. Cobb, Jr. (eds.). *The Later Heidegger and Theology.*
    New York : Harper & Row, 1963.
——. *The New Hermeneutic.* New York : Harper & Row, 1964.
Ryle, Gilbert. *The Concept of Mind.* London : Hutchinson & Company, 1949.
——. *Dilemmas.* London : Cambridge University Press, 1954.
Santoni, Ronald E. (ed.). *Religious Language and the Problem of Religious Knowledge.*
    Bloomington : Indiana University Press, 1968.
Schilling, Harold K. *Science and Religion.* New York : Scribners, 1962.
Shapere, Dudley (ed.). *Philosophical Problems of Natural Science.* New York : The
    Macmillan Company, 1965.
Shibles, Warren A. *Analysis of Metaphor in Light of W. M. Urban's Theories.* The
    Hague : Mouton, 1971.
Smith, John E. *Experience and God.* New York : Oxford University Press, 1968.
——. *Reason and God.* New Haven : Yale University Press, 1961.
Strawson, Peter. *Individuals : An Essay in Descriptive Metaphysics.* New York :
    Doubleday Anchor Books, 1965.
Tavard, G.H. *Paul Tillich and the Christian Message.* New York : Scribners, 1962.
Thomas, J. Heywood. *Paul Tillich : An Appraisal.* Philadelphia : Westminster Press,
    1963.
Tillich, Paul. *Dynamics of Faith.* New York : Harper & Row, 1957.
——. *Systematic Theology.* 3 vols. Chicago : The University of Chicago Press, 1951-63.
——. *Theology of Culture,* ed. R.C. Kimball. New York : Oxford University Press,
    1964.

Toulmin, Stephen. *Foresight and Understanding.* Bloomington : Indiana University Press, 1961.

——. *The Philosophy of Science.* New York : Harper Torchbooks, 1960.

——. *The Uses of Argument.* Cambridge : Cambridge University Press, 1964.

Urban, Wilbur. *Beyond Realism and Idealism.* London : Allen & Unwin, 1949.

——. *Humanity and Deity.* London : Allen & Unwin, 1951.

——. *The Intelligible World : Metaphysics and Value.* London : Allen & Unwin, 1929.

——. *Language and Reality.* New York : The Macmillan Company, 1961.

Van Buren, Paul. *The Secular Meaning of the Gospel.* New York : The Macmillan Company, 1965.

Wheelwright, Phillip. *The Burning Fountain.* Bloomington : Indiana University Press, 1954.

Whitehead, A. N. *Adventures of Ideas.* New York : The Macmillan Company, 1955.

——. *Symbolism.* New York : The Macmillan Company, 1927.

Wilder, Amos N. *The Language of the Gospel : Early Christian Rhetoric.* New York : Harper & Row, 1964.

Williams, Daniel Day. *The Spirit and the Forms of Love.* New York : Harper & Row, 1968.

Wisdom, John. *Other Minds.* Oxford : Blackwell, 1953.

Wittgenstein, Ludwig. *Philosophical Investigations,* trans. G. E. M. Anscombe. New York : Macmillan, 1953.

——. *Tractatus Logico-Philosophicus,* trans. Pears and McGuiness. London : Routledge, 1961.

Zuurdeeg, Willem. *An Analytical Philosophy of Religion.* Nashville : Abingdon Press, 1958.

B. Articles

Buri, Fritz. "The Problem of Non-Objectifying Thinking and Speaking in Contemporary Theology", *Distinctive Protestant and Catholic Themes Reconsidered,* ed. Robert Funk. New York : Harper & Row, 1967. Pp. 136-151.

Carnap, Rudolf. "Die Überwindung der Metaphysik durch die logische Analyse der Sprache", *Erkentniss,* Vol. II, No. 4. Pp. 237-255.

Coulson, Charles E. "The Similarity of Science and Religion", *Science and Religion,* ed. Ian G. Barbour. New York : Harper & Row, 1968. Pp. 57-77.

Driver, Tom F. "The Latent Image: Literary Sources of Theological Understanding", *Union Seminary Quarterly Review,* Vol. XXII, No. 2 (Winter 1968). Pp. 169-181.

Evans, Donald. "Differences Between Scientific and Religious Assertions", *Science and Religion,* ed. Ian G. Barbour. New York : Harper & Row, 1968, Pp. 101-133.

Feigl, Herbert. "Philosophical Tangents of Science," *Current Issues in the Philosophy of Science,* eds. Herbert Feigl and G. Maxwell. New York : Holt, Rinehart, and Winston, 1961. Pp. 1-17.

Ferré, Frederick. "Metaphors, Models, and Religion", *Soundings,* Vol. LI, No. 3 (Fall 1968). Pp. 327-345.

——. "Science and the Death of 'God'," *Science and Religion,* ed. Ian G. Barbour. New York : Harper & Row, 1964. Pp. 134-156.

Ford, Lewis E. "Three Strands of Symbolism", *Journal of Religion,* Vol. XLVI, No. 1 (January 1966). Pp. 104-127. Paul Tillich's "Reply" to this article, pp. 186-188.

Ford, Lewis E. "Tillich and Thomas : The Analogy of Being", *Journal of Religion*, Vol. XLVI, No. 2 (April 1966). Pp. 229-245.

Foster, Michael. "Contemporary British Philosophy and Christian Belief", *Christian Scholar* (Fall 1960). Pp. 185-198.

Hare, R. M. "Theology and Falsification", *New Essays in Philosophical Theology*, eds. A. G. N. Flew and Alasdair MacIntyre. London : SCM Press, 1955. Pp. 96-130.

Heisenberg, Werner. "The Representation of Nature in Contemporary Physics", *Symbolism in Religion and Literature*, ed. Rollo May. New York : George Brasiller, 1960. Pp. 215-232.

Macquarrie, John. "Heidegger's Earlier and Later Work Compared", *Anglican Theological Review* (January 1967). Pp. 3-16.

May, Rollo. "The Significance of Symbols", *Symbolism in Religion and Literature*, ed. Rollo May. New York : George Brasiller, 1960. pp. 11-49.

Mc Intyre, John. "Analogy", *Scottish Journal of Theology*, 12:1 (1959). Pp. 1-20.

McLean, George F.,O.M.I. "Symbol and Analogy", *Paul Tillich in Catholic Thought*, ed. Thomas O'Meara. Dubuque, Iowa : Priority Press, 1965. Pp. 145-183.

Nagel, Ernest. "The Nature and Aim of Science", *Philosophy of Science Today*, ed. Sidney Morgenbesser. New York : Basic Books, 1967. Pp. 3-13.

Nielson, Niels C. "Analogy as a Principle of Theological Method Historically Considered" *The Heritage of Christian Thought*, eds. R. E. Cushman and E. Grislis. New York : Harper & Row, 1965. Pp. 197-219.

Ott, Heinrich. "Language and Understanding", *Union Seminary Quarterly Review*, Vol. XXI, No. 3 (March 1966). Pp. 275-93.

——. "The Problem of Non-Objectifying Thinking and Speaking in Theology", *Distinctive Protestant and Catholic Themes Reconsidered*, ed. Robert W. Funk. New York : Harper & Row, 1967. Pp. 112-135.

——. "What is Systematic Theology?" *The Later Heidegger and Theology*, eds. J. M. Robinson and J. B. Cobb, Jr. New York : Harper & Row, 1963. Pp. 77-111.

Polanyi, Michael. "Notes on Professor Grünbaum's Observations", *Current Issues in the Philosophy of Science*, eds. H. Feigl and G. Maxwell. New York : Holt, Rinehart, and Winston, 1961. Pp. 52-54.

Quine, Willard E. "Necessary Truth", *Philosophy of Science Today*, ed. Sidney Morgenbesser. New York : Basic Books, 1967. Pp. 45-54.

Schilling, Harold K. "The Threefold Nature of Science and Religion", *Science and Religion*, ed. Ian G. Barbour. New York : Harper & Row, 1968. Pp. 78-100.

Smith, John E. "Being, Immediacy, and Articulation", *The Review of Metaphysics*, Vol. XXIV, No. 4 (June 1971). Pp. 593-613.

Tillich, Paul. "Existential Analysis and Religious Symbols", *Four Existentialist Theologians*, ed. Will Herberg. Garden City, New York : Doubleday Anchor Books, 1958. Pp. 41-45.

——. "The Meaning and Justification of Religious Symbols", *Religious Experience and Truth*, ed. Sidney Hook. New York : New York University Press, 1961. Pp. 3-11.

——. "The Religious Symbol", *Myth and Symbol*, ed. F.W. Dillistone. London : S.P.C.K., 1966. Pp. 15-34.

Tillich, Paul. "Theology and Symbolism", *Religious Symbolism*, ed. F. E. Johnson. New York : Harper & Brothers, 1955. Pp. 107-116.

Weigel, Gustave, S.J. "Myth, Symbol and Analogy", *Religion and Culture*, ed. W. Leibrecht. New York : Harper & Brothers, 1959. Pp. 123-128.

——. "The Theological Significance of Paul Tillich", *Paul Tillich in Catholic Thought*, ed. Thomas O'Meara. Dubuque, Iowa : Priority Press, 1965. Pp. 1-23.

Wisdom, John. "Gods", *Proceedings of the Aristotelian Society*. 1944-45. Pp. 76-86.

C. OTHER SOURCES

Buri, Fritz. "Symbol and Analogy". An unpublished essay.

Buri, Fritz and Heinrich Ott. "The Language Problem in Contemporary Theology". An English colloquium given at the University of Basel, Summer 1967.

Driver, Tom F. "Investigation and Revelation'". A seminar given at Union Thelogical Seminary, New York, Spring 1967.

Frei, Hans. "Analogy and the Spirit in the Theology of Karl Barth". An unpublished essay.

Macquarrie, John. "The Problem of Theological Language". A seminar given at Union Theological Seminary, New York, Spring 1966.

Ricœur, Paul. "The Word and the Words—The Levels of Significance in Language and the Relation to Biblical Theology". A lecture given at Union Theological Seminary, New York, Fall 1966.